Beginning Mark Logic with XQuery and MarkLogic Server

Andy Zhang

Champion Writers

Atlanta – Beijing – Harbin – Washington

Beginning Mark Logic with XQuery and MarkLogic Server
First Edition
Copyright © 2009 by Andy Zhang

International Standard Book Number:
ISBN-13: 978-1-60830-015-0
ISBN-10: 1-60830-015-3

Printed in the United States of America.

Disclaimer
The author of this book is not affiliated with any software maker and/or its affiliates. Therefore, the views and opinions expressed in this book do not represent the views and opinions of any software maker and/or its affiliates.

The information presented in this book is for reference only. The author(s) and publisher strive to provide accurate information. Several factors will create different user experiences than the one presented in this book. These factors include variations of software versions, patches, operating systems, configurations, and customizations. This book is not warranted to be error-free or up-to-date.

Reference resources listed in this book, such as website addresses, may have changed after this book was published.

The author(s) and the publisher shall have neither liability nor responsibility to any person or entity with respect to any loss or damages arising from the information contained in this publication.

for Jim, who continues to inspire me.

Who Should Read This Book

This book is an introduction to MarkLogic Server and XQuery. The content of this book is designed for the reader who has no knowledge of MarkLogic Server and XQuery. We hope this book will help our readers to acquire some essential skills and knowledge so they can become comfortable working with these technologies. We simply assume readers have some basic knowledge about XML to understand the examples in these chapters.

This book is not intended to help readers who have already worked with MarkLogic Server and XQuery for a while. Most information in this book is focused on the very basics. The materials in this book also place more emphasis on development than administration.

We Love to Hear from You!

Every reader of this book has something to say that we may learn from. Your opinions and comments are invaluable to us. While every precaution has been taken in the preparation of this book, there remains the possibility that errors or omissions still exist. If you find errors or omissions in this book, please check out the publisher's website and review all documented errata. If you do not find your issue on that list, please submit your comments to us, and we will update our website and correct all of the known issues in the next release.

Please note that the author(s) is unable to help you with any technical issues related to the topics included in this book. Due to the volume of messages we receive from our readers, we are unable to respond to every message; however, please be assured that your message will be carefully read, considered, and provided with a response when warranted.

When contacting us, please visit publisher's website at:

http://www.championwriters.com

How This Book is Organized

This book is divided into three parts. Part I is a brief introduction for MarkLogic Server including features for MarkLogic Server 4.x versions, forest, database, and geospatial functions.

Part II is focused on XQuery programming language and this part is for readers who want to learn XQuery. Another important feature of part II is that readers can practice along with the examples in XQuery development environment. Building a solid foundation of using XQuery is an essential skill for working with MarkLogic Server.

Part III is focused on specific features of MarkLogic Server. These chapters are intended to help readers to develop solutions for MarkLogic after the readers have learned how to work with XQuery from Part II.

Contents at a Glance

Table of Contents

Conventions Used in This Book

The following conventions are used in this book:

Italic is used for:
- Program Names, pathnames, and filenames
- Web addresses (URLs)
- Book or article titles

Constant Width is used for:
- Source code examples
- SQL statements

Bold is used for
- Emphasis
- Menu item or command

Please pay attention to the following icons:

 Warning: this message should be carefully reviewed to prevent issues or problems.

 Tips: This message provides you some shortcuts or efficient ways to solve problems.

 Real World: Real world working experience summary for the related topic.

 Notes: important information to remember.

 Security: features that related to application security.

 Resources: online or offline resources.

 Tools: special tools for application development, integration, or testing.

PART I

1

Introducing MarkLogic XML Server

Since the early and mid 1990s, XML implementations and usage have been skyrocketed. From government agencies to private enterprises, from academic environments and to non-profit organizations, XML is found almost everywhere. XML is endorsed by the World Wide Web Consortium (W3C) as an open standard for data markup and exchange. Exponential growth of XML implementations has resulted in business requirements for store, search, exchange, and deliver information effectively and efficiently.

Information management is the process of collecting and managing of information from one or multiple sources then distributing that information to users. Mark Logic positions itself in this niche market by providing so called "extreme information management" — innovative, dynamic, and scalable ways to manage XML data. The cornerstone of Mark Logic is its MarkLogic Server — an XML Server.

In this chapter, we are going to cover some key features of MarkLogic Server including the architecture of XML server, content enrichment, search, geospatial data, and notification. We will also briefly introduce the role of XQuery with MarkLogic Server.

Some Features of XML Server

With XML server such as MarkLogic Server, users can accomplish tasks that traditionally take more programming and server resources to accomplish. The main characteristic of XML Server is to store contents in a single and centralized repository. Users can access XML and other data by using XQuery language. Further, MarkLogic server provides numerous additional functionalities that are beyond the capabilities of XQuery. The key attractive features of XML servers are:

--Interoperability. Since XML data is plain text and markup, transformation can be integrated into the process, XML server has great interoperability with other systems and applications. XML applications are extremely popular with cross-platform systems and Internet applications.

--Accurate Search. Users can perform search and locate content with pinpoint accuracy. Also, the user can perform extensive full text search by running complex queries.

--Speed. When implemented properly, XML server can usually offer performance gain by providing information faster.

--Analysis and Reporting. To help the user understand information in logical and useful ways, XML server can be fine-tuned with indexes and other mechanisms to facilitate analysis and reporting.

--Multiple Content Types in Real Time. XML server is capable of transforming content into multiple format on the run — Word, HTML, PDF, RSS feeds, etc. Also, XML server can provide content that target different devices including mobile devices. MarkLogic ToolKit for Microsoft Word brings dynamic delivery and reuse capabilities of MarkLogic into Word.

A Typical XML Server Implementation

A typical XML server is usually composed of four layers: services, application logic, search and analytics, and database. In this section we are going to review the key functions for each layer.

Application logic layer is where the enterprise application and XQuery lives. For example, XQuery transforms a SharePoint list according to the user's business logic. The application logic layer is where most business requirements implement actions such as input validation, data filtering, and transaction processing.

Search and Analytics layer can provide facets, extensive, altering, and geospatial search capabilities. At the search and analytics layer, users can perform the search for their requested phrases and create reports for further analysis.

Database layer is where XML, text, binary data resides. Please note that programming code can also be stored in the database. Since the database is heart and soul of XML server, implementation, cluster, failover, synchronization, and replication actions occur here. Much of the MarkLogic server administration and programming skills are focused on this layer.

Services layer provides interface and services to user applications. For example, a web service that delivers data to the user application. Most content transformation and enrichment are happening in this layer such as converting XML data into Excel file format so the user can use the Spreadsheet data.

As you can see, XML server structure has its similarities and differences comparing the typical web server implementation. A successful implementation of XML server can offer higher speed, reduced software development, and serves more users. The demand for XML server has been increasing. MarkLogic server is one XML server in the industry, it is located in Saint Carlos, California, Mark Logic was the fourth fastest growing company in Silicon Valley between 2008 and 2009.

Figure 1-1

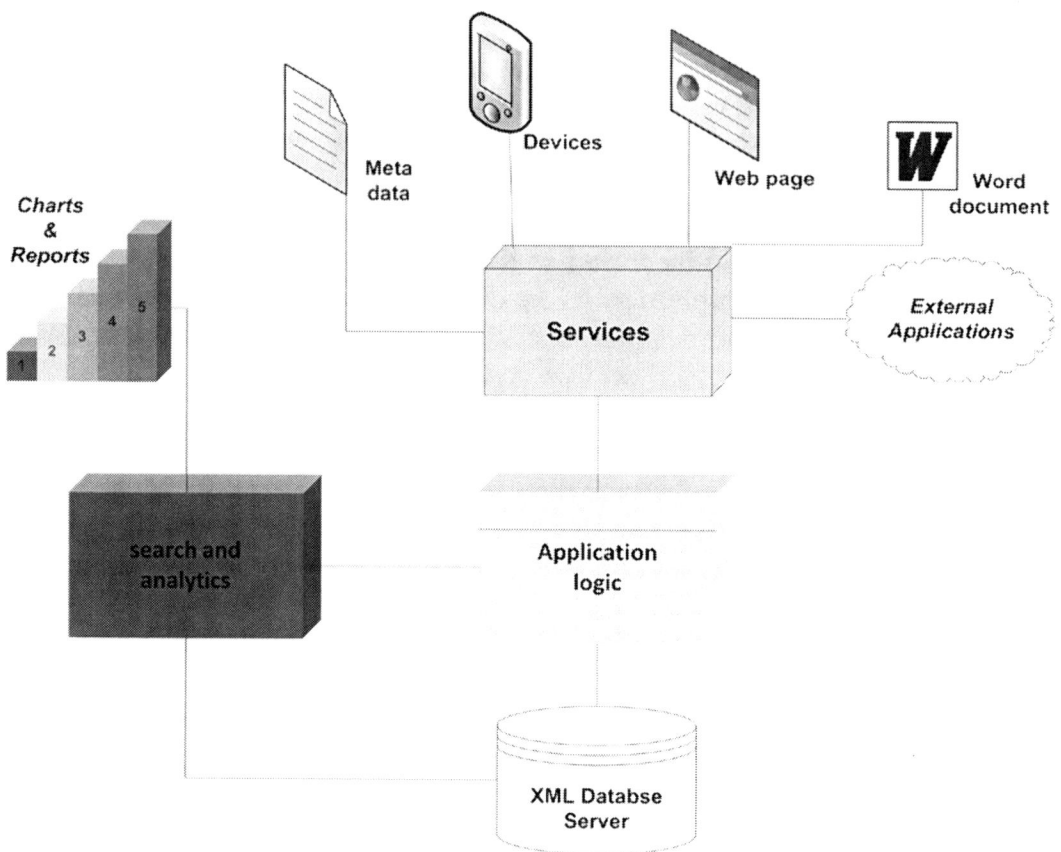

Content Enrichment

Content enrichment is to mark important data in order to improve its visibility in the document. For example, highlight a sales region in a sales report and add pie charts; emphasize a group of people in a document; feature some products in a catalog, and mark special policies that are important in a policy statement.

Implemented correctly, content enrichment can deliver striking results that further facilitates decision-making and improve document usage.

Figure 1-2

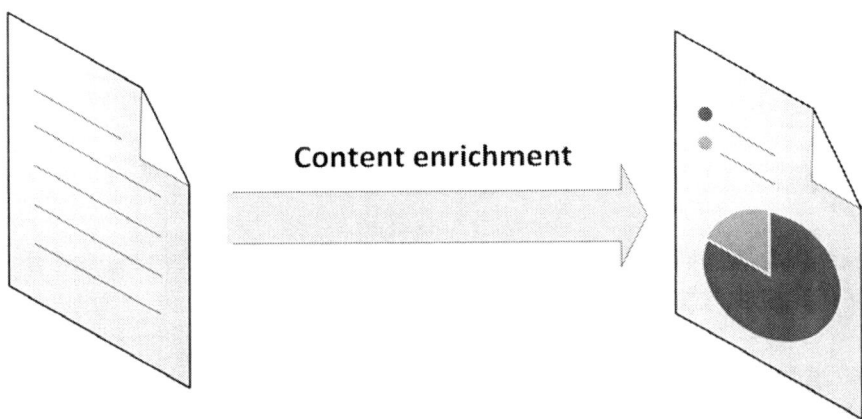

Content enrichment is to mark important data in order to improve its visibility in the document. For example, highlight a sales region in a sales report and add pie charts; emphasize a group of people in a document; feature some products in a catalog, and mark special policies that are important in a policy statement.

Implemented correctly, content enrichment can deliver striking results that further facilitates decision-making and improve document usage.

Geospatial Capabilities

Users can benefit from geospatial capabilities from XML Server implementation by searching for locations or specific geographical points within content or dynamically group content by location. MarkLogic server has build-in support for geospatial data types. This is a unique feature that distinguishes XML Server from many other relational databases.

Here are some key features for geospatial capabilities:

- Multiple selection range types. User can select a point, a radius from a selected location, a box, or even a polygon. Range selection can be combined with structured, full-text, or meta-data search.

- Geospatial index. Users can create geospatial index for high speed queries.

- Real-time analytics. Geospatial data can be integrated with analytic tools to provide real-time analytics.

- Geospatial data can be combined with alerts.

- User can combine with geospatial data with entity enrichment to further enhance the presentation of geospatial data.

You can go to http://www.geodata.gov to find specific data, maps, images, and other geospatial data.

Figure 1-3

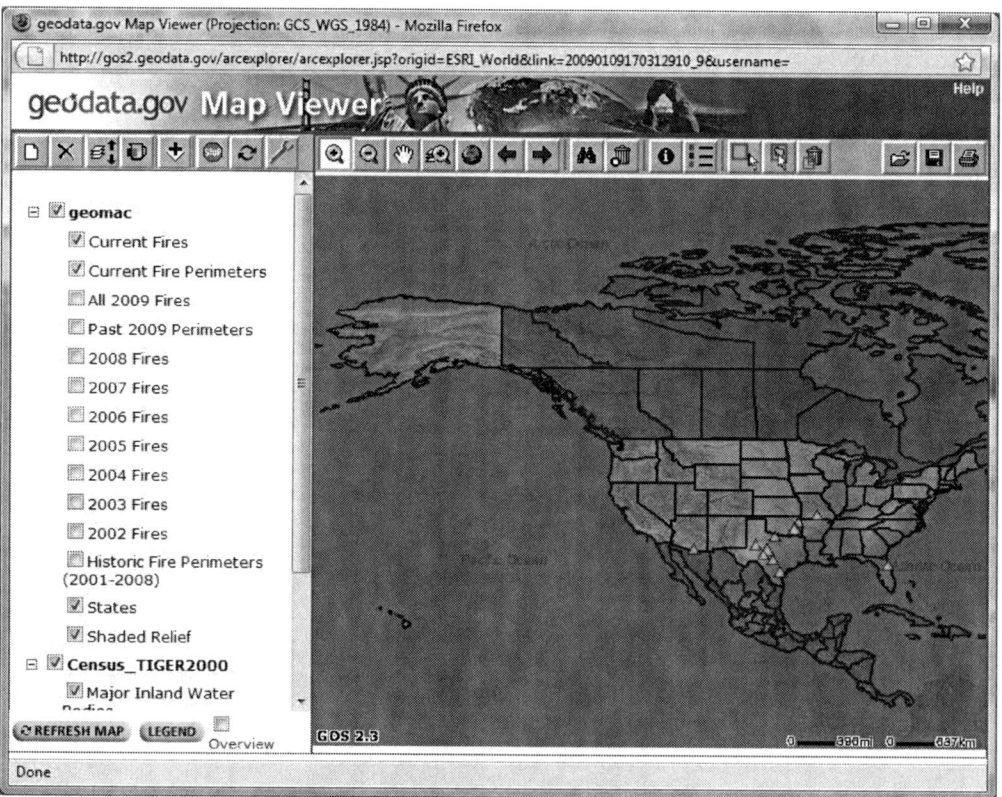

Search

The ability to find useful information is one the most important tasks for users. XML server can offer powerful, fast, and extended search capabilities. When users perform search, they are looking for relevant data within the correct context. Search is usually the beginning of a process of discovery, analysis, and learning. Here are some highlights of search features with XML server:

- Precision content. User can locate the exact content with the search text.
- Granular search. User can drill down to many levels when searching relevant content.
- Contextual display. Once a search result is found, user can see contextual content for the search result.
  For example, when you search for "sick leave", you will find the following content path: Employment Benefits → Policies → Sick Leave
- Results are dynamically rendered.

MarkLogic server also offers:

- Integrated XML and text search
- Relevance tuning
- Thesaurus support
- Entity extraction and enrichment
- Foreign language support
- Language processing (stemming, tokenization, and spell check)

Analytic

MarkLogic server can offer meaningful, deep, and actionable analysis. Users can gain insights into both high-level and granular level data, and then discover relationships and patterns. When user can combine the power of search and analytics together, they can find the meaningful information and gain understanding of their findings. Many scientific discoveries are based on our analytic abilities to connect the dots. MarkLogic Server can offer real-time and scalable performance for analytic functionalities.

Figure 1-4

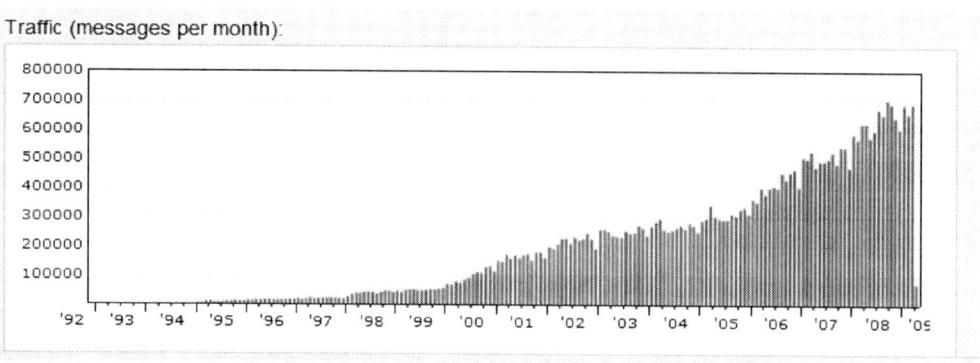

In general, analytic can help us:

- Count and aggregate things. For example, we can count the number of each products sold and how many customers in each region.
- Discover relationships and co-occurrence. For example, we can discover relationships between people, and between people and their environment.

One of the great features for MarkLogic Servers is allow users to bucket data. You can bucket all kind of data — strings, numeric values, date and time, geospatial indexes, etc. This feature alone can facilitate analytic abilities across data types. Also, MarkLogic Server comes with standard lexicon features and some new features such as enforce "order" of lexicons and proximity.

Real Time Notification

Notification is an essential part of our lives for preventing disasters, improving workflow, establishing critical communications, and much more. MarkLogic server can proactively monitors new documents and records to take actions based on user-defined rules and logic. Users will receive information precisely meet their specifications. Notification within MarkLogic server can be based on action triggers--taking action when query altered, data updated, or content changed.

Figure 1-5

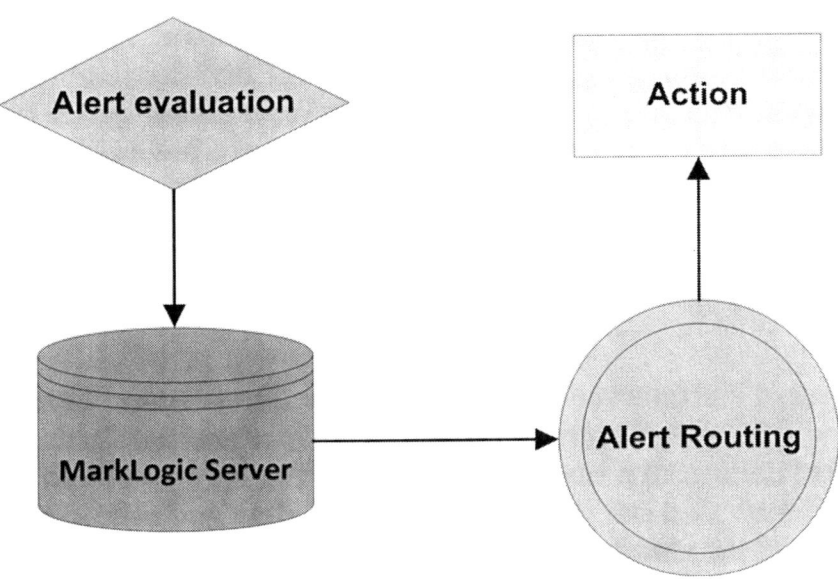

Notification that is integrated with MarkLogic Server can send out classical alerts such as Email, SMS, Pager, and standing queries. In addition, users can setup more advanced alerts by adding rule-based categorization, filtering and routing, cueing, and others. Users can also integrate notification system with their applications to deliver business analysis such as summarization, fuzzy categorization, theme detection, and tracking. Implemented properly, users can setup notification with MarkLogic server for real-time querying of large collections of XML data.

MarkLogic Connector for SharePoint

In the past several years, SharePoint has gained so much attention and usage. Today, many organizations are heavily relying on SharePoint portal sites for sharing their documents, managing their groups, communicating with team members, and establishing their online communities. Users can be empowered to create websites, develop website content, upload documents, create lists, and performing other activities in SharePoint.

MarkLogic Connector for SharePoint provides out of the box integration between SharePoint and MarkLogic server. The MarkLogic Connector offers functionalities for the user to add document services to an existing MarkLogic Server deployment—check-in, check-out, and other basic document services. Also, MarkLogic Connector has a mirroring capability from SharePoint Server 2007 to MarkLogic server and pushes content at any stage of a business workflow. Users can take advantage of MarkLogic functionalities once documents are stored in MarkLogic server.

Role of XQuery

To unleash the power of XML server such as MarkLogic Server, users have to utilize a programming language such as XQuery to retrieve and manipulate XML data. In this book, we dedicated a large amount of effort to help you learn some essential skills of XQuery. You can use the sample XML data and following the XQuery examples to get the results you are seeking. Every effort has been made to ensure your learning process is as easy as possible.

Many users who are working on MarkLogic Server will benefit from the knowledge of XQuery. Even MarkLogic administrators can greatly benefit from XQuery skills.

Summary

In this chapter, we provided a high-level overview of XML server architecture. Then we reviewed some key features for MarkLogic Server technology: content enrichment, geospatial features, search and analytic, real-time notification, and MarkLogic connector to SharePoint. We also discussed the role of XQuery. With proper implementation, MarkLogic Server is an exciting technology that can help users to perform rapid application development, accelerate cross-platform data sharing, and dynamically deliver document in multiple formats.

2

Introducing MarkLogic Administration

We start this chapter with some basic information about the MarkLogic server. First, we will cover what operating systems can host MarkLogic server and how swap space is critical for your server performance. Second, we introduce MarkLogic Server administrative interface. You can perform many server administrative tasks from the MarkLogic Server administrative interface. We then introduce forest—a collection of documents.

Operating Systems

There are several operating systems which can host MarkLogic Server and MarkLogic database. It is entirely up to your organization to decide which operating system is the best choice. This flexibility certainly is a good feature in the marketplace with diversified server choices.

One of the key considerations in selecting the operating systems is administration and development skills in your organization for each operating system. Installing, programming, maintaining, and upgrading MarkLogic requires solid skills for your selected operating system.

Table 2-1

Operating Systems
Red Hat Enterprise Linux 4.0 and 5.0 (x86)
Red Hat Enterprise Linux 4.0 and 5.0 (x64)
Sun Solaris 9 and 10 (64-bit SPARC)
Sun Solaris 10 (x64)
Microsoft Windows Server 2008 (x86)
Microsoft Windows Server 2008 (x64)
Microsoft Windows XP with SP2
Microsoft Windows 2003 Server (x86)
Windows 2003 Server 64-bit Edition (x64)
Microsoft Windows Vista 32-bit Edition (x86)
Windows Vista Server 64-bit Edition (x64)

 For more information on operating system requirements and installation information, you can find MarkLogic Installation Guide at the following document library:
http://xqzone.marklogic.com/pubs/4.0/default.xqy

Swap Space

From our working experience with MarkLogic, swap space is one of the most crucial factors for MarkLogic performance. When possible, your system administrator should configure a large amount of swap space. The rule-of-thumb is that you should consider configuring your swap space equal to twice the amount of physical memory. This applies to UNIX and Windows operating systems. For example, if your Windows Server 2008 has 20 GB of memory, you should consider configuring your swap space to 40 GB. Sufficient swap space allows MarkLogic server to deliver better performance during the peak usage hours.

Administrative Interface

Once you have MarkLogic Server properly installed, you should be able to conduct many administrative tasks from MarkLogic Server administrative interface. This administrative interface is running as a web application. This web application is usually configured on a designated port such as 8001. Once you logged into the administrative interface, you should see a screen looks similar to Figure 2-1.

Figure 2-1

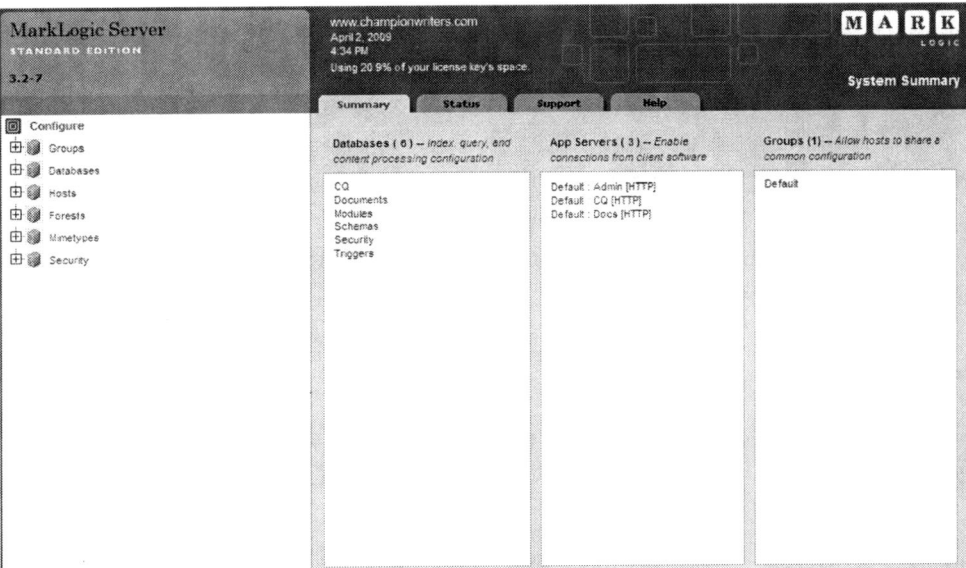

MarkLogic Server administrative interface is a powerful tool that allows you to perform essential MarkLogic administration tasks such as: create new group, backup and restore MarkLogic database, create new forests, and manage security settings. There are some tasks for MarkLogic server that you have to perform via command line tool, but majority administrative tasks are performed from this MarkLogic Server administrative interface.

Here are some server administrative tasks you can perform from the MarkLogic Server administrative interface:

- Creating new group and managing existing groups
- Creating new forest and managing existing forests
- Creating new database and managing existing databases
- Configuring security settings
- Configuring server, namespaces, and schemas
- Backup and restore
- Monitoring system state and performance

Introducing MarkLogic Forest

What is MarkLogic forest? You can consider MarkLogic forest as a document library. A forest can contain many kinds of documents—PDF files, images, XML documents, and more. The feature which makes MarkLogic forest unique is the ability to attach to MarkLogic database. When you attach a forest to a database, the two entities join together and you can use XQuery to select information from the database and from the forest.

To create a new forest, you can enter forest name (required), host, and data directory. The following figure shows the screen for creating a forest.

Figure 2-2

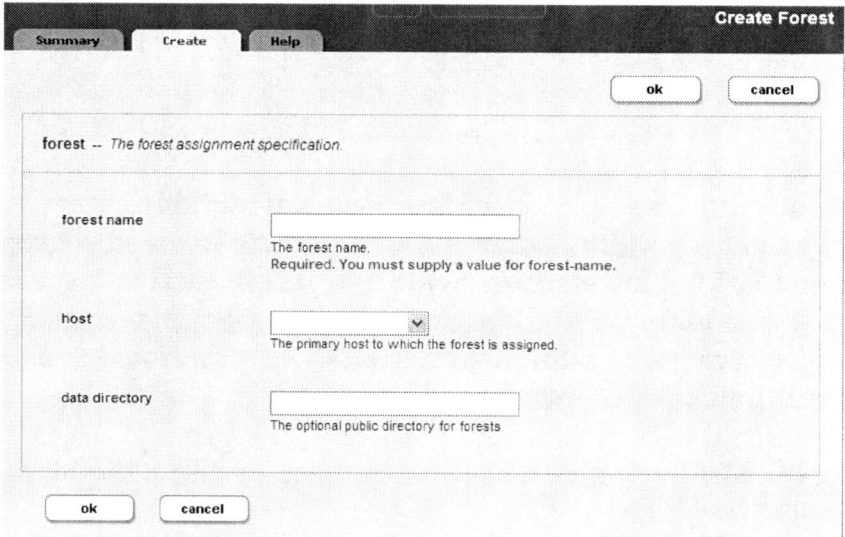

Data corruption and system failures can happen anytime, therefore it is a good idea to backup your forest. From the MarkLogic Server administrative interface, you can manually perform a forest backup or create a scheduled forest backup task. When you perform forest backup, the content within your forest is saved in your designated directory. To ensure your forest is in a consistent state with your database, you can perform a complete database backup.

Introducing MarkLogic Database

A MarkLogic database consists of one or more forests. If you are coming from relational database background, please keep in mind that MarkLogic database is very different from a typical RDBMS. A MarkLogic database functions like a classroom — it can host many students and allow teacher to interact with many students at once. Each MarkLogic database can have many forests and MarkLogic servers can connect with MarkLogic database and interact with all the forests in that database. XDBC, HTTP, and WebDAV servers can connect to the MarkLogic database and retrieve information from it.

Figure 2-3

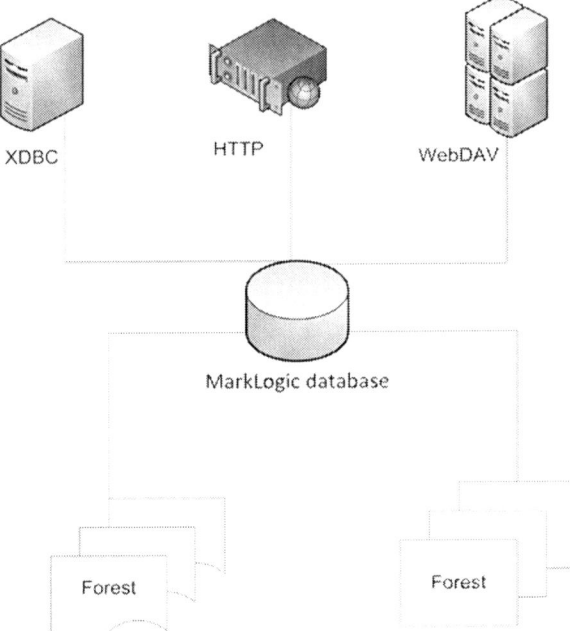

When you have installed MarkLogic server, you should see five default databases: Documents, Modules, Triggers, Schema, and Security. Documents database is where you store your XML and some other types of documents. To work with your XML documents, you need a programming language—XQuery to interact with your XML data. The Modules database contains XQuery code files. You can store triggers in the Triggers database. By default, a MarkLogic database stores its security settings in the Security database and its database schema information in the Schema database. It is recommended that you keep this default setting as is.

Figure 2-4

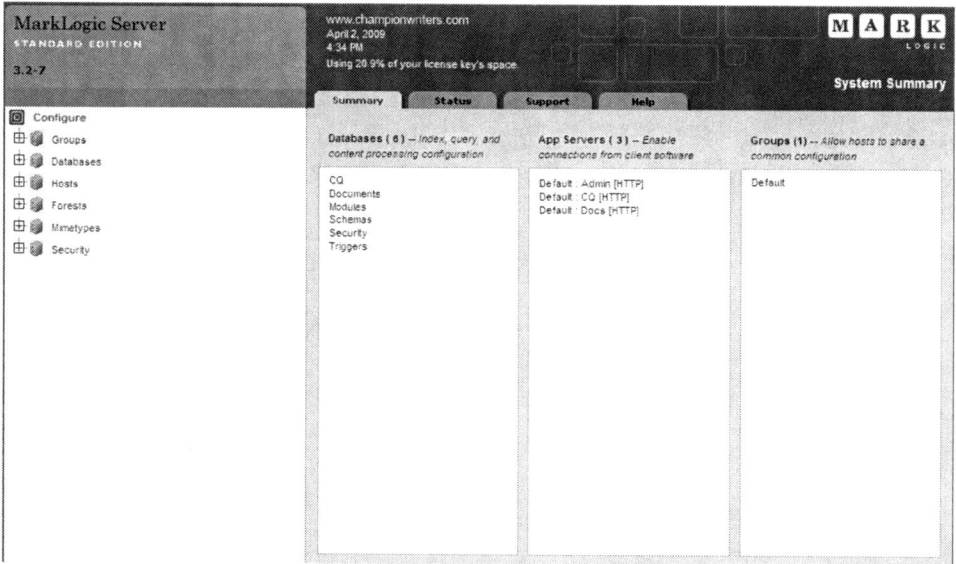

So for any given MarkLogic database, you should expect to see there is one associated security database, schema database, and triggers database. When you click on the Configuration tab for a database, you should see the associated databases.

Database Configuration Settings

Database configuration settings determine the functions of different aspects of the MarkLogic database. These configuration settings can be grouped into seven categories: administrative, indexing, reindexing, documents and directories, merge control, memory and journal, and others. The administrative configuration settings contain some of the most basic information for the database such as database name.

Indexing configuration settings determines how the database is indexed. The essential purpose for indexing is to improve performance on searches. So many indexing configuration settings are related to searches. For example, indexing configuration contains settings such as default language, word search options, element value positions, and trailing wildcard searches.

If you make changes to the existing indexing configuration settings, the changes will take effect if reindexing is enabled. You can enable reindexing by setting **reindexer enable** to **true**. Once reindexing is enabled, any changes to the indexing configuration will automatically initiate a background reindexing task. Therefore, reindexing configuration settings is closely related to indexing configuration settings and it can affect whether existing database will be reindexed.

To control how documents and directories are being created in the MarkLogic database, you can adjust configuration settings for documents and directories such as directory creation, maintain last modified, and inherit permission.

You can determine when and how to perform database merges through the merge control configuration settings. For example, you can set a blackout period that prevents any merge actions while upgrading a related database.

Usually the configuration settings that you need to pay the least attention to is the memory and journal configuration settings. These settings are come with the installation and rarely needs changes or updates. They determine functions such as system memory usage limit, transactional journal settings, and how to recover a database when transaction fails.

There are configuration settings that do not belong to the first six categories such as expunge locks. These configuration settings are categories as others.

Figure 2-5

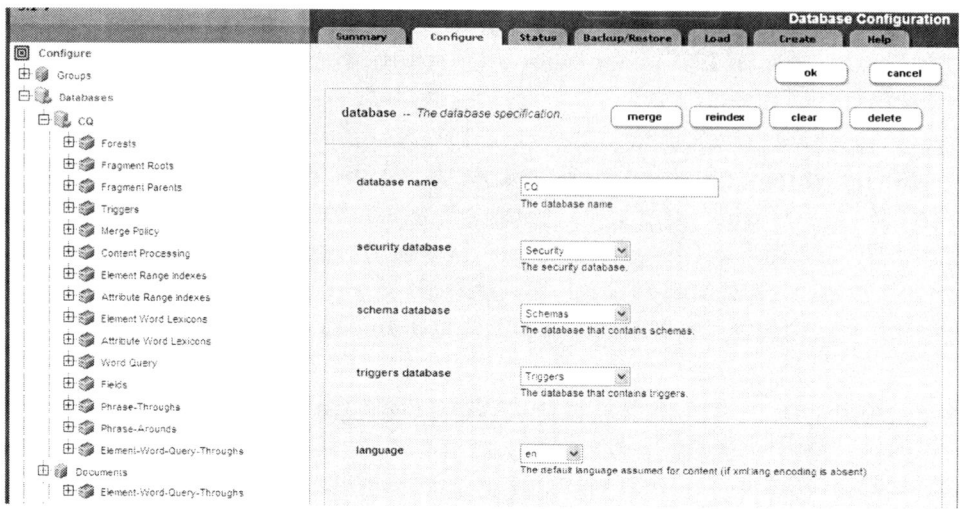

Create Database

Creating a new MarkLogic database is a breeze. Perhaps the most time consuming part is planning—to determine why you need to create a new database and how you are going to use it. At the MarkLogic administration interface, you can click on **Databases**, then clicking on the **Create** tab. You should see a database specification screen with most database configuration settings with default settings. Unless there is a very good well-thought technical reason, you should go ahead accept these default settings. The only information you need to enter is the database name. As soon as you click on OK, you have created a new MarkLogic database.

Figure 2-6

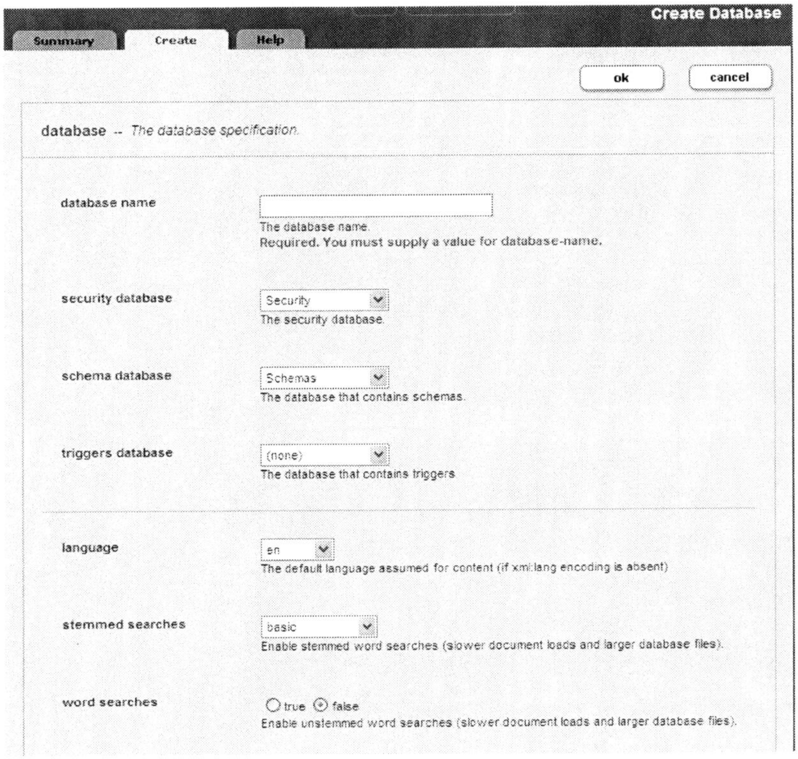

Database Status

Once your database has been created, you can check your database status by clicking on the **Status** tab. You should be able to see a snapshot of database status such as size, attached forest, backup and recovery state. You can also review forest information such as host, state, documents, fragments, stands, size, and free space.

When you are experiencing issues with your MarkLogic database, you should consider reviewing the database status first. MarkLogic database status screen usually offers good information to help you troubleshoot and analyze database health.

Figure 2-7

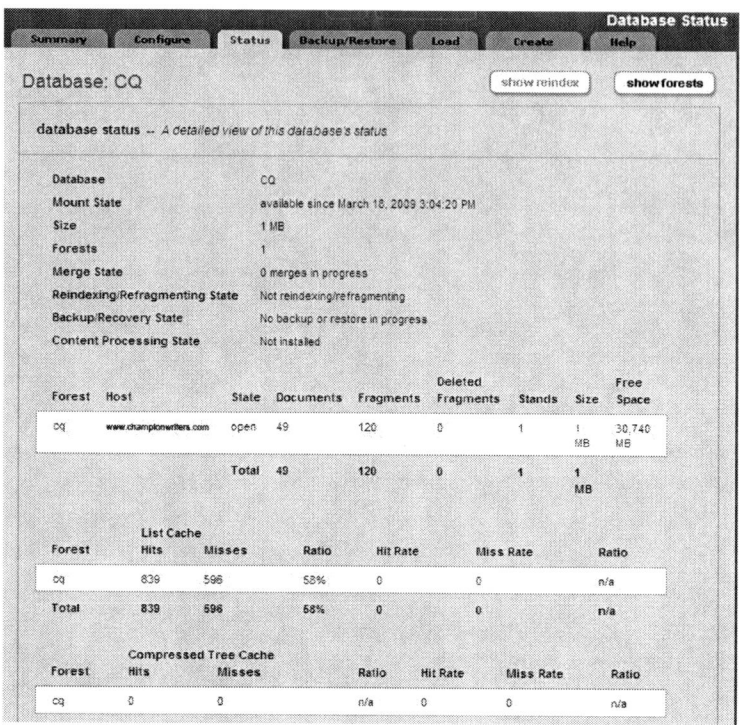

Load Documents

You can load documents directly into a database by going to the **Load** tab. If you only want to load certain type of documents, you can add a filter into the load requirement. For example, if you only want to load XML documents, you can add the following filter: *.xml. When you load documents from a given directory, only documents which meet the filter requirement will be loaded into the database you have specified.

 Your MarkLogic administrative account must have permissions to the document directory that you want to load documents into the database.

Backup and Restore

Occasionally, you will need to backup or restore your MarkLogic database. To ensure creating a consistent backup copy of your database, MarkLogic server will go through the following phases while performing backup of a database: validation, copy, and synchronization. The transaction starts right after the validation phase and ends after the synchronization phase. It is important to point out that your backup copy of your MarkLogic database is platform dependent. In other words, you should backup your database onto the same operating system as your running system.

To start your backup or restore process, you can click on Backup/Restore tab, then enter your backup or restore directory name. Once you are ready, you can click on OK to kick off the process.

 For more information about MarkLogic database backup and restore, please reference MarkLogic Administrator's Guide at: http://developer.marklogic.com/pubs/4.0/default.xqy

Figure 2-8

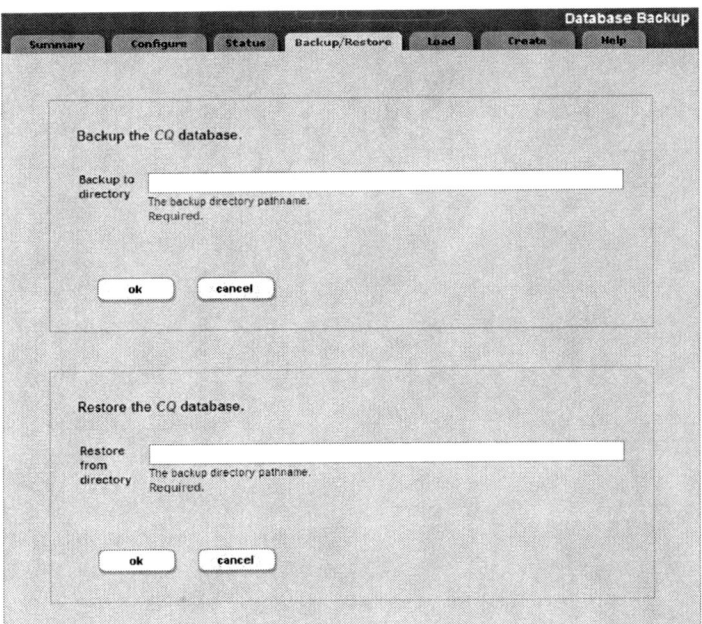

Summary

In this chapter, we covered some essential tasks for administering MarkLogic. We first started with server installation requirements and swap space. Then we introduced the administrative interface. From the administrative interface, you can perform many mission critical functions for MarkLogic server such as creating, configuring, and monitoring different aspects of the MarkLogic server.

MarkLogic forest can contain many documents of different types. You can attach a forest to a MarkLogic database. The last section of this chapter covers several topics about MarkLogic database: how to create, monitor, configure, backup, and restore database. MarkLogic developers usually work with XML documents by using XQuery. Soon we are going to start to help you get familiar with XQuery.

PART II

3

Accessing Documents

For years, I have been improving methods of helping people to learn technologies such as XQuery. It seems teaching and helping others to learn has always been part of my life. When I was in the fourth grade, one of my teachers was impressed with my ability to create sample questions during the class; she actually asked me to help her come up with some exam questions. When I was in college, I tutored countless people who were attending the same classes as me in various subjects—economics, statistics, computer science, college algebra, and many others. Even with different subjects and a diverse audience, I discovered two important findings for learning difficult material:

First, people learn better when they are involved. Class participation, hands-on sessions, and constructive discussions are great ways of helping people learn new materials. When a student sits in an isolated corner looking outside the classroom window, it is doubtful he or she is absorbing the material presented by the instructor. To help you stay involved while reading this material, I have created sample XML files for practice along with the materials presented in the chapters. When you find yourself writing XQuery function that works, you gain confidence and interest to learn more. That confidence will help you solve difficult problems in your job or make you feel knowledgeable during a technical interview. So I highly recommend you actually practice with each example.

Second, people retain more knowledge when they learn the material in tiny increments. Perhaps nobody can learn a complex programming language in one day—we all need to adjust our pace of learning and understanding new material in order to succeed. People are often overwhelmed by the sheer volume of new material and quickly give up if they perceive a learning task is too daunting. From my early days of writing technical books and training materials, I tried to cram as much useful information as possible into each chapter. My ambitious plan created exactly the opposite effect from what I desired—people retain far less materials when they read a 50-page chapter than a 10-page chapter. So I learned my lessons the difficult way and decided to lower the barrier of entry. Here, each chapter is very manageable and small compared to many other books out there. You can expect to finish reading it and practice the examples within a short timeframe.

Another important feature is the structure of the chapters. I spent much of my planning phase thinking how to teach people to learn XQuery in a logical, incremental, and gradual manner, so the learning curve is not very steep. Unless you are proficient in the materials presented in some chapters, it is beneficial to follow the sequence of the chapters.

In this chapter, we will begin to learn how to bring XML documents into your workspace by using XQuery. First, you need some software application to unleash the powerful XQuery. You have probably heard many times about Integrated Development Environment (IDE). When developing XQuery, it is well worth the investment to get a useful software application that can help your development process with color coding, syntax checking, debugging, and other features. It will save you a lot of time and headache. So we will look at a couple of popular options in the marketplace. Second, we will look at how to retrieve documents from different paths by using XQuery. Being able to interact with documents from various locations and sources is an important task for you when working with XQuery. It is also usually the first step you need to take, i.e., open the document.

Tools for XQuery Development

IIf you perform a search in a search engine like Google with "XQuery IDE" as your search phrase, you should find many matching software applications that support your XQuery development. Some of them are free tools too. You can decide which software application is best suited for your style. In terms of learning the material from this book, it really doesn't make much difference from one application to another. If your work environment dictates one particular software application for XQuery development, then you will most likely want to use it for your real production development.

Here are some popular software applications that many developers use for XQuery development:

Oxygen XML Editor
http://www.oxygenxml.com

Stylus XQuery Editor
http://www.stylusstudio.com

Altova Professional XML Suite
http://www.altova.com

You can see a sample screenshot for Oxygen XML Editor in Figure 1-1.

Figure 3-1

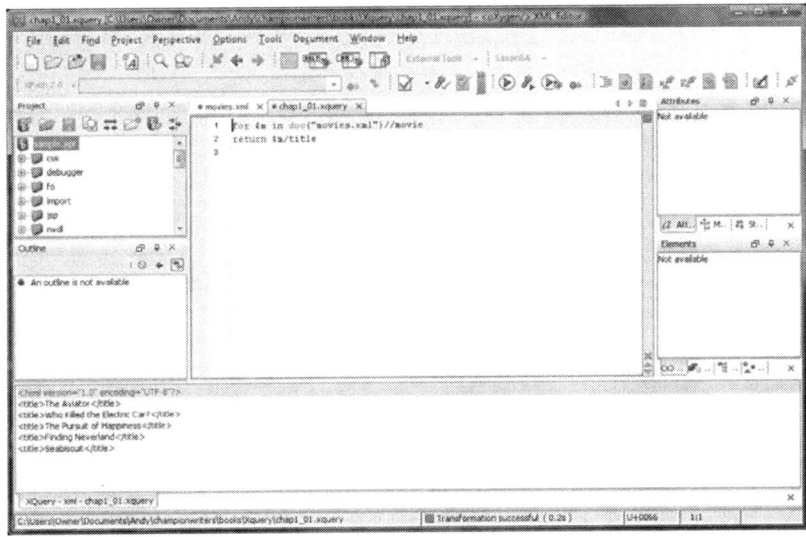

Once you are ready to test your XQuery expressions, you can execute your XQuery expression and see the result showing in the result pane. This is a rewarding way of learning XQuery by seeing your data being transformed.

Accessing Documents

XQuery is a powerful functional programming language. In a nutshell, XQuery is composed of expressions. Every expression evaluates a sequence of items, including atomic values or nodes. The expression syntax is superficially procedural. If you are familiar with XPath, you will find XQuery is loaded with XPath expressions. If you have not been using XPath, this book provides you with many examples of XPath expressions in XQuery for selecting information from XML documents.

With your XQuery development installed and ready to go, it is time to start working with some documents.

Access XML Document in the Same Folder

Suppose you have an XML file named movies.xml. To open an XML document located in the same folder as your XQuery file, you can use the following expression:

doc("movies.xml")

Figure 3-2

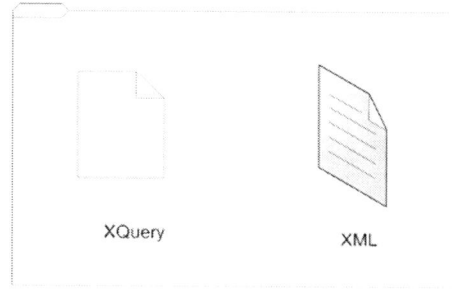

XQuery   XML

Access XML Document in a Different Folder

It is usually a good practice to group your XQuery files into a separate folder than your XML documents. For example, you want to access a document inside the "Entertainment Report" folder named movies.xml. To access XML documents from a different folder, you can provide a full path in your XQuery expression like this:

doc("file:///c:/Projects/Entertainment%20Report/Data/movies.xml")

NOTE
Please note that white spaces in the folder name should be replaced with "%20" to avoid any misinterpretation.

Figure 3-3

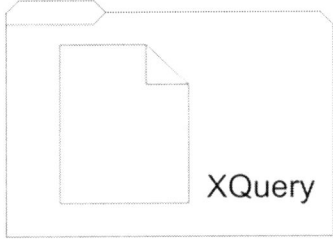

Entertainment Report

Access XML Document from the Internet

What if you want to process an XML file from the Internet? For example, you want to interact with an XML file that is hosted by another company. When you connect to the Internet and are able to browse to an XML document with a valid URL, then you can access the document by using an XQuery expression similar to the following:

doc("http://www.championwriters.com/books/XQuery/chap1/movies.xml ")

Figure 3-4

Summary

Believe or not, being able to interact with XML documents by using XQuery expression is not a trivial accomplishment. In this chapter, you have built your XQuery development foundation by researching and installing development software, and then opening XML documents with XQuery expressions. With your document successfully opened, you are now ready to perform more tasks with XQuery.

4

Basic Expressions

For many people, the collapse of the World Trade Center towers in New York City and the attack on the Pentagon in the Washington, D.C., area was a tragic and unforgettable lifetime event. For many Washington-area residents, what happened about one year later became the most terrifying days in their lives. In October 2002, people were being shot in random places. A student was shot in front of his school, a driver was shot at a gas station, and a customer was shot in front of a Home Depot store. There was no safe place, and you never knew who was going to pull the trigger behind you. For more than three weeks, the entire region was gripped with fear. People had to duck their heads and move around when filling up the gas tank, pedestrians walked in a zigzag pattern on the sidewalk, parents were worried their kids would be the next victims. When the media reported the sniper was driving a white van, many drivers got nervous when a white van was nearby. Twenty-three days later, someone spotted the snipers in a blue car and reported them to the police, with the entire region finally feeling relieved.

The reason those two snipers dominated the media coverage and terrified millions of people was largely due to the fact that they were difficult to find.

If you have a large XML file with a lot of data and complex structure, finding a crucial piece of information can very challenging. In this chapter, we are going to use some basic XQuery expressions to help you locate the information you need. Our sample XML is very simple and you can still learn useful techniques with this sample file by using XQuery.

Our Input File

In this chapter, we are going to use a sample XML file called movies.xml. Here is the movies.xml content with a list of movies and their titles, release dates, genres, prices, plots, and inventory information:

```
<?xml version="1.0"?>
<movies>
    <movie ID="1">
        <title>The Aviator</title>
        <release>December 25, 2004</release>
        <genre>Biography|Drama</genre>
        <price>12.95</price>
        <instock>2</instock>
        <plot>A biopic depicting the early years of
legendary director and aviator Howard Hughes' career, from
the late 1920s to the mid-1940s.</plot>
    </movie>
    <movie ID="2">
        <title>Who Killed the Electric Car?</title>
        <release>August 4, 2006</release>
        <genre>Documentary</genre>
        <price>14.95</price>
        <instock>3</instock>
        <plot>A documentary that investigates the birth
and death of the electric car, as well as the role of
renewable energy and sustainable living in the future.</
plot>
    </movie>
    <movie ID="3">
        <title>The Pursuit of Happiness</title>
        <release>December 16, 2006</release>
        <genre>Biography|Drama</genre>
        <price>19.95</price>
        <instock>1</instock>
        <plot>A struggling salesman takes custody of his
```

```
son as he's poised to begin a life-changing professional
endeavor.</plot>
    </movie>
    <movie ID="4">
        <title>Finding Neverland</title>
        <release>November 24,  2004 </release>
        <genre>Biography|Drama|Family</genre>
        <price>12.95</price>
        <instock>2</instock>
        <plot>The story of J.M. Barrie's friendship with a
family who inspired him to create Peter Pan.</plot>
    </movie>
    <movie ID="5">
        <title>Seabiscuit</title>
        <release>July 25,  2003</release>
        <genre>Drama|History|Sport</genre>
        <price>19.95</price>
        <instock>1</instock>
        <plot>True story of the undersized Depression-era
racehorse whose victories lifted not only the spirits of the
team behind it but also those of their nation.</plot>
    </movie>
</movies>
```

Once you saved this file in your local development environment, you are good
to go.

Find a Movie by Identifier

XQuery is a powerful functional programming language. In a nutshell, XQuery is
composed of expressions. Every expression evaluates a sequence of items, including
atomic values or nodes. The expression syntax is superficially procedural. If you are
familiar with XPath, you will find XQuery is loaded with XPath expressions. If you
have not been using XPath, this book provides you with many examples of XPath
expressions in XQuery for selecting information from XML documents.
As you can see from our movies.xml file, each movie has a unique identifier. For

example, *Finding Neverland* has ID=4.

Open your favorite XML editor application that you installed in Chapter 1 and start a new XQuery file. If you have saved movies.xml in the same folder as your XQuery file, you can try this XQuery expression:

```
for $m in doc("movies.xml")//movie[@ID=1]
return $m
```

The $m is a variable that stores your selected movie information. From Chapter 1, you learned how to open a document with doc() function. The XPath expression "//movie[@ID=1]" meaning find any movie for me with ID=1. When you run your XQuery, you should see results like this:

```
<movie ID="1">
        <title>The Aviator</title>
        <release>December 25, 2004</release>
        <genre>Biography|Drama</genre>
        <price>12.95</price>
        <instock>2</instock>
        <plot>A biopic depicting the early years
of legendary director and aviator Howard Hughes' career,
from the late 1920s to the mid-1940s.</plot>
        </movie>
```

If you can see your results similar to what you read here, congratulations! You are now programming in XQuery.

Find All Movie Titles

For some reason, your customer wants to see all the movie titles you have. It is really a simple task in XQuery to select all the movie titles:

```
for $m in doc("movies.xml")//movie
return $m/title
```

You see, the first part of our XQuery expression is identical to our previous example. This time instead of selecting movies by identifier, you select all movies. The $m variable contains all movies. When you want to display only the titles, you use "$m/title" to get results like this:

```
<title>The Aviator</title>
<title>Who Killed the Electric Car?</title>
<title>The Pursuit of Happiness</title>
<title>Finding Neverland</title>
<title>Seabiscuit</title>
```

Figure 4-1

Conditionals

Just when you are ready to hand your list of movies to your customer, your boss interrupted you. "Please only give a list of movies that have more than one copy in stock," he said. Now, you have to regenerate your list with conditionals. So you added conditionals into your XQuery expression like this:

```
for $m in (doc("movies.xml")//movie)
```

```
return if ($m/instock > 1)
then $m/title
else ()
```

Now if you run your XQuery expression, you should see that your list of movies has been reduced:

```
<title>The Aviator</title>
<title>Who Killed the Electric Car?</title>
<title>Finding Neverland</title>
```

Summary

In this chapter, we introduced our first sample XML file and how to use XQuery expressions to select the data you are looking for by identifier or by title. Then we discussed how to use conditionals in your XQuery expression. You have accomplished a lot in such a short time.

5

Predicates

When working with XML documents, XQuery makes heavy use of XPath to match and select XML data. If XQuery is a driver and XPath is a car, XQuery use XPath to reach where it wants to go. They can work seamlessly together to create powerful expressions. There is little wonder that both XQuery 1.0 and XPath 2.0 belong to the same W3C working group.

In this chapter, we are going to learn how to use predicates. What are predicates? You can consider predicates as data filters. When you use predicates in your XQuery, you can screen and select only the data that meet your defined rules. For example, you can select only those items on sale or you can select only items priced less than $20.

Our Sample File

In this chapter, we are going to use a sample file named breakfast.xml with a list of breakfast items and their corresponding prices. I hope you are not hungry while reading this chapter.

```
<?xml version="1.0" encoding="UTF-8"?>
<Items>
    <Item ID="1">
        <Name>Bagel</Name>
        <Price>1.25</Price>
```

```
        </Item>
        <Item ID="2">
            <Name>Orange Juice</Name>
            <Price>1.50</Price>
        </Item>
        <Item ID="3">
            <Name>Southwest Omelet</Name>
            <Price>7.25</Price>
        </Item>
        <Item ID="4">
            <Name>Pancakes</Name>
            <Price>4.75</Price>
        </Item>
        <Item ID="5">
            <Name>Milk</Name>
            <Price>1.25</Price>
        </Item>
        <Item ID="6">
            <Name>Two Eggs</Name>
            <Price>1.50</Price>
        </Item>
    </Items>
```

Select by Value

Predicates give you the power to select an element node by value. For example, you can select a single breakfast item by its name, such as "Orange Juice."

```
    for $i in (doc("breakfast.xml")//Items/Item[Name =
"Orange Juice"])
    return $i
```

The result you get is:

```
<Item ID="2">
        <Name>Orange Juice</Name>
```

```
        <Price>1.50</Price>
</Item>
```

You can also select an element node by its member child's value. For example, you can find all breakfast items that are equal to $1.50.

```
for $i in (doc("breakfast.xml")//Items/Item[Price = 1.50])
return $i
```

The results show all items with the price equal to $1.50, which includes Orange Juice and Two Eggs:

```
<Item ID="2">
        <Name>Orange Juice</Name>
        <Price>1.50</Price>
</Item>
<Item ID="6">
        <Name>Two Eggs</Name>
        <Price>1.50</Price>
</Item>
```

Similarly, you can also select items more expensive than $1.50. In this case, you can use the following XQuery expression:

```
for $i in (doc("breakfast.xml")//Items/Item[Price > 1.50])
return $i
```

The result shows there are two items that are more expensive than $1.50:

```
<Item ID="3">
        <Name>Southwest Omelet</Name>
        <Price>7.25</Price>
</Item>
<Item ID="4">
        <Name>Pancakes</Name>
        <Price>4.75</Price>
```

```
</Item>
```

Select by Attribute

If you know an attribute, you can directly use predicates to return the exact item. For example, you can use the following XQuery expression to select it:

```
for $i in (doc("breakfast.xml")//Items/Item[@ID=3])
return $i
```

Sure enough, you get the following result back:

```
<Item ID="3">
        <Name>Southwest Omelet</Name>
        <Price>7.25</Price>
</Item>
```

If you want to find all elements with attribute ID, you can use the following XQuery expression:

```
for $i in (doc("breakfast.xml")//Items/Item[@ID])
return $i
```

In our sample file, every breakfast item has an ID attribute. So we get the following result:

```
<Item ID="1">
        <Name>Bagel</Name>
        <Price>1.25</Price>
    </Item>
<Item ID="2">
        <Name>Orange Juice</Name>
        <Price>1.50</Price>
    </Item>
<Item ID="3">
        <Name>Southwest Omelet</Name>
```

```
        <Price>7.25</Price>
    </Item>
<Item ID="4">
        <Name>Pancakes</Name>
        <Price>4.75</Price>
    </Item>
<Item ID="5">
        <Name>Milk</Name>
        <Price>1.25</Price>
    </Item>
<Item ID="6">
        <Name>Two Eggs</Name>
        <Price>1.50</Price>
    </Item>
```

Positional Predicates

If you know the numeric position of the element you want to select, you can use positional predicates. When you have a list of elements that need to be processed, you can specify which element you want to select, for example, the fourth breakfast item on the list. You can use the following XQuery expression:

```
for $i in (doc("breakfast.xml")//Items/Item[4])
return $i
```

You should get the following result:

```
<Item ID="4">
        <Name>Pancakes</Name>
        <Price>4.75</Price>
    </Item>
```

Please note that if you want to select the fifth element in the document, you can use the following XQuery expression:

```
for $i in (doc("breakfast.xml")//Items/Item)[5]
return $i
```

In XQuery expressions, everything inside the parentheses is evaluated first. So in this case, we get a list of breakfast items, and then select the fifth one. Our result shows:

```
<Item ID="5">
        <Name>Milk</Name>
        <Price>1.25</Price>
    </Item>
```

The Position Function

In XQuery expressions, you can add position functions to select elements based on position within the context sequence. You can select items with position greater than 4 by using:

```
for $i in (doc("breakfast.xml")//Items/Item[position() > 3])
return $i
```

You may have noticed that the position function syntax is: position(). When your XQuery expression runs, you will get the following items with position greater than 3:

```
<Item ID="4">
        <Name>Pancakes</Name>
        <Price>4.75</Price>
    </Item>
<Item ID="5">
        <Name>Milk</Name>
        <Price>1.25</Price>
    </Item>
<Item ID="6">
        <Name>Two Eggs</Name>
        <Price>1.50</Price>
```

```
</Item>
```

The Last Function

As its name implies, the last function evaluates and select the last element in the sequence.

```
for $i in (doc("breakfast.xml")//Items/Item[last()])
return $i
```

From our sample XML document, we will get the following item:

```
<Item ID="6">
        <Name>Two Eggs</Name>
        <Price>1.50</Price>
    </Item>
```

Multiple Predicates

When necessary, you can combine multiple predicates together to get the result you are looking for. For example, you can select an item by ID and price.

```
for $i in (doc("breakfast.xml")//Items/Item[@ID = 4][Price =
4.75])
return $i
```

You should see your result looks like this:

```
<Item ID="4">
        <Name>Pancakes</Name>
        <Price>4.75</Price>
    </Item>
```

Summary

By now, you are probably starting to feel comfortable with XQuery expressions. Once you gain some hands-on experience in XQuery, you will probably agree this is a powerful language that can help you find what you are looking for from XML documents quickly and easily.

In this chapter, we covered the topic of predicates. Predicates are filters that are placed in the path expressions to help you narrow down the result set. First, you learned how to select element nodes by value or child element value. Then, you could select element nodes by attribute. Positional predicates allowed you to select elements by their position in the sequence. Finally, you learned that you can combine multiple predicates into the same XQuery expression.

6

Introducing FLWOR

If you were impressed by what you can do with predicates from the previous chapter, you are going to learn another powerful XQuery expression—FLWOR (pronounced "flower"). So what does FLWOR stand for? It means "for, let, where, order by, return" keywords in the XQuery expression. Please note that they are always in lower case. Also, they comprise one expression, not five!

FLWOR expression is most commonly used for managing, sorting, rearranging, or transforming XML data. You can build complex results in a single query with FLWOR expression.

Simple FLWOR Expression

To illustrate how to use FLWOR expression, we are going to use a sample file named car.xml with a list of vehicle parts. A typical auto store has many parts, and keeping track of these parts is crucial to the store's operation. Our sample file looks like this:

```
<?xml version="1.0" encoding="UTF-8"?>
<parts>
    <part region="NE">
        <name>Windshield Wiper</name>
        <color>Black</color>
```

```
            <code>EZI283095</code>
        </part>
        <part region="NE">
            <name>Tire</name>
            <color>Black</color>
            <code>TIN4592033</code>
        </part>
        <part region="SE">
            <name>Engine Oil</name>
            <color>Light Yellow</color>
            <code>OIL192396</code>
        </part>
        <part region="SW">
            <name>Break Light</name>
            <color>Red</color>
            <code>BLR763920</code>
        </part>
    </parts>
```

Before we start writing a FLWOR XQuery expression, we can first look at the basic structure of FLWOR expression:

for

>Normally, you want to use "for" to loop through the XML element nodes.

let

>You can assign the value of a variable by using "let."

where

To select the element you are looking for, you can use "where" to filter or narrow down your selection.

order by

>You can use the "order by" expression to sort your results the way you like it.

return

>This is where the action takes place: You use "return" to get your results

as output. It is time to practice our first FLWOR expression. With our car.xml file ready, you can try the following XQuery expression:

```
for $car_part in (doc("car.xml")//part)
let $part_name := $car_part/name
where $car_part/@region = "NE"
order by $part_name
return $part_name
```

Once you run this XQuery expression, you should see the following results:

```
<name>Tire</name>
<name>Windshield Wiper</name>
```

This XQuery expression may appear to be complex, but it is really easy to understand. The "for" clause sets up a list of parts from the car.xml file. With the part list ready, the "let" clause assigns part names to the **$part_name** variable. Since you only care to see parts in the northeastern region, you set your selection filter in the "where" clause. Inside "order" clause, you decided to sort your output by **$part_name**. Finally, you use "return" to produce your output.

Assign Multiple Values

FLWOR expression has its flexibility. For example, you can have "let" clause first. Also, you can assign multiple variables in the FLWOR expression.

```
let $car_part := (doc("car.xml")//part)
for $part_name in distinct-values($car_part/name),
    $part_color in distinct-values($car_part[name = $part_
name]/color)
order by $part_color
return <inventory name="{$part_name}" color="{$part_color}"
/>
```

When you run this XQuery expression, you should see results like this:

```
<inventory color="Black" name="Windshield Wiper"/>
<inventory color="Black" name="Tire"/>
<inventory color="Light Yellow" name="Engine Oil"/>
<inventory color="Red" name="Break Light"/>
```

You may have noticed "distinct-values" XQuery function. When you use this function, you will get distinct atomic values from the XML data you have selected.

Assign Range

Inside FLWOR expression, you can assign a range of integers to define the number of iterations. The integer range is used in "for" clause. For example, there are eight students in a dancing class. You can easily write the following XQuery to create eight student IDs:

```
for $s in 1 to 8
return <ID>{$s}</ID>
```

When you run this XQuery, you should get the following result:

```
<ID>1</ID>
<ID>2</ID>
<ID>3</ID>
<ID>4</ID>
<ID>5</ID>
<ID>6</ID>
<ID>7</ID>
<ID>8</ID>
```

Reverse Range

You can create a list of student IDs in descending order by using reverse range. To use reverse range, you can simply add "reverse" XQuery function. Our previous example can be modified into:

```
for $s in reverse(1 to 8)
return <ID>{$s}</ID>
```

When you run this XQuery expression, you should see student IDs are now in descending order:

```
<ID>8</ID>
<ID>7</ID>
<ID>6</ID>
<ID>5</ID>
<ID>4</ID>
<ID>3</ID>
<ID>2</ID>
<ID>1</ID>
```

Nested Loop

If you have two instructors teaching the eight-student dancing class, you can create a nested loop in XQuery to assign both instructors to each student. Here is an example of nested loop in XQuery:

```
for $s in reverse(1 to 8)
for $t in ("Johnson", "Schafer")
return <student>Student ID is {$s} and instructor is {$t}</student>
```

After you run this XQuery expression, you should see the following result:

```
<student>Student ID is 8 and instructor is Johnson</student>
<student>Student ID is 8 and instructor is Schafer</student>
<student>Student ID is 7 and instructor is Johnson</student>
<student>Student ID is 7 and instructor is Schafer</student>
<student>Student ID is 6 and instructor is Johnson</student>
<student>Student ID is 6 and instructor is Schafer</student>
<student>Student ID is 5 and instructor is Johnson</student>
<student>Student ID is 5 and instructor is Schafer</student>
```

```
<student>Student ID is 4 and instructor is Johnson</student>
<student>Student ID is 4 and instructor is Schafer</student>
<student>Student ID is 3 and instructor is Johnson</student>
<student>Student ID is 3 and instructor is Schafer</student>
<student>Student ID is 2 and instructor is Johnson</student>
<student>Student ID is 2 and instructor is Schafer</student>
<student>Student ID is 1 and instructor is Johnson</student>
<student>Student ID is 1 and instructor is Schafer</student>
```

Perhaps the most amazing effect of this XQuery expression is to see how fast you can create well-formed XML data. XQuery language can offer outstanding efficiency in working with XML.

Summary

In this chapter, we covered an important XQuery syntax — FLWOR. With this powerful XQuery expression, you can select and filter data. First, we used a simple FLWOR expression to select data from our XML data file. Then, we covered the topic of how to assign multiple values. Finally, we discovered how to use range, reverse range, and nested loops. You can create many variations of FLWOR expressions and they can be very powerful.

7

Joining

When you analyze data from different sources, you will most likely have to join the data. Another most frequently used feature of FLWOR expression is to join data.

Right after midnight on March 24, 1989, the supertanker Exxon Valdez ran aground on Bligh Reef in Prince William Sound, Alaska. Soon, the supertanker spilled 40 million liters of crude oil into the sea and beaches. Among the immediate casualties were 250, 000 sea birds, 2, 800 sea otters, 300 harbor seals, 22 killer whales, and countless fish eggs. It was the largest spill in U.S. waters.

The environmental impact of this oil spill was profound. Prior to the oil spill, there were two identified pods of whales. One of them was comprised of 22 whales before the spill, and after the pod lost all of its females at reproductive age after the spill, the number was dwindled down to seven or eight members. Scientists predicted this pod of whales would soon be extinct.

In this chapter, we will use XQuery to join two XML files: One contains Pacific herring population data in 1988 (prior to the spill); the other one contains Pacific herring population data in 2009 (twenty years after the spill). Please note that our sample data are not actual statistics. More comprehensive data can be obtained from the National Oceanic and Atmospheric Administration.

Two-Way Inner Join

In this section, we will compare the population for Pacific herring between 1988 and 2009 by using inner join with XQuery.

Our 1988 sample XML data look like this:

```
<?xml version="1.0" encoding="UTF-8"?>
<species>
    <specie ID="1001">
        <name>Pacific herring</name>
        <number>12000000</number>
        <unit>tons</unit>
        <year>1988</year>
    </specie>
</species>
```

Our 2009 sample XML data look like this:

```
<?xml version="1.0" encoding="UTF-8"?>
<species>
    <specie ID="1001">
        <name>Pacific herring</name>
        <number>20000</number>
        <unit>tons</unit>
        <year>2009</year>
    </specie>
</species>
```

Figure 7-1

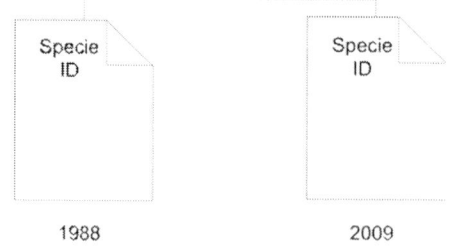

Joining

To join these two sets of data, you can join them with their species ID. Here is our sample XQuery expression for two-way join:

```
for $pre_spill in doc("1988_alaska_data.xml")//specie,
        $post_spill in doc("2009_alaska_data.xml")//
specie[@ID= $pre_spill/@ID]
        return <specie name="{$pre_spill/name}"
                pre_spill_number="{$pre_spill/number}"
                post_spill_number="{$post_spill/number}"
                measure_unit="{$post_spill/unit}" />
```

Two-way join is very common, so let's examine how it works. We first select the species in 1988 data and then we select 2009 data. While selecting the 2009 data, we indicate that the species ID in 2009 data joins with species ID in 1988 data. Then we create the output as we desired. Once you run this XQuery expression, you should see both sets of data are now joined into one:

```
<specie name="Pacific herring" pre_spill_number="12000000"
post_spill_number="20000"measure_unit="tons"/>
```

Three-Way Joins

After analyzing the results of the Pacific herring population, we have the following sample XML data to help us to perform our analysis:

```
<?xml version="1.0" encoding="UTF-8"?>
<species>
    <specie ID="1001">
        <conclusion>decreased</conclusion>
    </specie>
</species>
```

We can join all three files together with three-way joins to show the 1988 data, 2009 data, and conclusion.

```
for $pre_spill in doc("1988_alaska_data.xml")//specie,
    $post_spill in doc("2009_alaska_data.xml")//specie,
    $analysis in doc("alaska_analysis.xml")//specie
where $pre_spill/@ID = $post_spill/@ID and $post_spill/@ID =
$analysis/@ID
return <specie name="{$pre_spill/name}"
        pre_spill_number="{$pre_spill/number}"
        post_spill_number="{$post_spill/number}"
        conclusion="{$analysis/conclusion}"
        measure_unit="{$post_spill/unit}" />
```

In this XQuery expression, we joined three XML files together to get comparison data and conclusion. When you run this XQuery expression, you should see:

```
<specie name="Pacific herring" pre_spill_number="12000000"
post_spill_number="20000"
        conclusion="decreased" measure_unit="tons"/>
```

Perform Outer Joins

When you are joining data together, you can either perform inner joins — only return results that have matches from all joined files, or you can perform outer joins — return all results including the ones don't have matched items in all joined files.

For example, if we have 1988 data for killer whales but a lack of 2009 data, then our 1988 data look like this:

```
<?xml version="1.0" encoding="UTF-8"?>
<species>
    <specie ID="1001">
        <name>Pacific herring</name>
        <number>12000000</number>
        <unit>tons</unit>
        <year>1988</year>
    </specie>
```

Joining

```
<specie ID="1002">
    <name>Killer whales</name>
    <number>24</number>
    <unit>number</unit>
    <year>1988</year>
</specie>
</species>
```

Our 2009 sample XML data is unchanged from previous section. So if we need to get inclusive data from both years, we have to perform outer join. Here is a way you can perform outer join to both XML files:

```
for $pre_spill in doc("1988_alaska_data2.xml")//specie
return <specie name="{$pre_spill/name}" pre_spill_
number="{$pre_spill/number}">
{
    attribute post_spill_number
    {
        for $post_spill in doc("2009_alaska_data2.xml")//
specie
        where $pre_spill/@ID = $post_spill/@ID
        return $post_spill/number
    }
}
</specie>
```

As we expected, this XQuery expression returns both Pacific herring and killer whales:

```
    <specie name="Pacific herring" pre_spill_
number="12000000" post_spill_number="20000"/>
    <specie name="Killer whales" pre_spill_number="24" post_
spill_number=""/>
```

For killer whales, the post-spill number is empty. If you run the inner join XQuery expression, you will only see Pacific herring. So outer join gives you the entire list even though there is no match on the other XML file.

Summary

Joining data from different data sources give us the ability to combine data together. In this chapter, we covered inner joins and outer joins. We also covered three-way joins. If you want to select matched data, you can use inner joins. When you want to see inclusive data regardless if there is a match, then you can use outer joins. With the examples in this chapter, you should be able to create joins in your working environment.

8

Sorting

When there is a large amount of data, you want to sort and organize your XML data to make sense out of it. Using XQuery expressions, you can sort and group data very easily. We are going to use FLWOR expressions and add sorting into them.

Sorting Ascending

The 2008 epidemiology report (created by the CDC and George Washington University School of Health and Health Services) for Washington, D.C., indicates at least 3% of residents in the city have either HIV or AIDS. Public health officials consider anything higher than 1% as a "severe epidemic" and D.C. far surpassed that level. In fact, the rate of infection in D.C. is higher than in West Africa.

Our sample XML data contain some information from the epidemiology report and it looks like this:

```
<?xml version="1.0" encoding="UTF-8"?>
<regions>
    <region ID="DC">
        <disease type="HIV">
            <demographic>Black men</demographic>
            <infected>6304</infected>
```

```
        </disease>
        <disease type="HIV">
            <demographic>Black women</demographic>
            <infected>2520</infected>
        </disease>
        <disease type="HIV">
            <demographic>Hispanic men</demographic>
            <infected>2908</infected>
        </disease>
        <disease type="HIV">
            <demographic>Hispanic women</demographic>
            <infected>679</infected>
        </disease>
        <disease type="HIV">
            <demographic>White men</demographic>
            <infected>2521</infected>
        </disease>
        <disease type="HIV">
            <demographic>White women</demographic>
            <infected>194</infected>
        </disease>
    </region>
</regions>
```

To sort this XML data, you can run the following XQuery expression:

```
for $num in doc("epidemic.xml")//disease[@type="HIV"]
order by xs:integer($num/infected)
return <HIV demographic="{$num/demographic}"
infected="{$num/infected}" />
```

By default, the "order by" clause returns a list in ascending order. So you should see your result looks like this:

```
<HIV infected="194" demographic="White women"/>
<HIV infected="679" demographic="Hispanic women"/>
<HIV infected="2520" demographic="Black women"/>
```

```
<HIV infected="2521" demographic="White men"/>
<HIV infected="2908" demographic="Hispanic men"/>
<HIV infected="6304" demographic="Black men"/>
```

Sorting Descending

If you want to see the demographic group with highest infection rates to be listed first, you can slightly modify your XQuery expression into:

```
for $num in doc("epidemic.xml")//disease[@type="HIV"]
order by xs:integer($num/infected) descending
return <HIV demographic="{$num/demographic}"
infected="{$num/infected}" />
```

Once your sort your data in descending order, you should see your result looks like the following:

```
<HIV infected="6304" demographic="Black men"/>
<HIV infected="2908" demographic="Hispanic men"/>
<HIV infected="2521" demographic="White men"/>
<HIV infected="2520" demographic="Black women"/>
<HIV infected="679" demographic="Hispanic women"/>
<HIV infected="194" demographic="White women"/>
```

The **xs:integer** function simply converts a value into an integer. If we don't use this function, the result will be sorted like a string—which will be incorrect for what we wanted to be shown:

```
<HIV infected="679" demographic="Hispanic women"/>
<HIV infected="6304" demographic="Black men"/>
<HIV infected="2908" demographic="Hispanic men"/>
<HIV infected="2521" demographic="White men"/>
<HIV infected="2520" demographic="Black women"/>
<HIV infected="194" demographic="White women"/>
```

Multiple Sorting

Sometimes, we need to sort our list of data by more than one attribute. It is easy to use an XQuery expression to perform multiple sorting. If we can modify our data a little bit, change "White men" from "2521" to "2520." This means "White men" has the same infected number as "Black women." Now our data look like this:

```
<?xml version="1.0" encoding="UTF-8"?>
<regions>
    <region ID="DC">
        <disease type="HIV">
            <demographic>Black men</demographic>
            <infected>6304</infected>
        </disease>
        <disease type="HIV">
            <demographic>Black women</demographic>
            <infected>2520</infected>
        </disease>
        <disease type="HIV">
            <demographic>Hispanic men</demographic>
            <infected>2908</infected>
        </disease>
        <disease type="HIV">
            <demographic>Hispanic women</demographic>
            <infected>679</infected>
        </disease>
        <disease type="HIV">
            <demographic>White men</demographic>
            <infected>2520</infected>
        </disease>
        <disease type="HIV">
            <demographic>White women</demographic>
            <infected>194</infected>
        </disease>
    </region>
```

```
</regions>
```

We can now try to sort first by number of infected, then by demographic group name. Our XQuery expression looks like this:

```
for $num in doc("epidemic2.xml")//disease[@type="HIV"]
order by $num/infected descending, $num/demographic
return <HIV demographic="{$num/demographic}"
infected="{$num/infected}" />
```

Once we run this XQuery expression, our result looks like this:

```
<HIV infected="679" demographic="Hispanic women"/>
<HIV infected="6304" demographic="Black men"/>
<HIV infected="2908" demographic="Hispanic men"/>
<HIV infected="2520" demographic="Black women"/>
<HIV infected="2520" demographic="White men"/>
<HIV infected="194" demographic="White women"/>
```

Summary

In this chapter, we covered some techniques for sorting. By default, XQuery performs ascending sort. You can change your sort order into descending. Also, you can utilize multiple sort capabilities with XQuery. Sorting and grouping are often used together. Our next chapter covers the topic of grouping.

9

Grouping

To make sense of a large amount of data or objects, we like to group them. In this chapter, we are going to cover the XQuery expressions to help you to perform grouping tasks. Grouping works differently than sorting. To group your XML data, you first select the high level categories you want to group and then select lower level data elements for that category.

Within a typical university, there are professors, students, staff members, offices, departments, and courses. If there are over two hundred courses in the spring semester, students want to able to find the courses easily by departments. Our sample XML data is composed of a list of sample courses from several departments.

Figure 9-1

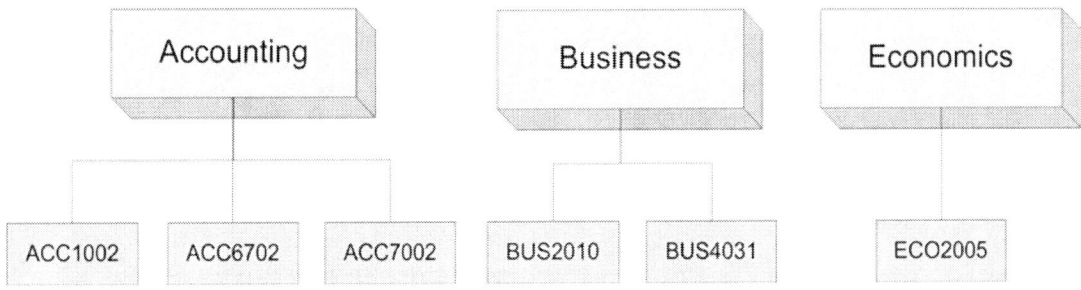

```
<?xml version="1.0" encoding="UTF-8"?>
<courses>
    <course dept="accounting">
        <number>ACC1002</number>
        <title>Principals of Accounting</title>
        <instructor>White, John</instructor>
    </course>
    <course dept="business">
        <number>BUS2010</number>
        <title>Organization Behavior</title>
        <instructor>Smith, Michael</instructor>
    </course>
    <course dept="economics">
        <number>ECO2005</number>
        <title>Microeconomics</title>
        <instructor>Hathaway, Julie</instructor>
    </course>
    <course dept="accounting">
        <number>ACC7002</number>
        <title>Taxation Accounting</title>
        <instructor>Brown, Sonya</instructor>
    </course>
    <course dept="accounting">
        <number>ACC6702</number>
        <title>Auditing</title>
        <instructor>Schafer, Frank</instructor>
    </course>
    <course dept="business">
        <number>BUS4031</number>
        <title>Advance Statistics</title>
        <instructor>Vaugh, Don</instructor>
    </course>
</courses>
```

To group courses into different departments, we can use nested FLWOR expressions such as this one:

Grouping

```
for $department in distinct-values(doc("courses.xml")//
course/@dept)
let $course := doc("courses.xml")//course[@dept =
$department]
order by $department
return <department name="{$department}">
    {
        for $c in $course
        order by $c/number
        return $c
    }</department>
```

If we run this XQuery expression with our sample data, we will see each department is listed separately and courses for that department are listed within.

```
<department name="accounting">
   <course dept="accounting">
        <number>ACC1002</number>
        <title>Principals of Accounting</title>
        <instructor>White, John</instructor>
    </course>
   <course dept="accounting">
        <number>ACC6702</number>
        <title>Auditing</title>
        <instructor>Schafer, Frank</instructor>
    </course>
   <course dept="accounting">
        <number>ACC7002</number>
        <title>Taxation Accounting</title>
        <instructor>Brown, Sonya</instructor>
    </course>
</department>
<department name="business">
   <course dept="business">
        <number>BUS2010</number>
        <title>Organization Behavior</title>
        <instructor>Smith, Michael</instructor>
```

```
    </course>
    <course dept="business">
        <number>BUS4031</number>
        <title>Advance Statistics</title>
        <instructor>Vaugh,  Don</instructor>
    </course>
</department>
<department name="economics">
    <course dept="economics">
        <number>ECO2005</number>
        <title>Microeconomics</title>
        <instructor>Hathaway,  Julie</instructor>
    </course>
</department>
```

The only redundancy in our previous result set is each course still list the name of the department. Sometimes, your may not like to see redundant data. So you can use the following XQuery expression to eliminate such redundancy:

```
for $department in distinct-values(doc("courses.xml")//
course/@dept)
let $course := doc("courses.xml")//course[@dept =
$department]
order by $department
return <department name="{$department}">
    {
        for $c in $course
        order by $c/number
        return <course title="{$c/title}" number="{$c/
number}" instructor="{$c/instructor}" />
    }</department>
```

When you run this XQuery expression, each course is listed without repeating the department information. As you progress along with this book, you can create your own XQuery expressions or modify our examples to get the results you are looking for.

```xml
<?xml version="1.0" encoding="UTF-8"?>
<department name="accounting">
   <course title="Principals of Accounting"
instructor="White,  John" number="ACC1002"/>
   <course title="Auditing" instructor="Schafer,  Frank"
number="ACC6702"/>
   <course title="Taxation Accounting" instructor="Brown,
Sonya" number="ACC7002"/>
</department>
<department name="business">
   <course title="Organization Behavior" instructor="Smith,
Michael" number="BUS2010"/>
   <course title="Advance Statistics" instructor="Vaugh,
Don" number="BUS4031"/>
</department>
<department name="economics">
   <course title="Microeconomics" instructor="Hathaway,
Julie" number="ECO2005"/>
</department>
```

Summary

If you have a SQL background, you may find it is strange how XQuery performs grouping. In XQuery expressions, there is no such thing as "Group By" like it is in SQL. Grouping in XQuery is performed by nested FLWOR expressions—you select the category you want to group with first, and then select the data for each category. This may seems a lot of efforts to perform grouping, but it usually works very well.

10

XQuery and Numbers

We all have to do some counting and calculations at some point of our lives—how much to spend on groceries, how much is a movie ticket, how many students in a class, etc. In this chapter we will use XQuery to work with numbers. There are many kinds of calculations you can perform by using XQuery and we will cover a few important ones. We will also introduce an important concept in XQuery—data type. In this chapter, we will discover some numeric data types.

Let's review our sample XML data file—movies_8.xml first. Inside this file, we have two numbers for each movie: unit price and number of units in stock. Our sample data file looks like this:

```
<?xml version="1.0"?>
<movies>
    <movie ID="1">
        <title>The Aviator</title>
        <release>December 25, 2004</release>
        <genre>Biography|Drama</genre>
        <price>12.95</price>
        <instock>2</instock>
        <plot>A biopic depicting the early years of
legendary director and aviator Howard Hughes' career, from
the late 1920s to the mid-1940s.</plot>
```

```
        </movie>
        <movie ID="2">
                <title>Who Killed the Electric Car?</title>
                <release>August 4, 2006</release>
                <genre>Documentary</genre>
                <price>14.95</price>
                <instock>3</instock>
                <plot>A documentary that investigates the birth
and death of the electric car, as well as the role of
renewable energy and sustainable living in the future.</
plot>
        </movie>
        <movie ID="3">
                <title>The Pursuit of Happiness</title>
                <release>December 16, 2006</release>
                <genre>Biography|Drama</genre>
                <price>19.95</price>
                <instock>1</instock>
                <plot>A struggling salesman takes custody of his
son as he's poised to begin a life-changing professional
endeavor.</plot>
        </movie>
        <movie ID="4">
                <title>Finding Neverland</title>
                <release>November 24, 2004 </release>
                <genre>Biography|Drama|Family</genre>
                <price>12.95</price>
                <instock>2</instock>
                <plot>The story of J.M. Barrie's friendship with a
family who inspired him to create Peter Pan.</plot>
        </movie>
        <movie ID="5">
                <title>Seabiscuit</title>
                <release>July 25, 2003</release>
                <genre>Drama|History|Sport</genre>
                <price>19.95</price>
                <instock>1</instock>
```

```
    <plot>True story of the undersized Depression-era
racehorse whose victories lifted not only the spirits of the
team behind it but also those of their nation.</plot>
    </movie>
</movies>
```

Four Numeric Types

There are four commonly used numeric types in XQuery: **xs:decimal, xs:double, xs:float,** and **xs:integer.** Let's review the basic definitions of each numeric type.

Decimal Type

The xs:decimal numeric type represents a subset of the real numbers that can contain decimal numerals. For example, -21.43 and 678967.5432.

Double Type

The xs:double numeric type represents 64-bit floating-point numbers. The format of xs:double data type is represented by a decimal number, then character E or e with an exponent. For example, 800 is formatted as 8E2, meaning 8×10^2.

 You may also encounter the following values for xs:double: NaN meaning not a number.

Float Type

The xs:float numeric type represents 32-bit floating-point numbers. The format of xs:float data type is represented by a decimal number (mantissa), then character E or e with an exponent. For example, -2E3, 667.43233E6, 62.78e-2, 69, and 0 are all valid float numeric numbers.

You may also encounter the following values for xs:float:
INF meaning infinity.
INF meaning negative infinity.
NaN meaning not a number.

Integer Type

The xs:integer is what you would expect from standard mathematical concept of the integer numbers: 2, 18, 94, -4, etc. No trailing decimals. No letter E or e. One interesting fact is xs:integer is a restricted type of xs:decimal. So anywhere you have a xs:decimal value, you can use xs:integer to trim off the decimal values and leaving you with numeric values with only digits.

Comparison

You can use numeric values for comparisons in your XQuery expressions. You can use either value comparison operator or general comparison operator. There are some differences for using the two types of comparison operators. When you use value comparison operators, every untyped operand will be treated like string.

 It is considered as a good practice by using explicit cast when performing value comparisons to avoid any ambiguity and unexpected results.

Table 10-1. Value Comparison Operators

Value Operators	Meaning
eq	Equal
ne	Not equal
lt	Less than
le	Less than or equal to
gt	Greater than
ge	Greater than or equal to

Table 10-2. General Comparison Operators

Value Operators	Meaning
=	Equal
!=	Not equal
<	Less than
<=	Less than or equal to
>	Greater than
>=	Greater than or equal to

With our movies_8.xml data file ready, you can try to run this XQuery expression to select all the movie titles with movie price greater than $14:

```
for $movie in doc("movies_8.xml")/movies/movie
let $title := $movie/title
where $movie/price >= xs:decimal(14.00)
order by $movie/title
return $title
```

When you run this XQuery expression, you should see the following results:

```
<title>Seabiscuit</title>
<title>The Pursuit of Happiness</title>
<title>Who Killed the Electric Car?</title>
```

Number Function

The previous example, we can use number function in our XQuery expression to indicate that movie price is a numeric value. If we use number function, the value is returned as xs:double by default.

```
for $movie in doc("movies_8.xml")/movies/movie
let $title := $movie/title
where number($movie/price) >= xs:decimal(14.00)
order by $movie/title
```

105

```
return $title
```

Of course, the result is as same as our previous example:

```
<title>Seabiscuit</title>
<title>The Pursuit of Happiness</title>
<title>Who Killed the Electric Car?</title>
```

Also, you can explicit cast the movie price into xs:decimal like this:

```
for $movie in doc("movies_8.xml")/movies/movie
let $title := $movie/title
where xs:decimal($movie/price) >= xs:decimal(14.00)
order by $movie/title
return $title
```

This is the preferred way of performing value comparisons by casting both operands into xs:decimal value type.

Arithmetic Calculations

XQuery supports the arithmetic operators including **+**, **-**, *****, **div**, **idiv**, and **mod**. The + operator adds two operands together. The - operand subtract the second operand from the first one. the * operator multiplies and the **div** operator performs division on any numeric type. The **idiv** operator requires integer arguments, and returns an integer as a result, rounding toward 0. The mod operator provides reminder after dividing the first operand by the second one.

If you want to start a sales event for all your movies, you can multiply your movie price by a discount amount. For example, the following XQuery expression will return movie prices with 30 percent off (70 percent of its original price).

```
for $movie in doc("movies_8.xml")/movies/movie
let $title := $movie/title,
    $sale_price := xs:decimal($movie/price) * .70
```

```
order by $movie/title
return <movie><title>{$title}</title><sale_price>{$sale_
price}</sale_price></movie>
```

When you run the XQuery expression, you should get the following result:

```
<movie>
   <title>
      <title>Finding Neverland</title>
   </title>
   <sale_price>9.065</sale_price>
</movie>
<movie>
   <title>
      <title>Seabiscuit</title>
   </title>
   <sale_price>13.965</sale_price>
</movie>
<movie>
   <title>
      <title>The Aviator</title>
   </title>
   <sale_price>9.065</sale_price>
</movie>
<movie>
   <title>
      <title>The Pursuit of Happiness</title>
   </title>
   <sale_price>13.965</sale_price>
</movie>
<movie>
   <title>
      <title>Who Killed the Electric Car?</title>
   </title>
   <sale_price>10.465</sale_price>
</movie>
```

Summary

In this chapter, we covered four main numeric types in XQuery: double, decimal, float, and integer. Each numeric type has its own format. We also covered how to compare numeric values. Also, we covered how to use the number function. Finally, we reviewed how to perform calculations.

11

XQuery and Strings

Perhaps the most frequently used data type is string. Able to work with string is an essential requirement for almost every programming language including XQuery. In this chapter, we are going to discuss some topics related to string manipulations, construction, and comparison.

Across the country, there are many homeowner associations. Each homeowner association maintains and manages many homes in the community. Our sample data, houses.xml, has a list of houses including association ID, home owner, address, year purchased, and some other information.

```
<?xml version="1.0" encoding="UTF-8"?>
<houses>
    <house>
        <association_id>AW4898</association_id>
        <model>Washington</model>
        <monthly_fee>325.00</monthly_fee>
        <address>2344 Upland Drive,  Springfield</address>
        <owner>Vishnu Mulla</owner>
        <purchased>1988</purchased>
    </house>
    <house>
        <association_id>AQ7322</association_id>
```

```
        <model>Madison</model>
        <monthly_fee>305.00</monthly_fee>
        <address>2348 Upland Drive, Springfield</address>
        <owner>Shazia Zobair</owner>
        <purchased>1992</purchased>
    </house>
    <house>
        <association_id>AW1876</association_id>
        <model>Washington</model>
        <monthly_fee>325.00</monthly_fee>
        <address>1900 Upland Drive, Springfield</address>
        <owner>Sue Zhao</owner>
        <purchased>1982</purchased>
    </house>
    <house>
        <association_id>AQ9003</association_id>
        <model>Madison</model>
        <monthly_fee>305.00</monthly_fee>
        <address>2112 Upland Drive, Springfield</address>
        <owner>Jim McDermott</owner>
        <purchased>1998</purchased>
    </house>
</houses>
```

The basic data type for string is xs:string. You can cast any type of value into xs:string or cast xs:string into other value types. For example, the following XQuery expression converts purchase year into xs:string:

```
for $house in doc("houses.xml")//house
let $house_purchased := xs:string($house/purchased)
order by $house_purchased descending
return <house><purchased>{$house_purchased}</purchased></house>
```

When we run this XQuery expression, we will get back the following results:
```
<house>
```

```
   <purchased>1998</purchased>
</house>
<house>
   <purchased>1992</purchased>
</house>
<house>
   <purchased>1988</purchased>
</house>
<house>
   <purchased>1982</purchased>
</house>
```

String Comparison

Imagine there are two types of house accounts with the homeowner association: accounts with direct deposit for monthly association dues and accounts without direct deposit. For the ones with direct deposit, the association ID starts with "AW" prefix. For accounts without direct deposit setup, the association ID starts with "AQ"prefix. When we want to select house account with direct deposit, we can select the accounts with association ID starts with "AW" prefix. Here is how we can use our XQuery expression to accomplish that:

```
for $house in doc("houses.xml")//house
let $association_id := xs:string($house/association_id),
    $direct_deposit := starts-with($association_id,  "AW")
return <house><ID>{$association_id}</ID>
             <automatic_payment>{$direct_deposit}</
automatic_payment>
       </house>
```

When we run our XQuery expression, we will get each house's association ID and automatic payment setup status:

```
<house>
   <ID>AW4898</ID>
   <automatic_payment>true</automatic_payment>
```

```
</house>
<house>
    <ID>AQ7322</ID>
    <automatic_payment>false</automatic_payment>
</house>
<house>
    <ID>AW1876</ID>
    <automatic_payment>true</automatic_payment>
</house>
<house>
    <ID>AQ9003</ID>
    <automatic_payment>false</automatic_payment>
</house>
```

Alternatively, we can use "match" comparison as well. For example:

```
for $house in doc("houses.xml")//house
let $association_id := xs:string($house/association_id),
    $direct_deposit := matches($association_id,  "AW")
return <house><ID>{$association_id}</ID>
              <automatic_payment>{$direct_deposit}</
automatic_payment>
        </house>
```

We should get back the results that are identical from the previous example:

```
<house>
    <ID>AW4898</ID>
    <automatic_payment>true</automatic_payment>
</house>
<house>
    <ID>AQ7322</ID>
    <automatic_payment>false</automatic_payment>
</house>
<house>
    <ID>AW1876</ID>
    <automatic_payment>true</automatic_payment>
```

```
</house>
<house>
    <ID>AQ9003</ID>
    <automatic_payment>false</automatic_payment>
</house>
```

There are a few other string comparisons you can try them out. They work in the similar fashion as our example. We have listed these string comparisons in table 9-1.

Table 11-1. String Comparison.

Name	Description	Example
compare	Perform comparison between two strings	compare("Wash", "Wash")
contains	Evaluate if one string contains another string	contains("Washington", "Wash")
matches	Evaluate if a string matches a regular expression	matches("Washington", "Wa")
starts-with	Evaluate if a string starts with another string	starts-with("Washington", "Wash")
ends-with	Evaluate if a string ends with another string	ends-with ("Washington", "ton")

As you may have guessed, all the examples from table 9-1 return **true.**

Substring

The **substring** function is available for evaluating a portion of a string. For example, the following XQuery expression takes a substring starting from the third character:

```
for $house in doc("houses.xml")//house
let $association_id := xs:string($house/association_id),
    $direct_deposit := matches($association_id, "AW"),
    $starts_third := substring($association_id, 3)
return <house><ID>{$association_id}</ID>
            <automatic_payment>{$direct_deposit}</
automatic_payment>
```

```
            <four_digits>{$starts_third}</four_digits>
      </house>
```

Once we run the XQuery expression, we should see the following results:

```
<house>
    <ID>AW4898</ID>
    <automatic_payment>true</automatic_payment>
    <four_digits>4898</four_digits>
</house>
<house>
    <ID>AQ7322</ID>
    <automatic_payment>false</automatic_payment>
    <four_digits>7322</four_digits>
</house>
<house>
    <ID>AW1876</ID>
    <automatic_payment>true</automatic_payment>
    <four_digits>1876</four_digits>
</house>
<house>
    <ID>AQ9003</ID>
    <automatic_payment>false</automatic_payment>
    <four_digits>9003</four_digits>
</house>
```

 Please note that the starting position for substring is starting at 1, not 0. This is a key difference with some other programming languages such as C#.

You can also specify the length of substring in your substring function. For example, the following XQuery expression returns 4 characters starting from the third character. The third parameter in the substring function is optional. The result of this XQuery expression is identical to the previous example.

```
for $house in doc("houses.xml")//house
```

```
let $association_id := xs:string($house/association_id),
    $direct_deposit := matches($association_id, "AW"),
    $starts_third := substring($association_id, 3, 4)
return <house><ID>{$association_id}</ID>
              <automatic_payment>{$direct_deposit}</
automatic_payment>
              <four_digits>{$starts_third}</four_digits>
        </house>
```

String Length

If you want to find out the length of a string, you can use **string-length** function. For example, you can use the following XQuery expression to return the length of association ID:

```
for $house in doc("houses.xml")//house
let $association_id := xs:string($house/association_id),
    $account_length := string-length($association_id)
return <house><ID>{$association_id}</ID>
              <ID_Length>{$account_length}</ID_Length>
        </house>
```

When you run the XQuery expression, you should see the following results:

```
<house>
   <ID>AW4898</ID>
   <ID_Length>6</ID_Length>
</house>
<house>
   <ID>AQ7322</ID>
   <ID_Length>6</ID_Length>
</house>
<house>
   <ID>AW1876</ID>
   <ID_Length>6</ID_Length>
</house>
```

```
<house>
   <ID>AQ9003</ID>
   <ID_Length>6</ID_Length>
</house>
```

Concatenating

When you ready to join strings together, you have two choices: **concat** or **string-join**. The following example shows how to use these two XQuery functions:

```
for $house in doc("houses.xml")//house
let $association_id := xs:string($house/association_id),
    $model := xs:string($house/model),
    $id_and_model := concat($association_id,  "-",  $model)
return <house><ID>{$association_id}</ID>
            <ID_Model>{$id_and_model}</ID_Model>
        </house>
```

Or you can use the following XQuery expression:

```
for $house in doc("houses.xml")//house
let $association_id := xs:string($house/association_id),
    $model := xs:string($house/model),
    $id_and_model := string-join(($association_id,  "-",
$model),  "")
return <house><ID>{$association_id}</ID>
            <ID_Model>{$id_and_model}</ID_Model>
        </house>
```

Both XQuery expressions return the following results:

```
<house>
   <ID>AW4898</ID>
   <ID_Model>AW4898-Washington</ID_Model>
</house>
```

```
<house>
   <ID>AQ7322</ID>
   <ID_Model>AQ7322-Madison</ID_Model>
</house>
<house>
   <ID>AW1876</ID>
   <ID_Model>AW1876-Washington</ID_Model>
</house>
<house>
   <ID>AQ9003</ID>
   <ID_Model>AQ9003-Madison</ID_Model>
</house>
```

Splitting

To split a string, you can use **tokenize** function with a regular expression. For example, we can split the house address into two strings: street address and city. Here is how to accomplish this task:

```
for $house in doc("houses.xml")//house
let $association_id := xs:string($house/association_id),
    $address := xs:string($house/address),
    $split_address := tokenize($address, ", ")
return <house><ID>{$association_id}</ID>
            <split_address>{$split_address}</split_
address>
       </house>
```

We will get back the following result:

```
<house>
   <ID>AW4898</ID>
   <split_address>2344 Upland Drive  Springfield</split_
address>
</house>
<house>
```

```
<ID>AQ7322</ID>
<split_address>2348 Upland Drive  Springfield</split_
address>
</house>
<house>
   <ID>AW1876</ID>
   <split_address>1900 Upland Drive  Springfield</split_
address>
</house>
<house>
   <ID>AQ9003</ID>
   <split_address>2112 Upland Drive  Springfield</split_
address>
</house>
```

Replacing

You can use **replace** function to replace portion or entire string with
something else. The replace function has three parameters: the original string,
the pattern, and the replacement string. Since all the houses are located
in Springfield, why don't we leave the city out of the address line? The
following example shows how to use this function to replace "Springfield"
with nothing:

```
for $house in doc("houses.xml")//house
let $association_id := xs:string($house/association_id),
    $address := xs:string($house/address),
    $repalce_address := replace($address,  ",  Springfield",
"")
return <house><ID>{$association_id}</ID>
             <replace_address>{$repalce_address}</replace_
address>
       </house>
```

When we run this XQuery expression, you should see the following results:

```
<house>
```

```
<ID>AW4898</ID>
    <replace_address>2344 Upland Drive</replace_address>
</house>
<house>
    <ID>AQ7322</ID>
    <replace_address>2348 Upland Drive</replace_address>
</house>
<house>
    <ID>AW1876</ID>
    <replace_address>1900 Upland Drive</replace_address>
</house>
<house>
    <ID>AQ9003</ID>
    <replace_address>2112 Upland Drive</replace_address>
</house>
```

Converting

You can convert string in several different flavors. For example, you can convert strings into all upper case or lower case.

Table 11-2. String Coversion

Name	Description
upper-case	Convert string into upper case
lower-case	Convert string into lower case
translate	Replace individual character with other individual character

Summary

In this chapter, we covered the topic of string. First, we introduced xs:string data type. Then we performed string comparison. You can use substring to retrieve a portion of a string and use string-length function to return the length of a string. Finally, we covered the topics of manipulating string including concatenating, splitting, replacing, and converting a string.

12

Navigating through the XML Document

In this chapter, we are going to cover the techniques of navigating through the XML document. Along with XQuery, we can use XPath to help us navigate our XML document to find the element or attribute we are seeking. XPath provides a set of common syntax and semantics for navigating through the hierarchical structure of an XML document.

Our sample document is named courses.xml. Within this document, there is a list of courses for several departments in the university.

```xml
<?xml version="1.0" encoding="UTF-8"?>
<courses>
    <course dept="accounting">
        <number>ACC1002</number>
        <title>Principals of Accounting</title>
        <instructor>White, John</instructor>
    </course>
    <course dept="business">
        <number>BUS2010</number>
        <title>Organization Behavior</title>
        <instructor>Smith, Michael</instructor>
    </course>
    <course dept="economics">
        <number>ECO2005</number>
```

```
        <title>Microeconomics</title>
        <instructor>Hathaway,  Julie</instructor>
    </course>
    <course dept="economics">
        <number>ECO2006</number>
        <title>Macroeconomics</title>
        <instructor>Vargo,  Andrew</instructor>
    </course>
    <course dept="accounting">
        <number>ACC7002</number>
        <title>Taxation Accounting</title>
        <instructor>Brown,  Sonya</instructor>
    </course>
    <course dept="accounting">
        <number>ACC6702</number>
        <title>Auditing</title>
        <instructor>Schafer,  Frank</instructor>
    </course>
    <course dept="business">
        <number>BUS4031</number>
        <title>Advance Statistics</title>
        <instructor>Vaugh,  Don</instructor>
    </course>
</courses>
```

The hierarchical structure of our XML document looks like Figure 10-1.

Figure 12-1

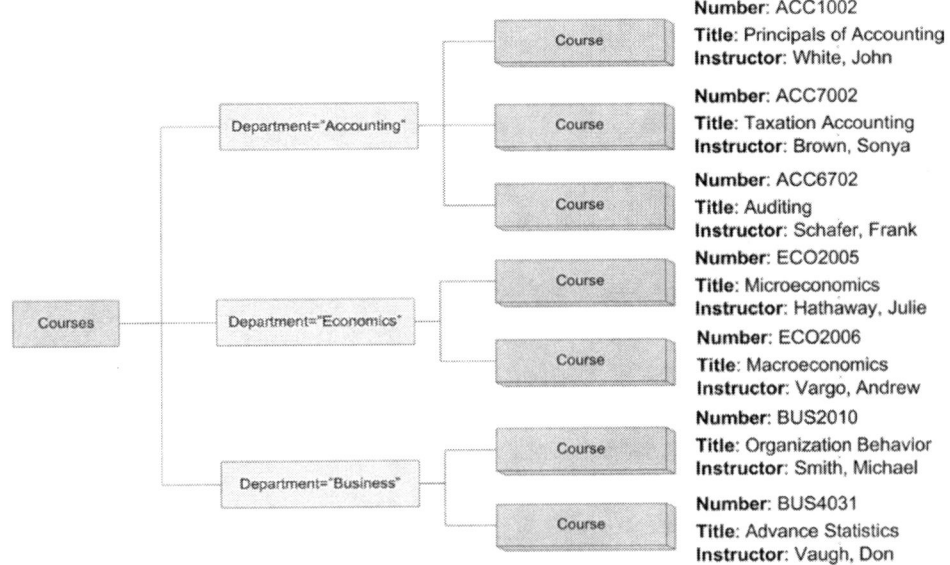

Finding Elements or Attributes

You can consider path expressions as roads leading to your destination. Path expression can be composed of one or many steps. Each step is separated by either a single slash "/" or double slashes "//." There are some differences incurred by using either the single slash or double slashes. Here are some examples:

Select the Outermost Element

Inside our sample XML document, you can find the outermost element is **Courses**. To select courses, you can use the following XQuery expression:

```
doc("courses.xml")/courses
```

When you run this XQuery expression, you should see the entire document displayed.

Select an Element with Precise Path

With the single slash, you can navigate to the exact level within hierarchical structure. For example, you can select a list of course numbers with the following XQuery expression:

```
for $num in doc("courses.xml")/courses/course/number
return $num
```

After you run this XQuery expression, you should see a list of course numbers:

```
<number>ACC1002</number>
<number>BUS2010</number>
<number>ECO2005</number>
<number>ECO2006</number>
<number>ACC7002</number>
<number>ACC6702</number>
<number>BUS4031</number>
```

Select Element Anywhere in the Document

If you want to select an element but don't want to be specific with the path, you can use double slashes. For example, we want to select a list of course titles without specifying the exact path to the titles. You can use the following XQuery expression:

```
for $titles in doc("courses.xml")//title
return $titles
```

When you run this XQuery expression, you should see results that similar to the following output:

```
<title>Principals of Accounting</title>
<title>Organization Behavior</title>
<title>Microeconomics</title>
<title>Macroeconomics</title>
```

```
<title>Taxation Accounting</title>
<title>Auditing</title>
<title>Advance Statistics</title>
```

Select Children

How can we select all children elements? For example, we may want to select all the courses for Accounting department. Here is the XQuery expression you can try:

```
for $acct_courses in doc("courses.xml")/courses/course[@
dept="accounting"]/*
return $acct_courses
```

When you run this XQuery expression, you should see all the courses in the Accounting department:

```
<number>ACC1002</number>
<title>Principals of Accounting</title>
<instructor>White,  John</instructor>

<number>ACC7002</number>
<title>Taxation Accounting</title>
<instructor>Brown,  Sonya</instructor>

<number>ACC6702</number>
<title>Auditing</title>
<instructor>Schafer,  Frank</instructor>
```

Select Grandchildren

To select grandchildren is just as easy as to select children. For example, we can select all the instructors for all the courses. To be clear, we have first generation: Courses, second generation: Individual Course, third generation: Instructor for that course. Here is the XQuery expression you can use:

```
for $instructor in doc("courses.xml")/courses/*/instructor
return $instructor
```

When you run this XQuery expression, you should see a list of instructors:

127

```
<instructor>White,   John</instructor>
<instructor>Smith,   Michael</instructor>
<instructor>Hathaway,   Julie</instructor>
<instructor>Vargo,   Andrew</instructor>
<instructor>Brown,   Sonya</instructor>
<instructor>Schafer,   Frank</instructor>
<instructor>Vaugh,   Don</instructor>
```

Axes

Almost like you are on the dance floor, you can step forward, backward, and side-ways with axis step within the XML document. Axis steps help you locate the element or attribute by using direction and relationships. This concept will make more sense as we move along with examples. Forward step helps you to select nodes after your current context node such as descendent. Reverse step helps you to select nodes prior your current context node such as parent. The table 10-1 lists axes available to use.

Table 12-1. Axes for XQuery.

Axis	Explanation
self::	The current context node
child::	Children of the current context node
descendant::	All types of descendants of the current context node including children and grandchildren
descendant-or-self::	The current context node and its descendant nodes
attribute::	Attributes for the current context node
following::	Nodes that follows the current context node excluding the descendants of the current context node
following-sibling::	All sibling nodes that follows the current context node
parent::	The immediate parent for the current context node
ancestor::	All ancestor nodes for the current context node including parents, grandparents, etc.
ancestor-or-self::	All ancestor nodes and the current context node
preceding::	All nodes that precede the current context node excluding ancestors
preceding-sibling::	All siblings that precede the current context node

The following example shows how to select a list of descendants by using XQuery:

```
for $course_num in doc("courses.xml")/courses/course/
descendant::number
return $course
```

When you run this XQuery, you should see the following results:

```
<number>ACC1002</number>
<number>BUS2010</number>
<number>ECO2005</number>
<number>ECO2006</number>
<number>ACC7002</number>
<number>ACC6702</number>
<number>BUS4031</number>
```

Figure 12-2

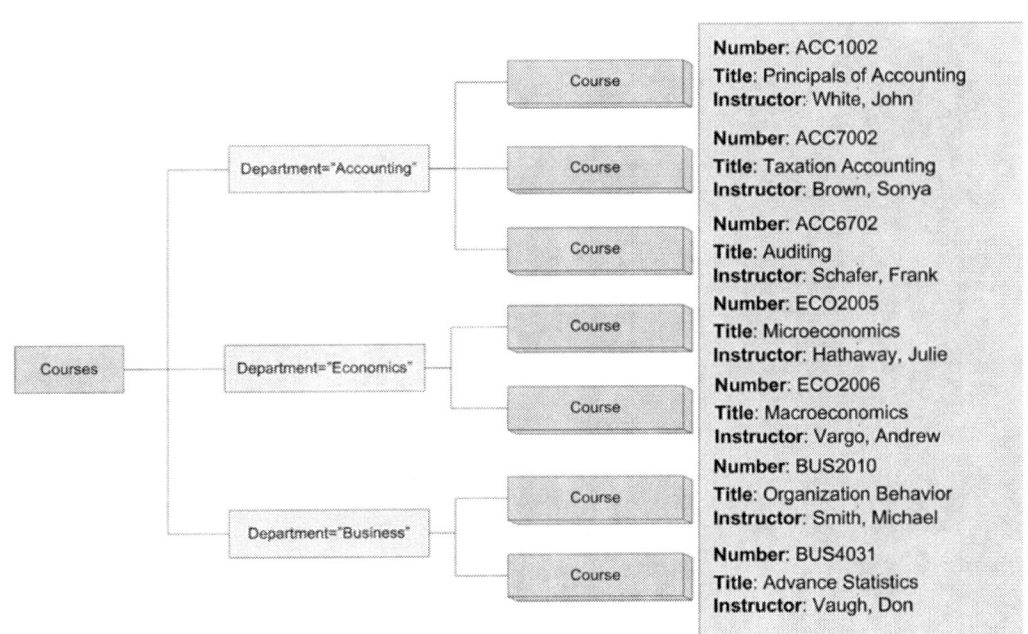

The last example we are going to look at is to select courses for the Economics department. We first select courses in the Economics department, then select the child nodes for this department. You can try the following XQuery:

```
for $course in doc("courses.xml")/courses/course[@
dept="economics"]/child::*
return $course
```

When you run this XQuery expression, you should get:

```
<number>ECO2005</number>
<title>Microeconomics</title>
<instructor>Hathaway, Julie</instructor>
<number>ECO2006</number>
<title>Macroeconomics</title>
<instructor>Vargo, Andrew</instructor>
```

Our illustrated steps are shown in Figure 10-3.

Figure 12-3

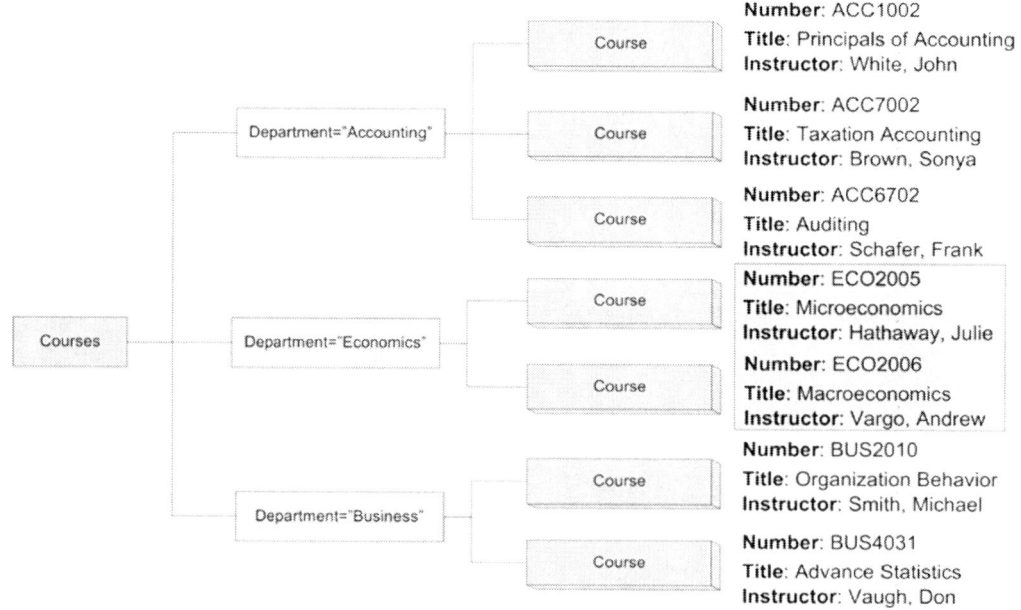

Summary

We discussed several ways of navigating through the XML document throughout this chapter. First, we covered how to select elements or attributes through path expressions. Then we learned how to used axes to select nodes in the hierarchical structure of an XML document. Hopefully, you have learned some techniques by using the examples in this chapter and able to expand more usage into your own XQuery expressions.

13

Types

Some programming language does not care about data types. For example, you can declare data type variant in VBScript. It can store numeric values, strings, and other data types. If you are coming from C# programming background, you know everything in C# is strongly-typed. XQuery is a strongly-typed language. When you retrieve data, call a function, or operator, XQuery is expecting a particular data type. Also, you are required to cast data into appropriate types when working with XQuery. For example, you will encounter an error if you try to divide a numeric value by a string. A strongly-typed language allows programmer or query creator to catch type errors at the design time, instead of run time.

There are occasions when XQuery will attempt to automatically cast the type for you if you have not declared a type. For example, you can send an untyped value to a modulus operator and the processor will attempt to cast the type into numeric value. To be on the safe side, it is a good programming practice to explicitly declare your data type.

Our sample document is named fitness.xml. Within this document, there is a list of fitness sessions offered by a health club. For each fitness session, there is a corresponding session id as attribute and five elements: session name, instructor, time, day, and maximum number of fitness club members can register.

```xml
<?xml version="1.0" encoding="UTF-8"?>
<sessions>
    <session id="1009">
        <name>Spinning</name>
        <instructor>Sandy</instructor>
        <time>7:30 a.m.</time>
        <day>Monday</day>
        <maximum>6</maximum>
    </session>
    <session id="1011">
        <name>Kickboxing</name>
        <instructor>Mike</instructor>
        <time>12:00 p.m.</time>
        <day>Tuesday</day>
        <maximum>12</maximum>
    </session>
    <session id="1015">
        <name>Yoga</name>
        <instructor>Lauren</instructor>
        <time>6:00 p.m.</time>
        <day>Thursday</day>
        <maximum>15</maximum>
    </session>
    <session id="1021">
        <name>Boot Camp</name>
        <instructor>James</instructor>
        <time>6:35 a.m.</time>
        <day>Friday</day>
        <maximum>8</maximum>
    </session>
    <session id="1025">
        <name>Pilates</name>
        <instructor>Lisa</instructor>
        <time>5:00 p.m.</time>
        <day>Wednesday</day>
        <maximum>15</maximum>
    </session>
```

Built-in Types

You can find a wide selection of simple data types that come with XQuery. These atomic types are called built-in types. Regardless you are using schemas to validate your source data or output results, you can freely use any or all of built-in types. At the top level of the type hierarchy, there are nineteen primitive built-in data types. The root of all built-in types are xs:anyAtomicType. You can cast data into this data type, it is a placeholder for other data types.

Figure 13-1.

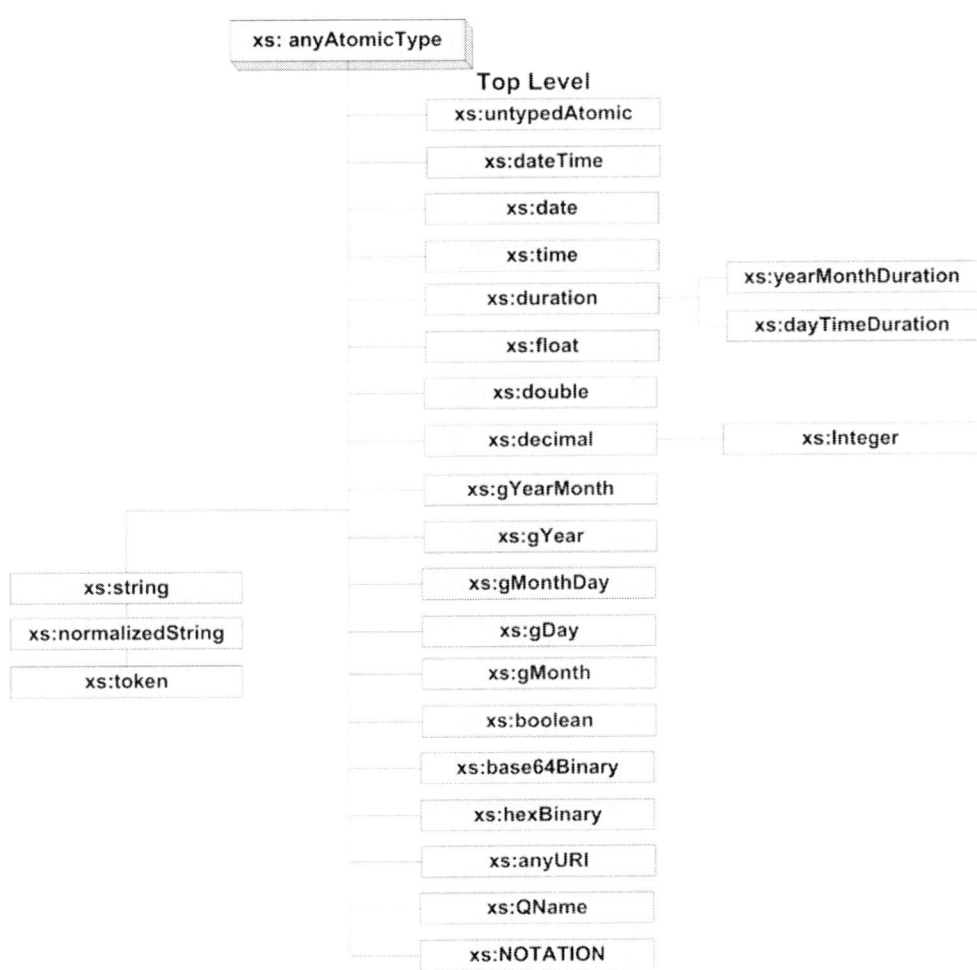

We can use the following XQuery expression to return maximum number of participants from our sample XML data:

```
for $maximum in doc("fitness.xml")/sessions/session/
xs:integer(maximum)
return <maximum_participant>{$maximum}</maximum_participant>
```

When we run this query, you should get the following results:

```
<maximum_participant>6</maximum_participant>
<maximum_participant>12</maximum_participant>
<maximum_participant>15</maximum_participant>
<maximum_participant>8</maximum_participant>
<maximum_participant>15</maximum_participant>
```

To simulate a data type error, you can try the following XQuery expression:

```
for $start in doc("fitness.xml")/sessions/session/
xs:time(time)
return <start>{$start}</start>
```

When you try to run this XQuery, you should get an error similar to this:

```
Invalid time "7:30 a.m." (hour must be two digits)
```

Luckily, we have another version of our XML file called fitness2.xml with starting time correctly formatted. It looks like this:

```
<?xml version="1.0" encoding="UTF-8"?>
<sessions>
    <session id="1009">
        <name>Spinning</name>
        <instructor>Sandy</instructor>
        <time>07:30:00</time>
        <day>Monday</day>
        <maximum>6</maximum>
```

```
        </session>
        <session id="1011">
            <name>Kickboxing</name>
            <instructor>Mike</instructor>
            <time>12:00:00</time>
            <day>Tuesday</day>
            <maximum>12</maximum>
        </session>
        <session id="1015">
            <name>Yoga</name>
            <instructor>Lauren</instructor>
            <time>18:00:00</time>
            <day>Thursday</day>
            <maximum>15</maximum>
        </session>
        <session id="1021">
            <name>Boot Camp</name>
            <instructor>James</instructor>
            <time>06:35:00</time>
            <day>Friday</day>
            <maximum>8</maximum>
        </session>
        <session id="1025">
            <name>Pilates</name>
            <instructor>Lisa</instructor>
            <time>17:00:00</time>
            <day>Wednesday</day>
            <maximum>15</maximum>
        </session>
</sessions>
```

With the following XQuery expression, you should no longer seeing an error:

```
for $start in doc("fitness2.xml")/sessions/session/
xs:time(time)
return <start>{$start}</start>
```

When you run this query, you should see the following results:

```
<start>07:30:00</start>
<start>12:00:00</start>
<start>18:00:00</start>
<start>06:35:00</start>
<start>17:00:00</start>
```

From our examples, you see XQuery is a strongly-typed language and it validates data according to the data type you specified.

Wildcard

Wildcard can be very useful for selecting information from XML file. You can use a wildcard "*" to match any node in an axis for the principal node type. Here are some examples:

/attribute::*
This XQuery expression should return all attribute nodes.

/child::*
     This XQuery expression should return all direct child nodes.

/descendant::*
     This XQuery expression should return all descendant element nodes.

The following XQuery expression tests how the wildcard works:

```
for $num in doc("fitness.xml")/sessions/session/descendant::*
return $num
```

When you run this XQuery expression, you should see all descendant element nodes.

```
<name>Spinning</name>
<instructor>Sandy</instructor>
<time>7:30 a.m.</time>
<day>Monday</day>
<maximum>6</maximum>
<name>Kickboxing</name>
<instructor>Mike</instructor>
<time>12:00 p.m.</time>
<day>Tuesday</day>
<maximum>12</maximum>
<name>Yoga</name>
<instructor>Lauren</instructor>
<time>6:00 p.m.</time>
<day>Thursday</day>
<maximum>15</maximum>
<name>Boot Camp</name>
<instructor>James</instructor>
<time>6:35 a.m.</time>
<day>Friday</day>
<maximum>8</maximum>
<name>Pilates</name>
<instructor>Lisa</instructor>
<time>5:00 p.m.</time>
<day>Wednesday</day>
<maximum>15</maximum>
```

Sequence Types

When you work with XML document, there are occasions you may need to select only certain types of nodes for your requirement. For example, you may only need to select elements or attributes. The following list contains some most common node types you can test in XQuery.

Table 13-1. Sequence Types in XQuery

Type	Description
element()	Matches any XML element
attribute()	Matches any attribute
comment()	Matches any comment
document-node()	Matches any document
text()	Matches any text node
node()	Matches any element, attribute, comment, text, or document
item()	Matches any node() and atomics

 There is another node type binary() that is used for matching BLOBs data. You can only use binary() match test when you work with MarkLogic server.

To understand how to use node test, we can try an example to select all descendant text for all fitness sessions:

```
for $num in doc("fitness.xml")/sessions/session/
descendant::text()
return $num
```

When you run this XQuery expression, you should get the following results:

```
Spinning
Sandy
7:30 a.m.
Monday
6

Kickboxing
Mike
12:00 p.m.
Tuesday
12
```

```
Yoga
Lauren
6:00 p.m.
Thursday
15

Boot Camp
James
6:35 a.m.
Friday
8

Pilates
Lisa
5:00 p.m.
Wednesday
15
```

Summary

In this chapter, we covered some basic information about data types in XQuery. Like many other programming languages such as C#, XQuery is a strongly-typed language. There are nineteen top level data types. In this chapter, we also discussed the wildcard and how to use a wildcard. Finally, we looked at the sequence types in XQuery and how to use them. There is a lot more information on data types and this chapter has barely scratched the surface.

14

Introducing Namespaces

By now, you have learned a lot of useful skills from our previous chapters. In this chapter, we are going to introduce another important part of XML and XQuery—namespaces. If you have worked on other programming languages such as C#, you probably know the importance of namespaces. Don't worry if you have no idea what namespaces mean. The fundamental functions for namespaces are used to clarify the proper root of vocabulary. For example, **path** has different meanings in different vocabularies. Without clearly indicating its namespace, we will introduce ambiguity into our code.

One essential concept to remember is that XML elements and attributes are always associated with a namespace. The World Wide Web Consortium (W3C) provides recommendations and standards for using namespaces. You can find more details from their publication Namespaces in *XML*.

 You can find W3C Namespaces in XML recommendation at: http://www.w3.org/TR/REC-xml-names/

Namespace URI

The process of referencing a namespace is similar to finding a website. You find websites by their corresponding web addresses—URLs. When you reference a namespace, you can use Uniform Resource Identifier (URI). In many cases, you will use a URI in the form of HTTP URL such as:

http://www.marklogic.com/xdmp

If you live on 7382 Walker Lane and your cousin lives on 7382 Wakefield Lane, the street names helps you to distinguish the different locations. The primary reason for using URI is to create a unique namespace that will not cause any confusion. An important fact to know is URI is different from URL. You can type a URL in a web browser and expect a website come up (well, most the time they will). Don't expect the same thing to happen with URI. Attempting to browse to a URI is not a good use of your time. URI is here to create distinction of namespaces. It is not a web address.

There is a special attribute just used for declaring the namespace prefix alias. This special attribute is **xmlns**. You can use an alias for elements and attributes. Once you have declared your alias, you can use your alias for that element and its content. Here is an example:

```
<hsp:hospital  xmlns:hsp="http://www.championwriters.com/
hospital"
                xmlns:rm="http://www.championwriters.com/
room">

        <hsp:name>Inova Alexandria</hsp:name>
        <rm:room>
                <rm:number>2813A</rm:number>
        </rm:room>
</hsp:hospital>
```

From the example above, we declared two namespace prefix aliases: **hsp** and **rm**. The **hsp** prefix alias is mapped to "http://www.championwriters.com/hospital" URI and **rm** prefix alias is mapped to "http://www.championwriters.com/room" URI. When you add **hsp** or **rm** in front of elements or attributes, they help to indicate where the namespaces belong.

Default Namespace

You can create a default namespace. Any element which does not have a prefix will use the default namespace. Perhaps this concept will make more sense if we use an example. The following code segment is different from the previous example to illustrate how to use a default namespace:

```
<hospital xmlns:hsp="http://www.championwriters.com/
hospital">
        <name>Inova Alexandria</name>
        <room>
            <number>2813A</number>
        </room>
</hospital>
```

Since hospital, name, room, and number do not have prefixes, they all belong to the default namespace. Namespace declaration can appear on any element and it is not required for the outermost element. When you have a namespace within another namespace, it can override the outer namespace or the default namespace. This is called "scope." To illustrate how namespace scope works, let's review the following example.

```
<hospital xmlns:hsp="http://www.championwriters.com/
hospital">
        <name>Inova Alexandria</name>
    <room xmlns:rm="http://www.championwriters.com/room">
            <number>2813A</number>
        </room>
</hospital>
```

In this example, we declared two namespaces: **hsp** and **rm**. Since **hsp** is the outer namespace then "name" will belong to the default namespace **hsp**. With inner namespace **rm**, the "number" element uses the **rm** default namespace and the default **hsp** namespace is being overridden.

 Namespace prefix should follow the same rules as XML names. They should start with a certain letter or underscore. Even when prefixes are arbitrary labels with no technical significance; it is a good idea to keep your namespace prefix short, preferably between two to four characters.

Namespaces in XQuery

XQuery element constructors use namespaces just like any other XML. You can use XQuery to process XML documents that contain one or more namespaces or you can use XQuery to produce elements or attributes with one or more namespaces. For XQuery element constructors, you can use namespaces as with the typical XML. The following XQuery expression demonstrates the usage of namespaces like typical XML:

```
let $session := <s:fitness xmlns:s="http://www.
championwriters.com/fit">
                  <s:name>Class Title</s:name>
               </s:fitness>
return $session
```

When you run this XQuery expression, you should see the following results:

```
<s:fitness xmlns:s="http://www.championwriters.com/fit">
   <s:name>Class Title</s:name>
</s:fitness>
```

You can also declare a namespace in the prolog section. This is also the recommended way of declaring namespace:

```
declare namespace s = "http://www.championwriters.com/fit";
let $session := <s:fitness>
                  <s:name>Class Title</s:name>
               </s:fitness>
return $session
```

When you run this XQuery expression, you should get the same result as the previous XQuery expression.

Pre-declared Namespace Prefixes

There are five namespace prefixes that are built into XQuery recommendations.

Introducing Namespaces

They can be freely used anywhere in your XQuery and you don't have to worry about their declaration. As you may have guessed, W3C created these recommendations.

Table 14-1 W3C Recommendations

Prefix	Namespace URI
xml	http://www.w3.org/XML/1998/namespace
xs	http://www.w3.org/2001/XMLSchema
xsi	http://www.w3.org/2001/XMLSchema-instance
fn	http://www.w3.org/2005/xpath-functions
local	http://www.w3.org/2005/xquery-local-functions

Table 14-2 Predefined Namespaces

Prefix	Usage	Namespace URI
cts	MarkLogic Server search functions (Core Text Services)	http://marklogic.com/cts
dav	Used with WebDAV	DAV:
dbg	Debug Built-In functions	http://marklogic.com/xdmp/debug
dir	MarkLogic Server directory XML	http://marklogic.com/xdmp/directory
err	namespace for XQuery and XPath errors	http://www.w3.org/2005/xqt-errors
error	MarkLogic Server error namespace	http://marklogic.com/xdmp/error
fn	XQuery standard function namespace	http://www.w3.org/2005/xpath-functions
local	local namespace for functions defined in main modules	http://www.w3.org/2005/xquery-local-functions
lock	MarkLogic Server locks	http://marklogic.com/xdmp/lock
map	MarkLogic Server maps	http://marklogic.com/xdmp/map
math	math Built-In functions	http://marklogic.com/xdmp/math

prof	profile Built-In functions	http://marklogic.com/xdmp/profile
prop	MarkLogic Server properties	http://marklogic.com/xdmp/property
sec	security Built-In functions	http://marklogic.com/xdmp/security
spell	spelling correction functions	http://marklogic.com/xdmp/spell
xdmp	MarkLogic Server Built-In functions	http://marklogic.com/xdmp
xml	XML namespace	http://www.w3.org/XML/1998/namespace
xmlns	xmlns namespace	http://www.w3.org/2000/xmlns/
xqe	Deprecated MarkLogic Server xqe namespace	http://marklogic.com/xqe
xqterr	XQuery test suite errors (same as err)	http://www.w3.org/2005/xqt-errors
xs	XML Schema namespace	http://www.w3.org/2001/XMLSchema

To see how to work with pre-declared namespaces and your own namespaces, you can try the following XQuery expression:

```
declare namespace s = "http://www.championwriters.com/fit";
let $len := fn:string-length("Champion Writers")
return  <s:length>{$len}</s:length>
```

When you run this XQuery expression, you should see the following result with the length of the string correctly returned without the namespace declaration in the XQuery expression:

```
<s:length xmlns:s="http://www.championwriters.com/fit">16</
s:length>
```

There are other pre-declared namespaces out there—depending on the environment with which you are working.. For example, when you work with MarkLogic XML server, you will have a lot more pre-declared namespaces to use. They provide many useful features. For example, **xdmp** can be used foran application server, and many other features. The Mark Logic pre-declared namespace prefix **cts** can be used for search, query constructors, and classifiers. Also, there are namespace prefixes that can be used for document conversion—

excel (convert to Excel), **msword** (Microsoft Word), **ppt** (PowerPoint), **pdf**, **xhtml**, and cs.

 For more information about Mark Logic pre-declared namespace prefixes, please visit:
http://developer.marklogic.com/pubs/3.1/apidocs/QNameBuiltins.html

Declare Function Namespace

You can use similar syntax to declare functions. When you declare functions, you have to use the keyword function. The following XQuery expression contains namespace declaration for functions:

```
declare default function namespace "http://www.
championwriters.com/functions";
declare namespace s = "http://www.championwriters.com/fit";

let $len := fn:string-length("Champion Writers")
return  <s:length>{$len}</s:length>
```

 It is considered bad programming practice to override the default function namespace. By default, you have functions available automatically from namespace http://www.w3.org/2005/xpath-functions. When you override the default function namespace, you are required to provide a prefix for every function. This includes the most basic functions such as **min** and **max**.

Import Modules

You can create library modules with XQuery and reuse your modules in other places. You can reduce query redundancy and create standardized library modules for all users. To use library modules, you can import modules in your prolog section. Here is an example:

```
import module namespace cw = "http://www.championwriters.
```

```
com/cw" at "http://www.championwriters.com/cw/common.xqy"
```

This import statement maps prefix **cw** to the "http://www.championwriters. com/cw" target module. The location is "http://www.championwriters.com/ cw/common.xqy" and it is right after the keyword **at**.

Summary

For some beginning level XQuery users, namespace can be a challenging topic. In this chapter, we covered some essential knowledge about namespace. In XQuery, namespaces are commonly used to distinguish the root of different vocabularies. There are five pre-declared namespaces that come from W3C recommendation. They are automatically available to you without the need for declaration.

In this chapter, we also covered the topic of how to declare function namespace and how to import modules. Library modules are useful to XQuery users because you can group functions or features into different modules and make them available to all other users. When they are ready to use, all they will need to do is to import these modules into their XQuery.

15

Date and Time

With XQuery, you can perform advanced functions to work with date and time. In this chapter, we are going to start with built-in data types for date and time. Then we will cover functions, time zones, and how to calculate durations.

 The International Standard for the representation of dates and times is ISO 8601. You can find more information at:
http://www.w3.org/TR/NOTE-datetime

Types

There are three built-in types for date and time in XQuery: xs:date, xs:time, and xs:dateTime. The xs:date type contains date information which includes year, month, and day. The xs:time type contains time information that includes hour, minute, and seconds. Also, you can add optional fraction of seconds in three digits. The third type is xs:dateTime which includes date and time information. Here are some examples of using these date and time types.

Table 15-1

Type	Format	Example
xs:date	YYYY-MM-DD	2009-10-11
xs:time	hh:mm:ss.sss	11:35:23, 10:08:33.212
xs:dateTime	YYYY-MM-DDT hh:mm:ss.sss	2010-01-19T08:33:19

Chapter 15

In this chapter, we start with the following XML file that contains several movie show times. The file is named showtime.xml and it contains the following data:

```xml
<?xml version="1.0" encoding="UTF-8"?>
<Showtime>
    <movie>
        <title>
            The Soloist
        </title>
        <date>
            2009-04-25
        </date>
        <time>
            14:10:00
        </time>
        <rating>
            PG-13
        </rating>
    </movie>
    <movie>
        <title>
            Earth
        </title>
        <date>
            2009-04-25
        </date>
        <time>
            11:15:00
        </time>
        <rating>
            NR
        </rating>
    </movie>
    <movie>
        <title>
            Slumdog Millionaire
```

```
        </title>
        <date>
            2009-04-25
        </date>
        <time>
            16:00:00
        </time>
        <rating>
            R
        </rating>
</movie>
<movie>
        <title>
            Hannah Montana: The Movie
        </title>
        <date>
            2009-04-25
        </date>
        <time>
            12:30:00
        </time>
        <rating>
            G
        </rating>
</movie>
<movie>
        <title>
            Monsters vs. Aliens
        </title>
        <date>
            2009-04-25
        </date>
        <time>
            17:35:00
        </time>
        <rating>
            PG
```

```
        </rating>
    </movie>
</Showtime>
```

To see how xs:time data type appears in action, you can create the following XQuery expression and run it against our showtime.xml file:

```
for $movie in doc("showtime.xml")//movie
let $showTime := xs:time($movie/time)
return <movie>{$movie/title}<showtime>{$showTime}</
showtime></movie>
```

When you execute this XQuery, you should get the following results:

```
<movie>
    <title>The Soloist</title>
    <showtime>14:10:00</showtime>
</movie>
<movie>
    <title>Earth</title>
    <showtime>11:15:00</showtime>
</movie>
<movie>
    <title>Slumdog Millionaire</title>
    <showtime>16:00:00</showtime>
</movie>
<movie>
    <title>Hannah Montana: The Movie</title>
    <showtime>12:30:00</showtime>
</movie>
<movie>
    <title>Monsters vs. Aliens</title>
    <showtime>17:35:00</showtime>
</movie>
```

To expand on our previous XQuery expression, you can add another variable with xs:date type to include the date. Here is our sample XQuery expression:

```
for $movie in doc("showtime.xml")//movie
let $showTime := xs:time($movie/time),  $showDate :=
xs:date($movie/date)
return <movie>{$movie/title}
               <date>{$showDate}</date>
               <showtime>{$showTime}</showtime>
        </movie>
```

This time when you run your XQuery expression, you should see both date and time are included in your results:

```
<movie>
    <title>The Soloist</title>
    <date>2009-04-25</date>
    <showtime>14:10:00</showtime>
</movie>
<movie>
    <title>Earth</title>
    <date>2009-04-25</date>
    <showtime>11:15:00</showtime>
</movie>
<movie>
    <title>Slumdog Millionaire</title>
    <date>2009-04-25</date>
    <showtime>16:00:00</showtime>
</movie>
<movie>
    <title>Hannah Montana: The Movie</title>
    <date>2009-04-25</date>
    <showtime>12:30:00</showtime>
</movie>
<movie>
    <title>Monsters vs. Aliens</title>
    <date>2009-04-25</date>
    <showtime>17:35:00</showtime>
</movie>
```

Functions

In addition to data types for date and time, XQuery also has several other available functions. Among them, you can use these functions along with data types in your XQuery expressions.

Table 15-2

Type	Format	Example
current-date	YYYY-MM-DD	2009-12-31
current-time	hh:mm:ss.sss	11:35:23, 10:08:33.212
current-dateTime	YYYY-MM-DDT hh:mm:ss.sss	2010-01-19T08:33:19

The following XQuery expression include the current-dateTime function:

```
for $movie in doc("showtime.xml")//movie
let $showTime := xs:time($movie/time),  $showDate :=
xs:date($movie/date)
return <movie>{$movie/title}
            <date>{$showDate}</date>
            <showtime>{$showTime}</showtime>
            <now>{current-dateTime()}</now>
      </movie>
```

When you run this XQuery expression, you should see results similar to the following:

```
<movie>
   <title>The Soloist</title>
   <date>2009-04-25</date>
   <showtime>14:10:00</showtime>
   <now>2009-04-25T13:06:17.492-04:00</now>
</movie>
<movie>
   <title>Earth</title>
```

```
   <date>2009-04-25</date>
   <showtime>11:15:00</showtime>
   <now>2009-04-25T13:06:17.492-04:00</now>
</movie>
<movie>
   <title>Slumdog Millionaire</title>
   <date>2009-04-25</date>
   <showtime>16:00:00</showtime>
   <now>2009-04-25T13:06:17.492-04:00</now>
</movie>
<movie>
   <title>Hannah Montana: The Movie</title>
   <date>2009-04-25</date>
   <showtime>12:30:00</showtime>
   <now>2009-04-25T13:06:17.492-04:00</now>
</movie>
<movie>
   <title>Monsters vs. Aliens</title>
   <date>2009-04-25</date>
   <showtime>17:35:00</showtime>
   <now>2009-04-25T13:06:17.492-04:00</now>
</movie>
```

Time Zones

XQuery has three functions for adjusting time zones: adjust-date-to-timezone, adjust-time-to-timezone, and adjust-dateTime-to-timezone. When adjusting time zone, it is important to know the baseline time zone is Coordinated Universal Time (UTC). So when you provide a time difference, XQuery assumes it is the deviation from the UTC.

Table 15-3

Type	Example
adjust-date-to-timezone	adjust-date-to-timezone(xs:date("2009-04-25"), xs:dayTimeDuration("-PT6H"))
adjust-time-to-timezone	adjust-time-to-timezone(xs:time("11:00:00"), xs:dayTimeDuration("-PT14H"))
adjust-dateTime-to-timezone	adjust-dateTime-to-timezone(xs:dateTime('2010-02-15T17:00:00'), xs:dayTimeDuration("PT5H"))

You can also use timezone-from-time, timezone-from-date, and timezone-from-dateTime function to figure which time zone is represented. When you use these functions, you have to provide the difference between this time zone and UTC. The following XQuery example shows how to use the function timezone-from-time:

```
for $movie in doc("showtime.xml")//movie
let $showTime := xs:time($movie/time),  $showDate :=
xs:date($movie/date)
return <movie>{$movie/title}
            <date>{$showDate}</date>
            <showtime>{$showTime}</showtime>
            <now>{current-dateTime()}</now>
            <timezone>{timezone-from-
time(xs:time("11:12:33-08:00"))}</timezone>
    </movie>
```

When you run this XQuery expression, you should get results similar to the following:

```
<movie>
    <title>The Soloist</title>
```

```
   <date>2009-04-25</date>
   <showtime>14:10:00</showtime>
   <now>2009-04-25T13:06:17.492-04:00</now>
   <timezone>-PT8H</timezone>
</movie>
<movie>
   <title>Earth</title>
   <date>2009-04-25</date>
   <showtime>11:15:00</showtime>
   <now>2009-04-25T13:06:17.492-04:00</now>
   <timezone>-PT8H</timezone>
</movie>
<movie>
   <title>Slumdog Millionaire</title>
   <date>2009-04-25</date>
   <showtime>16:00:00</showtime>
   <now>2009-04-25T13:06:17.492-04:00</now>
   <timezone>-PT8H</timezone>
</movie>
<movie>
   <title>Hannah Montana: The Movie</title>
   <date>2009-04-25</date>
   <showtime>12:30:00</showtime>
   <now>2009-04-25T13:06:17.492-04:00</now>
   <timezone>-PT8H</timezone>
</movie>
<movie>
   <title>Monsters vs. Aliens</title>
   <date>2009-04-25</date>
   <showtime>17:35:00</showtime>
   <now>2009-04-25T13:06:17.492-04:00</now>
   <timezone>-PT8H</timezone>
</movie>
```

Duration

Another important calculation you may need to perform is to calculate the time difference — duration. There are three types of durations you can use in XQuery: xs:duration, xs:yearMonthDuration, and xs:dayTimeDuration. Before we start using duration types, we have to understand the format of duration types. Duration type xs:duration has an expression which looks like "PnYnMnDTnHnMnS" and is somewhat cryptic. The xs:duration type contains number of years, months, days, hours, minutes, and seconds. The literal "P" indicating the starting point for the expression, and "n" can be replaced by numbers, you probably have guessed the rest — "Y" represents year, "M" represents month, "D" represents day, "T" represents time, "H" represents hour, the "M" after "H" represents minute, and "S" represents second.

Table 15-4

Type	Example
xs:duration	P3Y1M13DT12H21M16S
xs:yearMonthDuration	P1Y2M
xs:dayTimeDuration	P12DT8H23M12.5S

Summary

In this chapter, we started with built-in data types regarding date and time. We covered three data types: xs:date, xs:time, and xs:dateTime. We also introduced some functions such as current-date and current-time. These functions can be useful for date and time related information. Since people live in different time zones, so we also introduced ways to work with time zones in XQuery. Finally, we discussed the benefits of XQuery to calculate time durations.

16

Good XQuery Programming Practice

If you have programmed in other programming languages, you probably already know the importance of good programming practice—it can save you many hours of programming, testing, and maintenance. Since we have focused our efforts on learning many techniques of programming XQuery, it is time for us to discuss some useful tips from our XQuery programming experience. Keep in mind these recommendations and maybe you can develop your own list of best practices.

Iterative Coding

Every long journey starts with the first step. When programming XQuery, it is important to make sure every step is heading in the right direction. If you spend an hour writing lines and lines of XQuery expression without checking on them, it is likely you will have an issue somewhere in your code. Seasoned programmers often code small segments then check each segment before proceeding to the next one. Iterative coding is good practice and you should always consider testing small code segments. When you are ready, you can combine your segments together with a greater level of confidence.

For example, you can start with the simplest code segment first:

```
for $movie in doc("showtime.xml")//movie
return $movie
```

Then you can gradually add more complexity into your XQuery expression until you are satisfied with your output:

```
for $movie in doc("showtime.xml")//movie
let $showTime := xs:time($movie/time),  $showDate :=
xs:date($movie/date)
return <movie>{$movie/title}
                <date>{$showDate}</date>
                <showtime>{$showTime}</showtime>
                <now>{current-dateTime()}</now>
                <timezone>{timezone-from-
time(xs:time("11:12:33-08:00"))}</timezone>
        </movie>
```

Version Control

By now, you have already learned different ways of using XQuery to produce the same output. During your development time, you can make changes to your XQuery expressions frequently. Sometimes, you may want to revert back to a previous version. Many version control tools such as SVN and Visual Source Safe can save you time and effort in the process of switching to different versions.

 There are many flavors of SVN, one of my favorite is TortoiseSVN. You can download it from:
http://tortoisesvn.net/downloads

Here are some key benefits for using version control tools for you and your development team:

- Prevents accidental file loss
- Allows back-tracking to previous versions of code
- Enables user to view and analyze changes from version to version
- Tracks versions of entire projects

Strong Typing

If you want to catch your XQuery errors early, you should consider using strong typing. Writing strongly typed XQuery expressions is usually a good programming practice. For example, if you created a function with an input parameter, you should explicitly declare the data type for the parameter. This is an example of strong typing:

```
declare function get_sku_id ($product_id as xs:string)
```

Another interesting finding from working with XQuery is that text() can return a sequence, instead of a string. For example, the following XQuery expression can return a list of movie titles:

```
xs:string($movies/title)
```

To prevent such accident, you can try the following syntax:

```
String-join($movies/title,  "")
```

White Space and Indentation

You know white spaces and indentations are ignored in XQuery expressions, so feel free to use them to make your code more readable. Consider the following XQuery expression:

```
for $movie in doc("showtime.xml")//movie let $showTime
:= xs:time($movie/time),  $showDate := xs:date($movie/
date) return <movie>{$movie/title} <date>{$showDate}</date>
<showtime>{$showTime}</showtime> <now>{current-dateTime()}</
now> <timezone>{timezone-from-time(xs:time("11:12:33-
08:00"))}</timezone> </movie>
```

I am sure you would rather read the following XQuery expression instead:

```
for $movie in doc("showtime.xml")//movie
```

167

```
let $showTime := xs:time($movie/time),  $showDate :=
xs:date($movie/date)
return <movie>{$movie/title}
            <date>{$showDate}</date>
            <showtime>{$showTime}</showtime>
            <now>{current-dateTime()}</now>
            <timezone>{timezone-from-
time(xs:time("11:12:33-08:00"))}</timezone>
        </movie>
```

It is obvious white spaces and indentations can be immensely helpful.

Summary

In this chapter, we covered a few good programming practices for working with XQuery. You can always develop your own set of good programming practices as you gain more experience. We started with iterative coding style so you can produce small, manageable code segments and test them often. Then we discussed the importance of version control and how it can benefit developers and the development team.

Throughout this book, we covered several different data types and found that strong typing is also a good practice to help you catch errors early. Finally, we emphasized the usefulness of white spaces and indentations. With the knowledge you learned from this and previous chapters you will further advance your XQuery skills to improve your own programming.

PART III

17

Introducing MarkLogic Search

Helping you to find the information you are looking for can be a complex programming challenge. Many of us have found that websites or even search engines deliver many irrelevant search results. In this chapter, we are going to introduce MarkLogic Search. First, we will discuss how MarkLogic server determines relevance. Then we introduce the basic information about stemmed search. Each word has its stem and stemmed search is a default behavior for MarkLogic server. You can change this setting to fit your environment. There are two types of wildcards that you can use, both of them can be used more than once in a single search phrase.

Many users expect search results and the number of results from the search. In this chapter, we cover three counting methods: count, estimate, and remainder. Count is accurate but slower. Estimate is faster but not exact. Remainder can be used for search and counting the results at the same time.

Finally, we will cover highlight and contains functions. You can search and highlight your results when there is a match. Also, you can use the contains function to test whether there is a match.

Relevance

When users provide search input, they are looking for results that are relevant to their search conditions, therefor relevance is important. With MarkLogic, relevance is calculated as a percentage score. Results are ranked from the collection of items that meet the search condition.

First, appearance frequency counts. If a search phrase "labor law" appears 17 times in the text fragment and on average appears 6 times across full document set, then it receives a higher score. When a term appears more frequently than average in the text, MarkLogic thinks it is more relevant.

Second, when the text fragment is smaller, it scores higher. If a search phrase appears 17 times in a 500-word text fragment and appears 17 times in an 800-word fragment, the 500-word text fragment gets higher score.

To start your MarkLogic search process, you can use **cts:search** function. As you may remember from our previous chapters, **cts** prefix is usually used for MarkLogic search functions. Here is an example of how to use **cts:search:**

```
cts:search(//movies/title, "Mama Mia")
```

Inside the search function, we first pass the XPath statement, and then we add a search phrase. When you run this XQuery against your XML data, you should get a sequenced list of elements that are relevant to your search query.

You can also ask MarkLogic to return the top ten most relevant results by using XQuery syntax like this:

```
cts:search(//movies/title, "Mama Mia") [1 to 10]
```

If you are interested to see the actual ranking score of your returned relevant results, you can try the following XQuery expression:

```
for $movie in cts:search(//movies/title, "Mama Mia") [1 to 10]
return <result score="{ xdmp:score($movie) }">{ $movie
}</result>
```

 For more information about search, please reference:
http://developer.marklogic.com/howto/tutorials/technical-overview.
xqy#searching

Stemmed Search

By default, MarkLogic Server has enabled stemmed search. Each word has its roots—stems. With stemmed search, you can get results back based on the stems of words, not just the words themselves. For example, the following words are all have the stem: forget.

--forgetting
--forgot
--forgotten

Figure 17-1. Stemmed Search

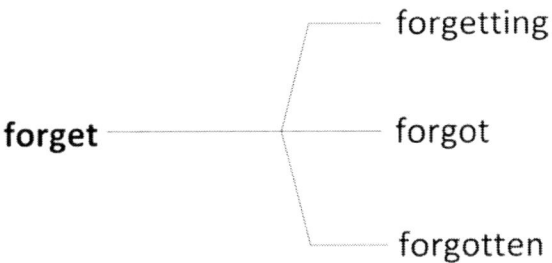

With stemmed search, your search term is compared with stems instead of exact words. In many cases, this can bring back better, more relevant results. If you feel stemmed search is not suitable for your local environment, you can turn this option off and only perform word search. There are three stemmed search options on MarkLogic Server: basic, advanced, and decompounding. Basic stem means each word indexed to one stem. This is the default behavior on MarkLogic Server. Advanced stem means each word indexed to one or multiple stems. The decompounding option means each word is indexed to one or multiple stems and each component of the words is also indexed.

Wildcard Search

There are two wildcards you can use: "*" (asterisk) and "?" (question mark). You can use "*" to match zero or multiple non-space characters. For example, "for*" will match the following words:

--for
--foreign
--form
--formidable
--foresight

You can use "?" to match exactly one non-space character. For example, the search phrase "?old" will match words with any single character followed by "old":

--cold
--bold
--sold
--mold
--gold

You can use more than one wildcards in your search string. For example, "??mp" will match words with any two leading characters and ends with "mp":

--lamp
--dump
--hump
--ramp
--limp

Figure 17-2. Wildcard Search

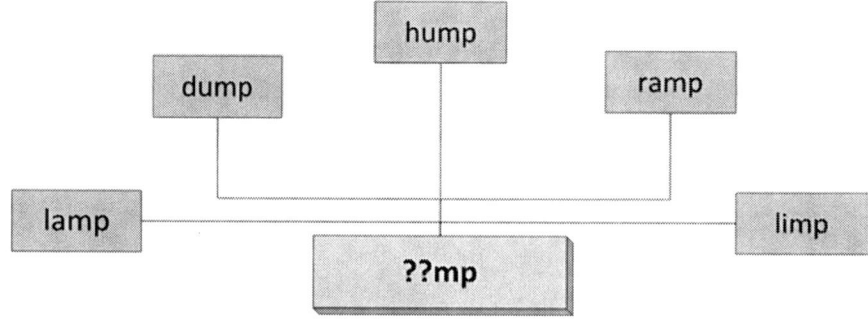

Wildcard search

Cou nt, Estimate, and Remainder

Sometimes you may need to know how many items there are in the result set or in a sequence. For example, you may want to know how many articles are available that contain your search phrase. There are three functions you can use to get this kind of statistic: fn:count, xdmp:estimate, and cts:remainder. Each of these functions has its characteristics so we will start with fn:count.

Count

If you need to get the exact number of how many items are in your result set or in a sequence, you can use fn:count function. The obvious benefit of using fn:count is that you will get the accurate number. The disadvantage of using fn:count is performance—it has to process data directly in order to get the results.

 Some MarkLogic programmer created a double counting logic, once for search, another time for counting the result of that search. This kind of approach can be expensive, especially when MarkLogic Server is busy serving other requests. Understanding the performance issue for fn:count is essential.

Estimate

When you don't need the exact number of how many items are in your result set or in a sequence, you should consider use xdmp:estimate. The obvious benefit for using xdmp:estimate is speed. Instead of counting each item, this function uses a more efficient way to return approximate value. You should expect very similar results between using fn:count and xdmp:estimate when working with indexed values. The results can have greater degrees of variation when working with different types of result sets or data types. So while fn:count is accurate the xdmp:estimate is faster.

Remainder

To avoid the double counting logic with fn:count in your search results, you should consider using cts:remainder. You can use cts:remainder to perform the search and counting the search results at the same time. This is ideal for obtaining search results and the count of your search results. If your website has several thousands of searches daily, the performance gain of using cts:remainder can add up quickly—faster searches and better response time.

 If your only goal to obtain the total number of your result set or a sequence, then xdmp:estimate is your better choice. Only use cts:remainder for situations when you need to perform search and get the total number of results from your search.

Highlight and Contains

When you are trying to search a block of text or a keyword, you may like to see your matched results highlighted. The cts:highlight function can be used to test and/or highlight the matching results. For example, the following XQuery expression should return movie titles matches search phrase "Electric Car."

```
let $movie := doc("movie.xml")
return cts:highlight($movie, "Electric Car",
<title>{$cts:text}</title>)
```

Another function you can consider to use is cts:contains. This function is useful when you try to evaluate and see if the word or phrase matches your query keyword. When a match is found, this function will return true, otherwise it will return false.

Summary

In this chapter, we introduced some MarkLogic search functions. When users perform search, they want to see the most relevant findings first. Luckily, MarkLogic Server already has some serious considerations for helping users. The key concepts behind relevance are frequency and fragment. When a word is found more times in one document than the other, the more frequent one has higher chance of being more relevant. When a keyword shows up in smaller fragments, it means that keyword has higher density in the document. This also contributes to higher chances of being more relevant.

We also covered stemmed search. Knowing stemmed search will help you to understand your search results. We also introduced wildcard search and two types of wildcards you can use. Then we discussed three counting functions: count, estimate, and remainder. Count is accurate, estimate is fast, and remainder can be a great candidate when you need to search and count at the same time. Finally, we covered highlights and contains. You can use these two functions to highlight and test your matched keywords.

18

Introducing Thesaurus

The thesauru functions is one of the reasons that makes MarkLogic Server search powerful. When users are searching the term operating systems, then the search results should return *Windows Server 2008, UNIX, Linux, Mac OS, and Solaris.* This has become typical expectation from users when they perform searches to see that the search engine not only matches the search phrase but is also intelligent enough to bring back results with synonyms.

You can load your own thesaurus documents onto the MarkLogic Server with your own thesaurus entries. Since each organization has its own vocabulary, you can use thesaurus functions to create a stunning, powerful website with MarkLogic that helps user to find relevant information quickly.

Figure 18-1

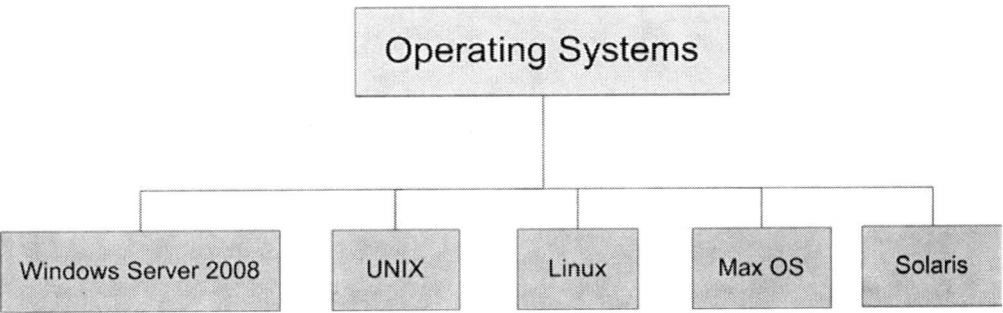

Please note that thesaurus is case-sensitive by default. So "Hello" is not the same as "hello" and it is not the same as "HELLO." In many cases this is a desired behavior. If your environment requires case-insensitive, then you can add case variation of words into thesaurus document. Another option is to convert user input into all lower case (or all upper case) and then add all lower case (or all upper case) words into your thesaurus document.

You can create and manage thesaurus documents on MarkLogic Server so your synonyms will be best suited for your specific environment and return relevant results for users. In this chapter, we will cover some basic functions of using thesaurus. First, we will discuss how to add and delete a thesaurus entry in the thesaurus document. Then, we will cover how to load a thesaurus document onto your MarkLogic Server.

Using Thesaurus

When you are ready to use any thesaurus functions in your XQuery, the first thing is to include its namespace declaration at your prolog section. Functions for thesaurus are using **thsr**: prefix. Here is an example of thesaurus namespace declaration:

```
import module namespace thsr="http://marklogic.com/
xdmp/thesaurus" at "/MarkLogic/thesaurus.xqy";
```

With your MarkLogic Server installed, you can find your thesaurus functions in the thesaurus.xqy module file. The path to this file is usually located at:

```
[MarkLogic_install_directory]/Modules/MarkLogic/
thesaurus.xqy
```

Depending on your installation path for MarkLogic Server, you can replace [MarkLogic_install_directory] with your actual MarkLogic Server installation directory.

For your own MarkLogic Server, you can have one or multiple thesaurus documents to serve your needs. To make sure a thesaurus document is valid, you should first check the thesaurus schema. Every thesaurus document must conform with this thesaurus schema. You can find your thesaurus schema file at the following default location:

```
[MarkLogic_install_directory]/config/thesaurus.xsd
```

 For more information on thesaurus functions, you can visit:
http://developer.marklogic.com

Adding a Thesaurus Entry

Adding a new thesaurus entry is a very straightforward process. Suppose your thesaurus document is named as "synonym.xml" and it is located inside the "references" directory. The URI for your thesaurus document is: "references/synonym.xml" and here is how to add an entry:

```
xquery version "1.0-ml";
Import module namespace thsr="http://marklogic.com/xdmp/
thesaurus" at "/MarkLogic/thesaurus.xqy";

thsr:set-entry("references/synonym.xml",
<entry xmlns="http://marklogic.com/xdmp/thesaurus">
    <term>Operating Systems</term>
    <synonym>
        <term>Windows Server 2008</term>
        <part-of-speech>noun</part-of-speech>
    </synonym>
    <synonym>
        <term>UNIX</term>
        <part-of-speech>noun</part-of-speech>
    </synonym>
    <synonym>
        <term>Linux</term>
        <part-of-speech>noun</part-of-speech>
    </synonym>
    <synonym>
```

```
        <term>Mac OS</term>
        <part-of-speech>noun</part-of-speech>
    </synonym>
    <synonym>
        <term>Solaris</term>
        <part-of-speech>noun</part-of-speech>
    </synonym>
</entry>)
```

Deleting a Thesaurus Entry

Deleting a thesaurus entry is also a simple process. If you have multiple instances of a term in the thesaurus document, then you can either delete all instances or delete a particular instance. For example, if we only have one entry for the term "Operating Systems" then deleting all instances is as same as deleting one instance. Here is the XQuery syntax to delete all instances of a term:

```
xquery version "1.0-ml";
Import module namespace thsr="http://marklogic.com/xdmp/
thesaurus" at "/MarkLogic/thesaurus.xqy";

thsr:remove-term("references/synonym.xml", "Operating
Systems")
```

If you want to delete just an instance out of multiple instance of a thesaurus entry, then you can use the same syntax above and add the instance index. For example the following syntax deletes the second instance of the term "Operating Systems":

```
xquery version "1.0-ml";
Import module namespace thsr="http://marklogic.com/xdmp/
thesaurus" at "/MarkLogic/thesaurus.xqy";

thsr:remove-term("references/synonym.xml", "Operating
Systems"[2])
```

There are many thesaurus functions available worth exploring. Here are some important ones: thsr:set-entry, thsr:add-synonym, thsr:remove-entry, thsr:remove-term, thsr:remove-synonym.

Thesaurus Document

There are two functions you can use to load a thesaurus document: **thsr:load** and **thsr:insert**. Since loading a large document can take some time and is sometimes too large to fit into in-memory list, you can divide your thesaurus document into multiple documents. Suppose you have a thesaurus document in your local directory that needs to be loaded, here is an example of how to load a thesaurus document:

```
xquery version "1.0-ml";
Import module namespace thsr="http://marklogic.com/xdmp/
thesaurus" at "/MarkLogic/thesaurus.xqy";

thsr:set-entry("c:\my documents\synonym.xml", "/references/
synonym.xml")
```

If there is already a synonym.xml that exists in the same directory on the MarkLogic server, then that will be overwritten by this file. If this is not your intention, you can first check and see if the same file exists. If there is already a document with the same name, you can rename your document and then load the renamed document.

 By default, the security setting for any thesaurus document corresponds to the user who is loading the thesaurus document. If that user's rights and privileges prevent reading or updating, then the permission must be modified. You can add a function call **xdmp:document-set-permissions** after the **thsr:load** operation.

Summary

In this chapter, we covered how to use thesaurus. MarkLogic Server empowers user to create new thesaurus entries and add new thesaurus documents. With these thesaurus functionalities, you can continuously build your thesaurus list that is best suited for your organization and provide your website visitors useful information they are seeking.

19

Introducing Lexicons

We all work in different types of organizations—commercial, non-profit, government, and others. Also, we all work in different industries such as manufacturing, education, graphic design, printing, software, healthcare, and military. So when MarkLogic server is being implemented into your specific environment, you will want to make it intelligent—knowing the specific vocabularies of your industry will help the user find the information they are seeking by understanding the real meanings of their keywords, and providing auto-completion features when users start to type some popular terms. User's will appreciate the usefulness and friendliness of your website with these features of MarkLogic.

Lexicons have been introduced since the MarkLogic Server 3.1 version. In a high-level, lexicons are a special type of dictionary that you can create for your MarkLogic Server. There are two types of lexicons: word lexicons and value lexicons. With proper use of lexicons, you can make your MarkLogic Server powerful and useful.

Word lexicons are dictionaries of word tokens. They are unique and case-sensitive. You can use word lexicons throughout a MarkLogic database. Also, you can use word lexicons in an element or an attribute defined by a QName.

Value lexicons are dictionaries of unique values. You can use value lexicons for a specific element or attribute with QName. There are many types of value lexicons: *value co-occurrences lexicon, geospatial lexicon, range lexicon, URI lexicon, and collection lexicon.*

Imagine you are search a pair of words in a specific range of a document, you can use *value co-occurrences lexicon* to help narrow down the scope and the words you are looking for. You can constrain your results to documents, directories, search results, collections, or any combination of these possible segments on MarkLogic Server. This can be very powerful.

When you want to associate a set of geospatial values with a geospatial index, you can use *geospatial lexicon*. As its name implies, *range lexicon stores* a range of values such as 1000 to 9999. URI lexicons store URIs for a given set of documents in the MarkLogic database. Finally, *collection lexicon* can be used to store collections in a database.

All lexicons share the following characteristics: they are unstemmed, case-sensitive, and diacritic-oriented. Word lexicons do not include any punctuation, value lexicons do.

Enable Lexicons

To start using lexicons, you should enable lexicon settings first. You can enable lexicons from the administration interface. If your MarkLogic database has no data, you can create and enable lexicon, then load your data. If you already have data in your MarkLogic database, you can create and enable lexicon, then reindex your database. Another option is to create and enable lexicon, then reload your data.

To create a word lexicon, you can click on the lexicon setting from your database administration interface. You can supply namespace URI, localname, and collation. To create an element value lexicon or element attribute value lexicon, you can specify element and attribute namespace URIs, localnames, the collation, and data type.

 For more information on how to setup lexicons on your MarkLogic Server, please review Administrator's Guide on http://developer.marklogic.com.

Figure 19-1 Enable Lexicons

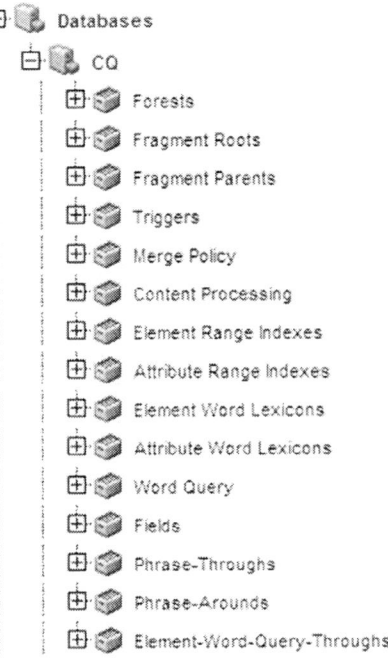

Lexicons

In this section, we are going to cover different types of lexicons. As we have discussed earlier, there are *word lexicons, value lexicons for element or attribute, value co-occurrences lexicon, geospatial lexicon, range lexicon, URI lexicon, and collection lexicon.*

 To use these lexicons, you should enable lexicons first. Otherwise, MarkLogic Server will throw exceptions.

Word Lexicon

One thing to keep in mind is that word lexicon spans across the entire database. You can use cts:words to return words from the word lexicon or use cts:word-match to return words from word lexicon that matches the supplied wildcard pattern.

For example, you can use the following XQuery expression to look for word "defense" in your MarkLogic database:

```
cts:word("defense")
```

Table 19-1

Function	Definition
cts:words	Returns words from the word lexicon.
cts:words-match	Returns words from the word lexicon that match the wildcard pattern.

Value Lexicon for Element or Element-Attribute

You can use element value lexicon or element-attribute lexicon to match values with specific elements or attributes. The following table shows a list of functions for this type of lexicon.

Table 19-2

Function	Definition
cts:element-values	Returns values from the specified element value lexicon(s).
cts:element-value-match	Returns values from the specified element value lexicon(s) that match the specified wildcard pattern.
cts:element-attribute-values	Returns values from the specified element-attribute value lexicon(s).
cts:element-attribute-value-match	Returns values from the specified element-attribute value lexicon(s) that match the specified wildcard pattern.

Value Co-occurrences Lexicon

When you are looking to find a value-element or value-attribute pair in a specific MarkLogic segment, you can use value co-occurrence lexicon. A MarkLogic segment can be documents, directories, search results, collections, or any combination of them. The following table shows a list of functions for this type of lexicon.

Table 19-3

Function	Definition
cts:element-value-co-occurrences	Returns value co-occurrences (that is, pairs of values, both of which appear in the same fragment) from the specified element value lexicon(s).
cts:element-attribute-value-co-occurences	Returns value co-occurrences from the specified element or element-attribute value lexicon(s).

Using value co-occurrence lexicon can help you find patterns from your data. This can enhance your analysis and provide you insights. For example, we can find co-occurrences between flu and regions having the flu by using the XQuery expression below:

```
xquery version "1.0-ml";
declare namespace e="http://marklogic.com/entity"

cts:element-value-co-occurrences(xs:QName("e:flu"), xs:QName("e:region"))
```

Geospatial Lexicon

There are a lot of functionalities for geospatial lexicons. You may remember from chapter one that we introduced geospatial boxes. You can provide ranges or values when working with geospatial lexicon. The following table shows a list of functions for this type of lexicon.

Table 19-4

Function	Definition
cts:element-attribute-pair-geospatial-boxes	Returns boxes derived from the specified element point lexicon(s).
cts:element-attribute-pair-geospatial-value-match	Returns values from the specified element attribute pair geospatial value lexicon(s) that match the specified wildcard pattern.
cts:element-attribute-pair-geospatial-values	Returns values from the specified element-attribute-pair geospatial value lexicon(s).
cts:element-attribute-value-geospatial-co-occurrences	Returns value co-occurrences from the specified element-attribute value lexicon with the specified geospatial lexicon.
cts:element-child-geospatial-boxes	Returns boxes derived from the specified element point lexicon(s).
cts:element-child-geospatial-value-match	Returns values from the specified element child geospatial value lexicon(s) that match the specified wildcard pattern.
cts:element-child-geospatial-values	Returns values from the specified element-child geospatial value lexicon(s).
cts:element-geospatial-boxes	Returns boxes derived from the specified element point lexicon(s).
cts:element-geospatial-value-match	Returns values from the specified element geospatial value lexicon(s) that match the specified wildcard pattern.
cts:element-geospatial-values	Returns values from the specified element geospatial value lexicon(s).
cts:element-pair-geospatial-boxes	Returns boxes derived from the specified element point lexicon(s).
cts:element-pair-geospatial-value-match	Returns values from the specified element pair geospatial value lexicon(s) that match the specified wildcard pattern.

cts:element-pair-geospatial-values	Returns values from the specified element-pair geospatial value lexicon(s).
cts:element-value-geospatial-co-occurrences	Returns value co-occurrences from the specified element value lexicon with the specified geospatial lexicon.
cts:geospatial-co-occurrences	Returns value co-occurrences from the geospatial lexicons.

Range Lexicon

You can use the range lexicon to select values within limits. The following table shows a list of functions for this type of lexicon.

Table 19-5

Function	Definition
cts:element-attribute-value-ranges	Returns value ranges from the specified element-attribute value lexicon(s).
cts:element-value-ranges	Returns value ranges from the specified element value lexicon(s).

URI Lexicon

The URI lexicon provides a summary list of document URIs in a given MarkLogic database. The following table shows a list of functions for this type of lexicon.

Table 19-6

Function	Definition
cts:uri-match	Returns values from the URI lexicon that match the specified wildcard pattern.
cts:uris	Returns values from the URI lexicon.

Collection Lexicon

The collection lexicon provides a list of collection URIs in a given MarkLogic database. The following table shows a list of functions for this type of lexicon.

Table 19-7

Function	Definition
cts:collection-match	Returns values from the collection lexicon that match the specified wildcard pattern.
cts:collections	Returns values from the collection lexicon.

Summary

In this chapter, we introduced lexicons. This is a new feature since the MarkLogic 3.1 version. With lexicons, you can discover relationships between data and gain insights with your data. This is one of reasons MarkLogic Server is so powerful while working with XML data.

We started this chapter with some basic information about lexicon. Then we discussed how to enable lexicon features on your MarkLogic database. Once your lexicon feature is enabled, you can use different types of lexicons. We introduced word lexicons and values lexicons. There are many types of value lexicons: *value co-occurrences lexicon, geospatial lexicon, range lexicon, URI lexicon, and collection lexicon.*

20

Spelling Functions

Over the years, more and more applications began to offer spelling functions—from web-based email clients to mobile applications. In this chapter, we are going to cover spelling functions in MarkLogic. You can create your own dictionary in MarkLogic and use your dictionary to help the user perform spell checks. When the user enters words that are not found in the dictionary, then you can create an application to alert the user that the words might spelled incorrectly. What spell check programs cannot detect however, is a word spelled correctly but being used in the wrong context.

Also, we are going to discuss how to suggest words to the user, how to create a dictionary document, and how to load the dictionary document to your MarkLogic Server.

Dictionary

By default, the MarkLogic sever will install the dictionary in the modules database. The dictionary is an XQuery file named spell.xqy and here is its typical location:

[MarkLogic_Install_Directory]/Modules/MarkLogic/spell.xqy

The *[MarkLogic_Install_Directory]* is the installation path for your MarkLogic Server.

New words are created each day for different fields and industries. For example, most programmers had not heard of "Silverlight" and "Expression Blend" as new web presentation technologies before 2007. You can add your own dictionary documents to MarkLogic Server with more words in addition to the default dictionary. Here is the required structure of your dictionary document:

```
<dictionary xmlns="http://marklogic.com/xdmp/spell">
    <metadata>
    </metadata>
    <word>Silverlight</word>
    <word>Expression Blend</word>
</dictionary>
```

In this example, we added two words into our dictionary document: "Silverlight" and "Expression Blend."

 For more examples of creating dictionary file, please visit:
http://developer.marklogic.com

Load Dictionary File

Once you have created your dictionary file, you can save it in your local directory. When you are ready, you can load your dictionary file onto the MarkLogic Sever. For example, you have created a dictionary file named "technology_words.xml" and saved in "c:\references\dictionary\" directory. Now you are ready to load it to your MarkLogic Server.

To load your dictionary file, there are two functions you can use: spell:load or spell:insert. Both of these functions can accomplish the same load task, so it doesn't matter which one you choose to use. Here is an example in XQuery expression:

```
xquery version "1.0-ml";
import module "http://marklogic.com/xdmp/spell" at
"MarkLogic/spell.xqy"
```

```
spell:load("c:\references\dictionary\technology_words.xml",
"/dictionary/technology_words.xml")
```

By default, dictionary documents are loaded into the following collections on MarkLogic Server: http://marklogic.com/xdmp/documents and http://marklogic.com/xdmp/spell.

 By default, the security setting for any thesaurus document corresponds to the user who is loading the thesaurus document. If that user's rights and privileges prevent reading or updating, then the permission must be modified. You can add a function call **xdmp:document-set-permissions** after the **spell:load** operation.

The following table has a summary of some spelling functions.

Table 20-1

Function	Definition
spell:add-word	Add the word $word to the dictionary at $uri.
spell:insert	Load the words in $dict into the dictionary at $uri.
spell:is-correct	Returns true() if the specified word is spelled correctly, otherwise returns false().
spell:load	Add the words from the file specified in $path to the dictionary at $uri.
spell:remove-word	Remove the word $word from the dictionary at $uri.
spell:suggest	Suggests a list of spellings for a word.

 When you get a chance, be sure to visit the MarkLogic Collaborative Code Workshop at the following web address:

http://developer.marklogic.com/code/default.xqy

From this workshop, you will find a section labeled **Dictionaries and Thesauri**. Within this section, there are three dictionaries (small, medium and large) and a thesaurus (very large) for use with MarkLogic Server.

Figure 20-1

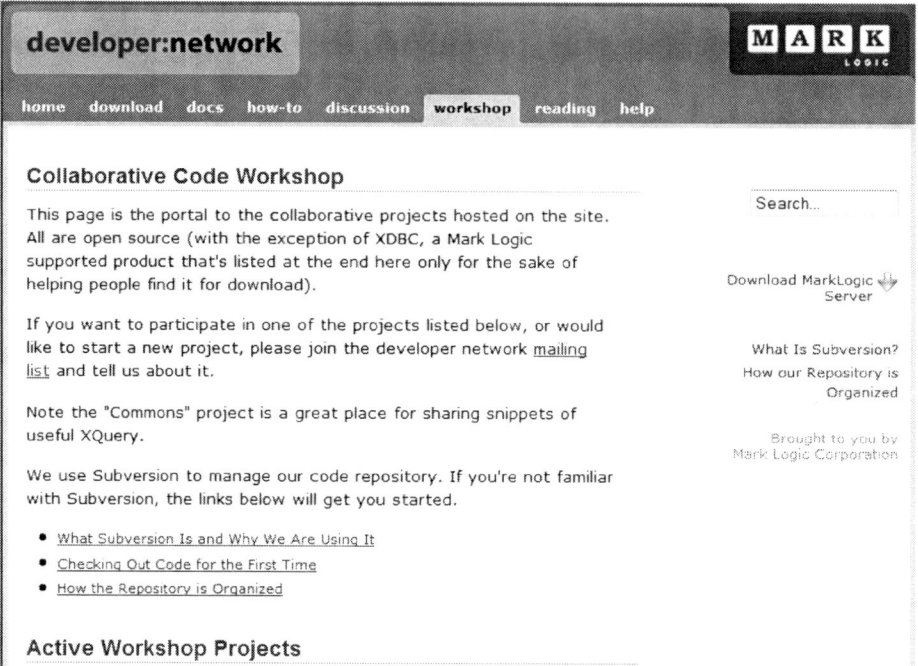

Add or Remove Words

Once you have loaded your dictionary file onto the MarkLogic Server, you may need to update the file by adding new words or remove existing words. To add new words, you can use **spell:add-word**. To remove existing words, you can use **spell:remove-word**. Here is an example of adding a new word "XAML" into our dictionary document:

```
xquery version "1.0-ml";
import module "http://marklogic.com/xdmp/spell" at
"MarkLogic/spell.xqy"

spell:add-word("/dictionary/technology_words.xml",
"XAML")
```

The following example shows how to remove a existing word "DateTimePicker" from our dictionary document:

```
xquery version "1.0-ml";
import module "http://marklogic.com/xdmp/spell" at
"MarkLogic/spell.xqy"

spell:remove-word("/dictionary/technology_words.xml",
"DateTimePicker")
```

Spelling

Once you have your dictionary documents created and loaded onto your MarkLogic Server, you can unleash the power of spelling function to check words and suggest words for users. To check spelling of a word, you can use **spell:is-correct** function. If the word is correct, it will return true. Otherwise, it will return false. Here is an XQuery expression showing how to use this function:

```
spell:is-correct("/dictionary/technology_words.xml",
"CalendarPicker")
```

 Please note that spelling functions are case-sensitive. So you should keep this in mind when you creating are new words, checking spelling, or suggesting words.

To suggest words to user, you can use **spell:suggest** function. Here is an XQuery expression illustrates how it works:

```
spell:suggest("/dictionary/technology_words.xml",
"DatePicker")
```

Summary

In this chapter, we covered some functions related to spelling. First, we discussed how to create a dictionary document. In order for your dictionary document to work properly, you should follow the correct structure. Then, we covered how to load your custom dictionary document to the MarkLogic Server. After you have loaded your dictionary document to your server, you can add or remove words to your document at anytime. With your dictionary file ready, you can check the spelling of words or suggest words to the user.

21

Working with Documents

Once you have started using MarkLogic Server, it will grow as you adding more content to it. From the MarkLogic Server's administration and programming perspective, there are three types of documents: XML, Binary, and Text. By now, you have gained some knowledge about XML documents by working with XQuery. As soon as XML documents are load onto the MarkLogic Server, they will be indexed. Once they are indexed, they are ready to be served for querying and can be searched quickly. This is one of strengths of MarkLogic Server.

Binary documents are also called BLOB format documents. They are some of the most popular files you work with on a day-to-day basis such as Word documents (.doc, .docx), PDF, PowerPoint (.ppt, pptx), and images (.jpg, .gif, .tiff). When you upload binary documents, they will be stored at the binary nodes.

 Please note that binary file has its size limits on MarkLogic Server. If your server is 32-bit machines, the upper limit for your document size is 128 MB. If your server is 64-bit machines, the upper limit for your document is 512 MB.

Text documents are plain text files that do not comply with XML conventions. For example, simple text files (.txt), cascading style sheets (.css), and source code files (.cs, .vb, .java). If a web page is not well formed, then the .html file should also be stored as text documents.

 Please note that text file has its size limits on MarkLogic Server. If your server is 32-bit machines, the upper limit for your document size is 16 MB.

If your server is 64-bit machines, the upper limit for your document is 64 MB.

Figure 21-1

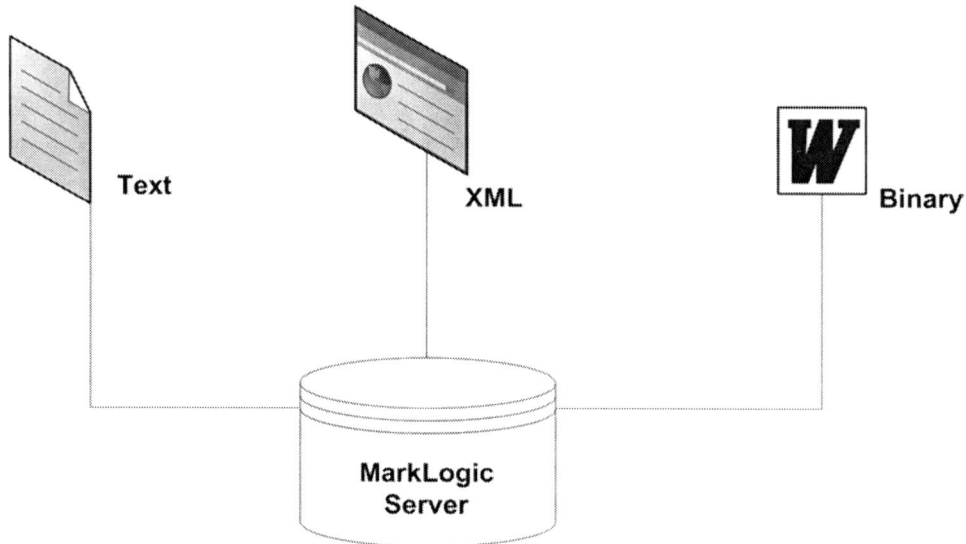

Loading Documents

To load a document onto the MarkLogic Server, you can use the **xdmp:document-load** function. During the process of loading your document, you can specify the source URI of your document such as your local drive and server options. Inside the server options section, you can specify the destination URI, file permission, which collection it should belong to, and the format of your document.

 It is highly recommended that you explicitly specify the document format as shown in our example. This way, there will be no surprises.

Here is an XQuery expression that loads a sample XML document named movie. xml onto the MarkLogic Server.

```
xdmp:document-load("c:\champion\movie.rss",
<options xmlns="xdmp:document-load">
        <uri>http://championwriters.com/movie.xml</uri>
        <permissions>{xdmp:default-permissions()}</
permissions>
        <collections>{xdmp:default-collections()}</
collections>
        <format>xml</format>
</options>)
```

You can also specify if you want to repair the document.

```
xdmp:document-load("c:\champion\movie.rss",
<options xmlns="xdmp:document-load">
        <uri>http://championwriters.com/movie.xml</uri>
        <repair>full</repair>
        <permissions>{xdmp:default-permissions()}</
permissions>
        <collections>{xdmp:default-collections()}</
collections>
        <format>xml</format>
</options>)
```

xdmp:document-insert and xdmp:document-get

In addition to the **xdmp:document-load** function, you can also use **xdmp:document-insert** and **xdmp:document-get.** What are the differences? You can load documents from your file system by using the **xdmp:document-load** function. You can use **xdmp:document-get** function to load a document from file system into the server memory. To insert something into an existing document or create a new document, you can use **xdmp:document-insert**. For example, you can use **xdmp:document-get** to get some nodes from a document, then use xdmp:document-insert to add that information to an existing document on the server. For a new document, you can use either **xdmp:document-load**, or the combination of **xdmp:document-get** and **xdmp:document-insert.**

Loading to Specific Collections

The previous examples load our document into the default collections. If you want to load your document into specific collections, you can try to use the following XQuery expressions:

```
xdmp:document-load("c:\champion\movie.rss",
<options xmlns="xdmp:document-load">
    <uri>http://championwriters.com/movie.xml</uri>
    <permissions>{xdmp:default-permissions()}</
permissions>
    <collections>movie_feeds</collections>
    <format>xml</format>
</options>)
```

Load to Specific Forests

Do you know that over 17 million Americans who have written a novel in 2008? Almost all publishers receive a large amount of manuscript submissions each week. If you are working with a large set of documents such as manuscripts, you may need to create several forests to store them. Let's assume your forests are grouped based on manuscript ID numbers. You can use xdmp:document-get to load the document into memory, then select the manuscript ID and put the document into the proper forest. Here is an example:

```
let $tempDoc := xdmp:document-get("c:\champion\
greatscript_tk.xml")
let $forest :=
if ($tempDoc//ID gt "200000")
then xdmp:forest("Review")
else xdmp:forest("Rejected")
return
xdmp:document-insert
("http://championwriters.com/greatscript_tk.xml",
    $tempDoc,
    xdmp:default-permissions(),
```

```
xdmp:default-collections(),
0,
$forest)
```

Working with Nodes

Adding Nodes

You can add nodes to an existing document. What you should keep in mind is the position of the current node. Every operation is relative. There are three functions that can help you to add nodes.

Insert a node before a node:

xdmp:node-insert-before($sibling as node(), $new as node())

Insert a node after a node:

xdmp:node-insert-after($sibling as node(), $new as node())

Insert a child node for a node:

xdmp:node-insert-child($sibling as node(), $new as node())

Replacing Nodes

You can replace a node by using **xdmp:node-replace** function. To replacing a node, here is an example:

xdmp:node-replace(doc("movie.xml")/movie/title, <name>No Country for Old Man</name>)

Deleting Documents

Deleting a document is a much simpler operation than loading a document. It usually requires only one line of code and here is an example in XQuery expression:

```
xdmp:document-delete("greatscript_tk.xml")
```

Saving Documents

On some occasions, you may want to save your documents. You can use xdmp:save function to save any type of document—XML, binary, and text. Here is an XQuery expression to illustrate how to save a document to a different location.

```
xdmp:save("temp.xml", doc("c:\champion\movie.xml"))
```

Summary

In this chapter, we covered another important topic—how to work with documents. MarkLogic Server becomes useful when you have great contents for your website users. There are three types of documents you can work with and almost all documents can be categorized into one of these types: XML, binary, and text.

We discussed how to load a document, including how to load a document into a specified collection and a specified forest. You can also add new nodes or change existing nodes. Finally, we covered how to save or delete a document.

22

Geospatial Functions

Many web applications allow you to perform some sort of geospatial search. The most common type of search is a zip code based search. When you type in a zip code and look for theaters or store locations near your zip code, the search engine is performing a search based on latitude and longitude coordinate values around that zip code. The coordinate values are based on the geospatial coordinate system mappings. Every spot on earth can be located by an intersection point of horizontal axis and vertical axis. The vertical axis is known as latitude. The horizontal axis is known as longitude. Geospatial coordinate system maps the earth with latitude and longitude numbers.

 Many map services, such as Google Maps and Global Positioning System (GPS), are using World Geodetic System (WGS 84). MarkLogic Server is also using this popular system for its geocoding basis.

 You can find more information such as documentation and earth orientation for World Geodetic System 1984 (WGS 84) at the website of Office of GEOINT Sciences:
http://earth-info.nga.mil/GandG/wgs84/

In this chapter, we are going to cover some geospatial queries available from MarkLogic Server including point query, box query, radius query, and polygon query.

Table 22-1

Function	Definition
cts:box	Returns a geospatial box value.
cts:box-east	Returns a box's eastern boundary.
cts:box-north	Returns a box's northern boundary.
cts:box-south	Returns a box's southern boundary.
cts:box-west	Returns a box's western boundary.
cts:circle	Returns a geospatial circle value.
cts:circle-center	Returns a circle's center point.
cts:circle-radius	Returns a circle's radius.
cts:distance	Returns the distance (in miles) between two points.
cts:point	Returns a point value.
cts:point-latitude	Returns a point's latitude value.
cts:point-longitude	Returns a point's longitude value.
cts:polygon	Returns a geospatial polygon value.
cts:polygon-vertices	Returns a polygon's vertices.

Point

You can use point query to match a single geographic point. The function to use is cts:point. As you may have already guessed, you can provide latitude and longitude values to this function in order to find the point. Here is the XQuery expression for using the point query:

```
cts:point(0.265757758585894E+02, -0.126453937478388E+03)
```

Another example is:

```
cts:point(-45.76, 54.66)
```

Figure 22-1

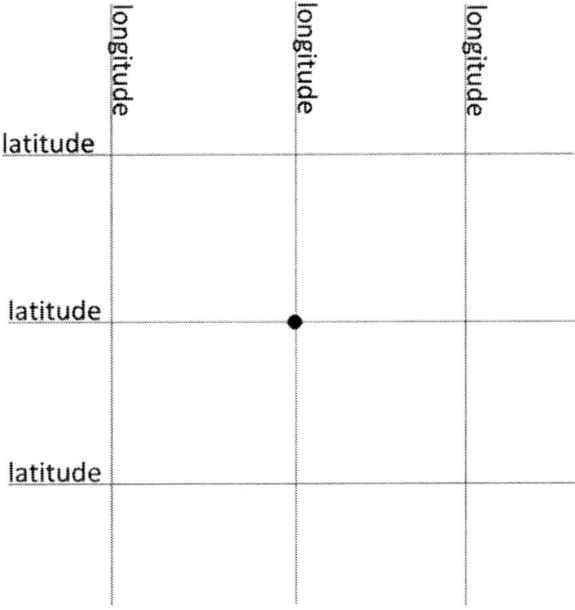

Box

Geospatial box is a very commonly used function. You can use four coordinates to create a region. The points are representing four corners of a box in the following sequence: south, west, north, and east. The **cts:box** function takes four parameters and all of them are float data type. When you provide southern boundary, western boundary, northern boundary, and eastern boundary into **cts:box** function, you will get a geographical boxed region.

Here is an example in XQuery expression:

cts:box(-136, 72, 32, 50)

Figure 22-2

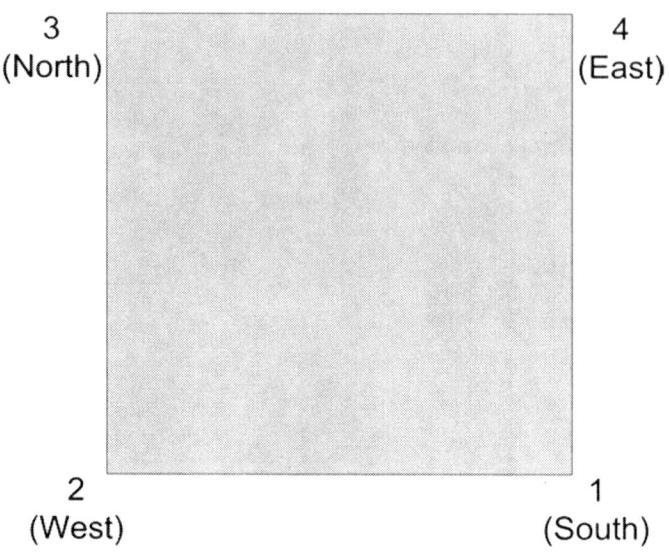

Circle

A geospatial circle starts with a point. From that point, we can draw a circle based on radius. Radius is measured in miles. If your value is in kilometers, for example, you need to convert the value into miles first. Once the circle is drawn, anything inside the boundary of the circle is the geospatial range we are focusing on. The cts:circle function takes two parameters: radius, and cts:point. Radius is a float number data type. Of course, cts:point contains two float numbers.

Here is an example using XQuery expression to create a geospatial circle with radius of 35 miles from the center point:

```
cts:circle(35, cts:point(21.88, 89.71))
```

To retrieve the center point from a geospatial circle, you can use cts:circle-center function. To retrieve the radius from a geospatial circle, you can use cts:circle-radius function.

Figure 22-3

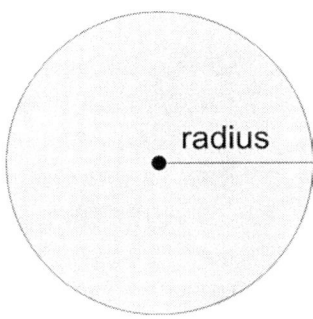

Polygon

Thanks to geospatial polygon, you can create a geospatial area with as many sides as you need to draw your boundaries. For example, you can draw an island with an 800-sided polygon. So polygon is n-sided. With polygon, you have much more flexibility and precision than over a circle or a box. To create a polygon, you can use cts:polygon function by providing all the necessary vertices. Vertices are points and you can use cts:point as parameter. Here is some information about vertices provided by MarkLogic documentation:

> The vertices of the polygon, given in order. No edge may cover more than 180 degrees of either latitude or longitude. The polygon as a whole may not encompass both poles. These constraints are necessary to ensure an unambiguous interpretation of the polygon. There must be at least three vertices. The first vertex should be identical to the last vertex to close the polygon.

 Usually, you should expect a typical 8-sided polygon runs faster than an 800-sided polygon on MarkLogic Server.

 Polygon must be compatible with the earth's sphere coordinate system. Otherwise, you can get an exception error.

 You can find more information on polygon at MarkLogic website: http://developer.marklogic.com

Here is an example with XQuery expression to create a polygon:

```
let $polygon_points :=
    (cts:point(0.628199253086420E+02, -0.273078578406509E+03),
     cts:point(0.628765400000000E+02, -0.273063772000000E+03),
     cts:point(0.628781400000000E+02, -0.273067972000000E+03),
     cts:point(0.628825650000000E+02, -0.273068365000000E+03),
     cts:point(0.628797400000000E+02, -0.273072172000000E+03),
     cts:point(0.628899400000000E+02, -0.273092573000000E+03),
     cts:point(0.628941400000000E+02, -0.273095573000000E+03),
     cts:point(0.628966710000000E+02, -0.273094173000000E+03),
     cts:point(0.628938400000000E+02, -0.273092628000000E+03),
     cts:point(0.629004400000000E+02, -0.273091273000000E+03),
     cts:point(0.629004200000000E+02, -0.273091273000000E+03),
     cts:point(0.628873100000000E+02, -0.273057872000000E+03),
     cts:point(0.628819400000000E+02, -0.273057572000000E+03),
     cts:point(0.628775800000000E+02, -0.273060872000000E+03),
     cts:point(0.628765400000000E+02, -0.273063772000000E+03)
    )
    return
    cts:polygon($polygon_points)
```

Summary

In this chapter, we covered some basic functions with geospatial search. First, we started with point. A point is a intersect spot with latitude and longitude. A geospatial box composed of four points. From these four points, you can create a boxed boundary for the geospatial area you are looking for. Similarly, a circle starts from its center point, then draw the circle based on its radius. Finally, we covered polygon. A polygon can be composed of n-sides. Polygon can be very flexible and you can create as many sides as you need.

23

MarkLogic Alerts

One of useful features for MarkLogic Server is that users can setup alerts. Some users like to be notified when important changes are made to the MarkLogic database, collection, or document. In this chapter, we will cover some basic knowledge about working with alerts. To understand how alert works in MarkLogic, it is essential to understand how reverse query works.

A typical user will interact with MarkLogic Server using XQuery or a web application that runs XQuery behind the scenes. Suppose our user, Susan, wants to find documents that contain her keyword "headache." She runs her XQuery to retrieve documents on the MarkLogic Server that contains her keyword. Soon afterward, MarkLogic performs its magic and gives Susan a list of documents. Susan was happy and her headache has gone away. So a when a typical query runs, MarkLogic Server matches documents to query.

Figure 23-1

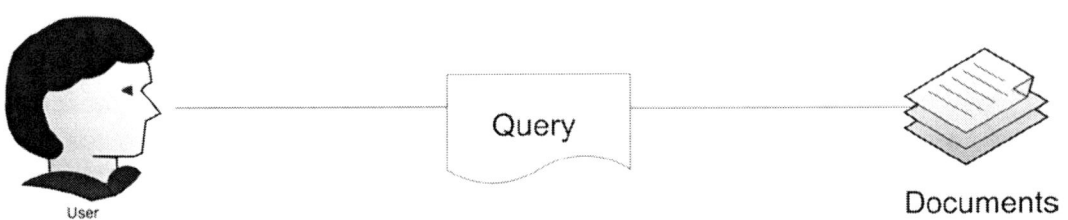

223

In order for MarkLogic server to create alerts based on this kind of action, MarkLogic Server has to be able to understand the consequences of using these queries. So when the user runs these queries, MarkLogic Server can match up the alert condition and send out alerts. Like its name implies, reverse query matches queries to documents.

Figure 23-2

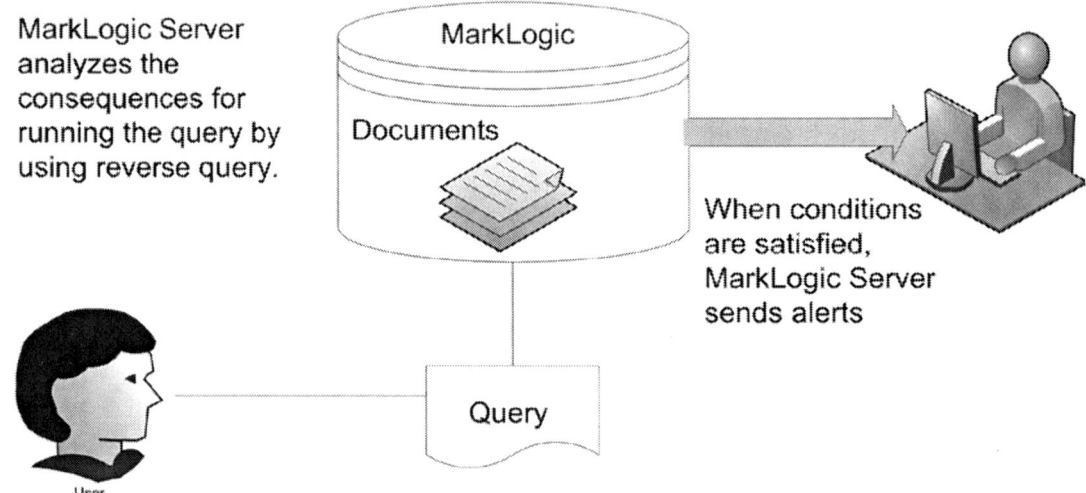

You can run reverse query by using cts:reverse-query function. Here is an XQuery expression that illustrates how to use reverse query:

```
let $query := <query>{cts:word-query("headache")}</query>
let $content := <definition>A headache is a condition of
pain in   the head; something or someone that causes
anxiety; a source of unhappiness.</definition>

return
cts:contains($query, cts:reverse-query($content))
```

 The default installation of MarkLogic Server comes with a basic sample alerting application. You can either use this sample application as your reference or add more features into it to meet your needs.

Alert Roles

There are two pre-defined user roles for MarkLogic alert applications. The first one is Alert-Admin role. This role is used for administrators who need all the rights and privileges. People with Alert-Admin role can perform a lot of privileged actions such as running any query that with rules attached.

 For security reasons, it is important to keep this role limited to people who are capable and responsible for the role.

The second pre-defined user role is **Alert-User** role. Users with this role can perform typical functions with alert API such as establishing alert configurations. This role is sufficient for users who want to create and use alerts. Alert-User role does not have full privileges as Alert-Admin role.

 An important item you should consider during the planning phase is who should receive the alert. Users will feel annoyed when they receive too many alerts or irrelevant alerts.

Besides Alert-Admin and Alert-User roles, there are two internal roles for Alerting API only: **alert-internal** and **alert-execution**. You should not grant these roles to users.

Creating Alerts

There are two aspects of creating alerts. First, you create alert configuration settings in the alert **config** XML file. These settings determine the settings and behaviors of your alerting application. Second, you specify actions for when an alert fires. As soon as the alert condition is satisfied, you want the alert to fire, then take proper actions to notify user such as sending an email to a user.

Figure 23-3

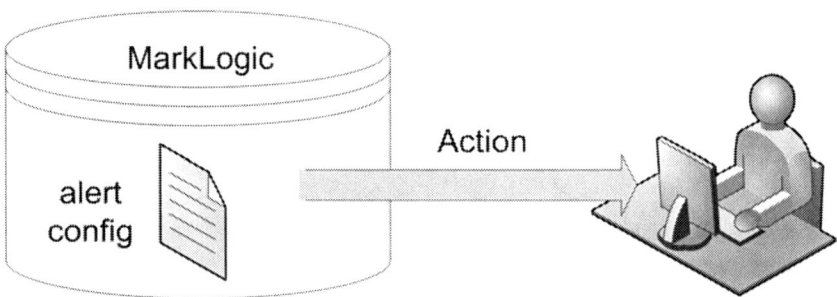

In MarkLogic, all alert functions are associated with **alert** namespace. In order to create a new alert configuration setting, you can use **alert:config-insert** function. There are many other functions available for creating alerts, setting, and actions as shown in Table 23-1. Here is example of alert:**config-insert** and **alert:make-config** functions using XQuery expression:

```
xquery version "1.0-ml";
import module namespace alert = "http://marklogic.com/
xdmp/alert"
          at "/MarkLogic/alert.xqy";

let $configuration_setting := alert:make-config(
"http://www.championwriters.com/alert/message-portal",
     "Message Portal",
     "Alerting configuration for messages from the
portal",
     <alert:options/>
     )
return alert:config-insert($configuration_setting)
```

 For more information about alert functions and syntax examples, please visit: http://developer.marklogic.com/pubs/4.0/apidocs/alerting.html

Table 23-1 Alert Functions

Function	Description
alert:action-get-description	This function returns the description of a given action.
alert:action-get-module	This function returns the module of a given action.
alert:action-get-module-db	This function returns the module database of a given action.
alert:action-get-module-root	This function returns the module root of a given action.
alert:action-get-name	This function returns the name of a given action.
alert:action-get-options	This function returns the options of a given action.
alert:action-insert	This function inserts the xml representing the action into the collection.
alert:action-remove	This function removes the named action from the database or throws an exception if the action does not exist.
alert:action-set-description	This function returns the action with the description of the action updated.
alert:action-set-module	This function returns the action with the module of the action updated.
alert:action-set-module-db	This function sets the module database of a given action.
alert:action-set-module-root	This function sets the module root of a given action.
alert:action-set-name	This function returns the action with the name of the action updated.
alert:action-set-options	This function returns the action with the options of the action updated.

alert:config-delete	Remove an alerting configuration identified by the specified URI.
alert:config-get	Gets the config associated with the specified URI.
alert:config-get-cpf-domain-ids	This function provides convenient access to the specified sub-element within an alerting config.
alert:config-get-cpf-domain-names	This function provides convenient access to the specified sub-element within an alerting config.
alert:config-get-description	This function provides convenient access to the specified sub-element within an alerting config.
alert:config-get-id	This function provides convenient access to the specified sub-element within an alerting config.
alert:config-get-name	This function provides convenient access to the specified sub-element within an alerting config.
alert:config-get-options	This function provides convenient access to the specified sub-element within an alerting config.
alert:config-get-trigger-ids	This function provides convenient access to the specified sub-element within an alerting config.
alert:config-get-uri	This function provides convenient access to the specified sub-element within an alerting config.
alert:config-insert	Inserts a config into the database.
alert:config-set-cpf-domain-ids	This function provides convenient access to the specified sub-element within an alerting config.

alert:config-set-cpf-domain-names	This function provides convenient access to the specified sub-element within an alerting config.
alert:config-set-description	This function provides convenient access to the specified sub-element within an alerting config.
alert:config-set-name	This function provides convenient access to the specified sub-element within an alerting config.
alert:config-set-options	This function provides convenient access to the specified sub-element within an alerting config.
alert:config-set-trigger-ids	This function provides convenient access to the specified sub-element within an alerting config.
alert:config-set-uri	This function provides convenient access to the specified sub-element within an alerting config.
alert:config-set-uri	This function provides convenient access to the specified sub-element within an alerting config.
alert:create-triggers	Create triggers that invoke the standard alerting trigger module.
alert:find-matching-rules	Returns a list of all rules associated with the specified config that match the specified document.
alert:get-actions	This function retrieves all the named actions in the specified config URI.
alert:get-all-rules	This function returns all rules visible to the current user.
alert:get-my-rules	This function returns all rules associated with the current user.

alert:invoke-matching-actions	Finds the rules that match the specified document and invokes their associated actions.
alert:make-action	This function creates the xml representing an action.
alert:make-config	Create an alerting configuration associated with a particular URI.
alert:make-log-action	Create a standard logging action named "log".
alert:make-rule	This function creates the XML representing a rule.
alert:remove-triggers	Remove triggers whose IDs are listed in the config.
alert:rule-action-query	This function creates a query to find rules with any of the specified actions.
alert:rule-get-action	This function returns the action of a given rule.
alert:rule-get-description	This function returns the description of a given rule.
alert:rule-get-id	This function returns the ID of a given rule.
alert:rule-get-name	This function returns the name of a given rule.
alert:rule-get-options	This function returns the options of a given rule.
alert:rule-get-query	Get the cts:query corresponding to the rule's query expression.
alert:rule-get-user-id	This function returns the user ID of a given rule.
alert:rule-id-query	This function creates a query to find rules with any of the specified IDs.

alert:rule-insert	This function inserts rule into the database associated with the specified alerting configuration.
alert:rule-name-query	This function creates a query to find rules with any of the specified names.
alert:rule-remove	This function removes the XML representing the rule from the collection.
alert:rule-set-action	This function returns the rule with the action updated.
alert:rule-set-description	This function returns the rule with the description of the rule updated.
alert:rule-set-name	This function returns the rule with the name of the rule updated.
alert:rule-set-options	This function returns the rule with the options of the rule updated.
alert:rule-set-query	Set the cts:query corresponding to the rule's query expression.
alert:rule-set-user-id	This function returns the rule with the user ID updated.
alert:rule-user-id-query	This function creates a query to find rules with any of the specified user IDs.
alert:spawn-matching-actions	Finds the rules that match the specified document and spawns their associated actions.

Alert Rules

An alert rule is a condition which determines whether a notification action is necessary. When the rule is satisfied, you can trigger your alert. For example, you can create a rule when user search for specific term such as "H1N1 flu" or other keywords. To create a rule, you can use **alert:make-rule** function. Here is an example using XQuery expression:

```
xquery version "1.0-ml";
import module namespace alert = "http://marklogic.com/
xdmp/alert"
            at "/MarkLogic/alert.xqy";

alert:make-rule(
    "H1N1 flu alert email",
    "Alert me to anything concerning H1N1 Swine flu",
    0,
    cts:or-query((
        cts:word-query("H1N1"),
     cts:word-query("Swine"),
        cts:word-query("flu"),
     cts:word-query("virus")
        )),
    "email",
    <alert:options>
        <alert:email-address>sample@championwriters.
com</alert:email-address>
    </alert:options>
  )
```

Summary

Alerting is a large topic. We introduced some basic information in this chapter. It is important to know how reverse query works. Alerting is based on the foundation of reverse query. To create and use alert functions, there are two pre-defined user roles: Alert-Admin and Alert-User. Understanding the difference is essential to make your application more secure. We also introduced how to create new alert configuration settings and how to create alert actions. Finally, we discussed how to create alert rules.

24

Error Handling

How to handle application errors gracefully and give useful information to the developers is an important decision for any enterprise web application. When website visitors or users are employing MarkLogic applications, their interaction is first started with XQuery, then MarkLogic Server runs the XQuery expression with app servers. The good news is - there are built-in functions in XQuery and there are configuration settings on the app server which can be helpful in handling the errors.

In this chapter, we will introduce some error handling functions and configuration settings. Hopefully, the information presented in this chapter can help you gain some insights on error handling with MarkLogic.

Figure 24-1

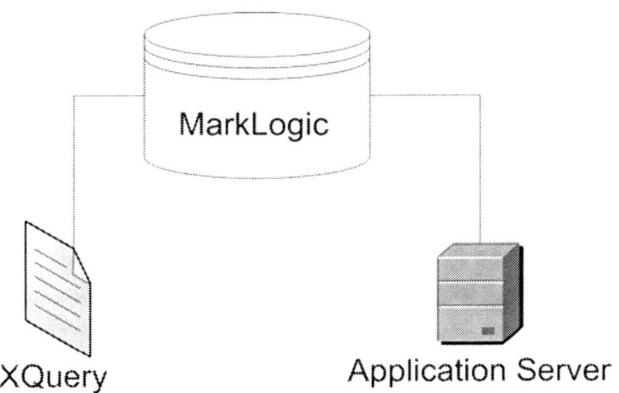

XQuery Error Functions

There are two error functions in XQuery that you should know: fn:error and fn:trace. The fn:error function throws an error and stops the execution of the program. The fn:trace function returns the value to trace and displays output onto the specified label. Here is an example using fn:error with XQuery expression:

```
xquery version "1.0-ml";
let $len := fn:string-length(doc("survey.xml")//Items/
Item)
return
(
if ( $len gt 2000 )
then ( fn:error(xs:QName("ERROR"), "greater than 2000
characters")
)
else ( "Less than or equal to 2000 characters" ) , ":
no error was thrown" )
```

Please note that if you are using 0.9-ml version, the function you should use is fn:err instead of fn:error.

Custom Error Pages

When the user requests a page and encounters an error, you must consider how to display the error page. If the resource that user is requesting is not available, then the user should see 503 resource unavailable error. In this case, no error handler is being invoked and user will see the 503 error right away. It makes sense that this type of error does not involve error handling. Many times when the user encounters an error, the error is related to the issues inside a page — whether it is a logical error or some other type of error. In this case, there is an exception and the error stack trace along with error code will be passed to the front-end.

The format setting is for displaying an error message and stack trace information is controlled by error.xsd schema. If you want to customize your error page, this is a place to start. Here is a simple error handling page example:

```
xquery version "1.0-ml";

declare variable $error:errors as node()* external;

xdmp:set-response-content-type("text/plain"),
xdmp:get-response-code(),
$error:errors
```

App Server Configuration

When you install MarkLogic Server, many configuration settings are selected by default. The default settings are usually good for most users. But there are exceptions and you may need to change app server configuration settings to meet your specific needs. To make changes to your app server configuration, you can go to Groups → Default → App Servers → YourServer.

Figure 24-2

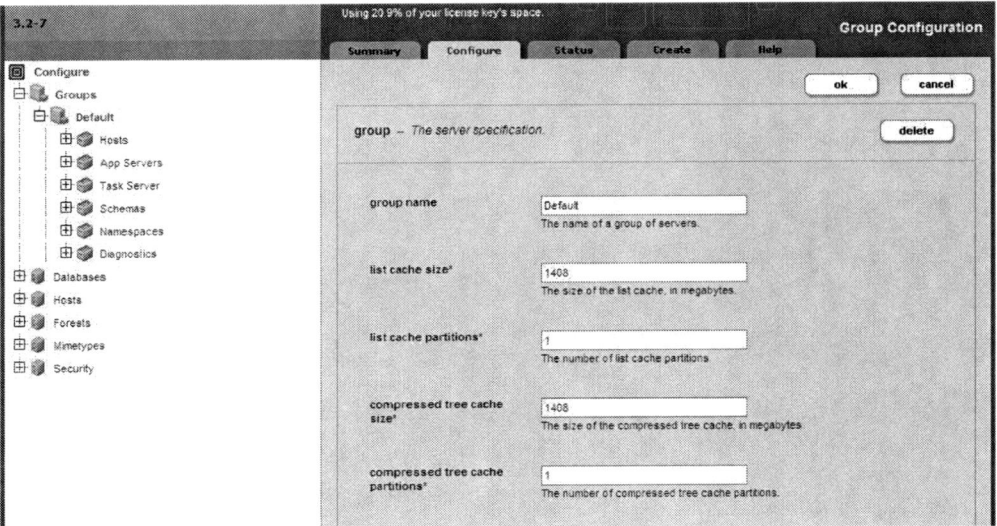

By default, the output encoding for MarkLogic Server is utf-8. If you need to change this setting, you can change it here. Also, this is the place you can change your SGML Mapping.

 For more information on SGML Mapping, you can reference to the Developer's Guide at the following website: http://developer.marklogic.com/

Summary

In these chapters, we introduced a few XQuery functions for error handling. The fn:error function is used for handling errors and fn:trace is used to perform trace and display information. Web site users will appreciate your efforts for displaying a user-friendly error message when an exception occurs. Since error page is an XQuery module for MarkLogic, you can add additional logic and then display more meaningful messages.

Appendix I

MarkLogic Functions

Source: http://developer.marklogic.com

Function	Definition
admin:appserver-add-namespace	Add one or more namespaces to an App Server configuration, which will predefine the namespace(s) for all requests evaluated against the App Server.
admin:appserver-add-request-blackout	This function adds a request blackout specification for a appserver to a configuration.
admin:appserver-add-schema	This function adds a schema binding definition to the existing schema binding definitions in the configuration for the specified App Server.
admin:appserver-copy	This function creates a new App Server specification with the same settings as the App Server with the specified ID.
admin:appserver-delete	This function deletes an App Server in the configuration.
admin:appserver-delete-namespace	This function deletes a namespace configuration from the configuration for the specified App Server.
admin:appserver-delete-request-blackout	This function deletes a request blackout specification for a appserver from a configuration.
admin:appserver-delete-schema	This function deletes a schema definition in the configuration for the specified App Server.

admin:appserver-get-address	This function returns the IP address of the App Server configuration.
admin:appserver-get-authentication	This function returns the authentication scheme (basic, digest, digestbasic, or application-level) configured for the specified App Server.
admin:appserver-get-backlog	This function returns the socket listen backlog setting for the specified App Server.
admin:appserver-get-collation	This function returns the collation URI set in the configuration for the specified App Server.
admin:appserver-get-compute-content-length	This function returns the value of whether the WebDAV server computes content length.
admin:appserver-get-concurrent-request-limit	This function returns the concurrent request limit for any user for the specified App Server.
admin:appserver-get-database	This function returns the ID of the database to which the App Server is set to execute queries against for the specified database.
admin:appserver-get-debug-allow	This function returns the value of debug allow setting configured for this App Server, where true indicates that the App Server will allow queries to be debugged, and false indicates that it will not.
admin:appserver-get-default-time-limit	This function returns the default time limit value configured for the specified App Server.
admin:appserver-get-default-user	This function returns the default user value configured for the specified App Server.
admin:appserver-get-default-xquery-version	This function returns the value of the default xquery version configured for the specified App Server.
admin:appserver-get-display-last-login	This function returns the value of the whether or not the appserver should display users' last login information.
admin:appserver-get-enabled	This function returns the enabled state for the specified App Server.
admin:appserver-get-error-handler	This function returns the path to the error handler configured for this App Server.
admin:appserver-get-group-id	This function returns the ID of the specified App Server's group.

admin:appserver-get-host-ids	This function returns the ID(s) of the hosts the specified App Server's is currently running on.
admin:appserver-get-id	This function returns the ID(s) of the specified App Server(s).
admin:appserver-get-keep-alive-timeout	This function returns the keep alive timeout value configured for the specified App Server.
admin:appserver-get-last-login	This function returns the ID of the database to which the App Server stores users' last login information.
admin:appserver-get-log-errors	This function returns the value of the log errors setting configured for this App Server, where true indicates that the App Server will send uncaught exceptions to the ErrorLog.txt file, and false indicates that it will not.
admin:appserver-get-max-time-limit	This function returns the max time limit value configured for the specified App Server.
admin:appserver-get-modules-database	This function returns the ID of the database set as the modules database for the specified database.
admin:appserver-get-name	This function returns the name of the appserver with the specified ID.
admin:appserver-get-namespaces	This function returns the value of any namespace definitions predefined for the specified App Server.
admin:appserver-get-output-encoding	This function returns the value for the output encoding setting for the specified App Server.
admin:appserver-get-output-sgml-character-entities	This function returns the value for the output sgml character entities setting for the specified App Server.
admin:appserver-get-port	This function returns the port for the specified App Server.
admin:appserver-get-pre-commit-trigger-depth	This function returns the pre commit trigger depth value configured for the specified App Server.
admin:appserver-get-pre-commit-trigger-limit	This function returns the pre commit trigger limit value configured for the specified App Server.
admin:appserver-get-privilege	This function returns the privilege ID for the specified App Server.

admin:appserver-get-profile-allow	This function returns the value of the profile allow setting configured for this App Server, where true indicates that the App Server will allow queries to be profiled, and false indicates that it will not.
admin:appserver-get-request-blackouts	This function returns the request blackouts specification for the specified appserver from the configuration.
admin:appserver-get-request-timeout	This function returns the request timeout value configured for the specified App Server.
admin:appserver-get-root	This function returns the root for the specified App Server.
admin:appserver-get-schemas	This function returns the value of any schemas definitions predefined for the specified App Server.
admin:appserver-get-session-timeout	This function returns the session timeout value configured for the specified App Server.
admin:appserver-get-static-expires	This function returns the value of the "expires" HTTP header for static content to expire after this many seconds port for the specified App Server.
admin:appserver-get-threads	This function returns the maximum number of threads configured for the specified App Server.
admin:appserver-get-type	This function returns the type of appserver with the specified ID.
admin:appserver-one-time-request-blackout	This function constructs a one-time request-blackout specification.
admin:appserver-recurring-request-blackout	This function constructs a request-blackout specification.
admin:appserver-set-address	This function changes the IP Address in the configuration for the specified App Server to the specified address.
admin:appserver-set-authentication	This function sets the authentication scheme in the configuration for the specified App Server.
admin:appserver-set-backlog	This function sets the value in the configuration of the backlog (the maximum number of pending connections allowed on the HTTP socket) for the specified App Server.

admin:appserver-set-collation	This function sets the default collation in the configuration for the specified App Server.
admin:appserver-set-compute-content-length	This function changes the value whether a WebDAV server computes content length.
admin:appserver-set-concurrent-request-limit	This function sets the limit on concurrent requests that any user may have on a particular appserver.
admin:appserver-set-database	This function sets the value in the configuration of the database for the specified App Server.
admin:appserver-set-debug-allow	This function sets the debug allow setting in the configuration for the specified App Server.
admin:appserver-set-default-time-limit	This function sets the default time limit (the maximum total amount of time to service a request before the App Server throws a timeout exception) in the configuration for the specified App Server.
admin:appserver-set-default-user	This function sets the default user (for use with application-level authentication) in the configuration for the specified App Server.
admin:appserver-set-default-xquery-version	This function sets the default XQuery version setting in the configuration for this App Server.
admin:appserver-set-display-last-login	This function sets the display last login setting in the configuration for the specified App Server.
admin:appserver-set-enabled	This function sets the enabled state in the configuration for the specified App Server.
admin:appserver-set-error-handler	This function sets the value of the path to the error handler in the configuration for the specified App Server.
admin:appserver-set-keep-alive-timeout	This function sets the keep-alive timeout (the maximum number of second for subsequent socket requests to time out) in the configuration for the specified App Server.
admin:appserver-set-last-login	This function sets the value in the configuration of the last login database for the specified App Server.
admin:appserver-set-log-errors	This function sets the log errors setting in the configuration for the specified App Server.

admin:appserver-set-max-time-limit	This function sets the max time limit (the maximum total amount of time to service a request before the App Server throws a timeout exception) in the configuration for the specified App Server.
admin:appserver-set-modules-database	This function sets the value in the configuration of modules database for the specified App Server to the specified database ID.
admin:appserver-set-name	This function changes the name of an existing App Server to the newly specified value.
admin:appserver-set-output-encoding	This function sets the value for the default output encoding in the configuration for the specified App Server.
admin:appserver-set-output-sgml-character-entities	This function sets the SGML character entity output setting in the configuration for the specified App Server.
admin:appserver-set-port	This function changes the port in the configuration for the specified App Server to the specified number.
admin:appserver-set-pre-commit-trigger-depth	This function sets the maximum depth (how many triggers can cause other triggers to fire, which in turn cause others to fire, and so on) in the configuration for the specifed App Server.
admin:appserver-set-pre-commit-trigger-limit	This function sets the value in the configuration for the maximum number of pre-commit triggers a single statement can invoke for the specified App Server.
admin:appserver-set-privilege	This function sets an execute privilege in the configuration for the specified App Server.
admin:appserver-set-profile-allow	This function sets the profile allow setting in the configuration for the specifed App Server.
admin:appserver-set-request-timeout	This function sets the value of the socket request timeout (the number of seconds before the socket times out) in the configuration for the specified App Server.
admin:appserver-set-root	This function changes the root for a specified App Server to the newly specified value.

admin:appserver-set-session-timeout	This function sets the session timeout value (in seconds) in the configuration for the specified App Server.
admin:appserver-set-static-expires	This function changes the value of the "expires" HTTP header for a specified App Server to the newly specified value.
admin:appserver-set-threads	This function sets the value in the configuration of the maximum number of threads for the specified App Server.
admin:database-add-backup	This function adds scheduled backup specifications for a database to a configuration.
admin:database-add-element-attribute-word-lexicon	This function adds an element attribute word lexicon to the specified database in the configuration.
admin:database-add-element-word-lexicon	This function adds an element word lexicon to the specified database in the configuration.
admin:database-add-element-word-query-through	This function adds an element word query through to the specified database in the configuration.
admin:database-add-field	This function adds the field specification to the specified database in the configuration.
admin:database-add-field-excluded-element	This function adds the field excluded element specification in the specified database in the configuration.
admin:database-add-field-included-element	This function adds the field included element specification tn the specified database in the configuration.
admin:database-add-field-word-lexicon	This function adds a word lexicon to the specified database in the configuration.
admin:database-add-fragment-parent	This function adds the specified fragment parent to the specified database in the configuration.
admin:database-add-fragment-root	This function adds the specified fragment root to the specified database in the configuration.
admin:database-add-geospatial-element-attribute-pair-index	This function adds a geospatial element attribute pair index to the specified database in the configuration.

admin:database-add-geospatial-element-child-index	This function adds a geospatial element child index to the specified database in the configuration.
admin:database-add-geospatial-element-index	This function adds a range element index to the specified database in the configuration.
admin:database-add-geospatial-element-pair-index	This function adds a geospatial element pair index to the specified database in the configuration.
admin:database-add-merge-blackout	This function adds a merge blackout specification for a database to a configuration.
admin:database-add-phrase-around	This function adds a phrase around to the specified database in the configuration.
admin:database-add-phrase-through	This function adds a phrase through to the specified database in the configuration.
admin:database-add-range-element-attribute-index	This function adds a range element attribute index to the specified database in the configuration.
admin:database-add-range-element-index	This function adds a range element index to the specified database in the configuration.
admin:database-add-word-lexicon	This function adds a word lexicon to the specified database in the configuration.
admin:database-add-word-query-excluded-element	This function adds the word query excluded element specification for the specified database to the configuration.
admin:database-add-word-query-included-element	This function adds the word query included element specification to the specified database in the configuration.
admin:database-attach-forest	This function attaches the specified forest to the specified database.
admin:database-copy	This function creates a new database specification with the same settings as the database with the specified ID.
admin:database-create	This function creates a new database specification.
admin:database-delete	This function deletes the configuration from the specified database(s).
admin:database-delete-backup	This function deletes scheduled backup specifications for a database from a configuration.

admin:database-delete-element-attribute-word-lexicon	This function deletes an element attribute word lexicon for the specified database from the configuration.
admin:database-delete-element-word-lexicon	This function deletes an element word lexicon for the specified database from the configuration.
admin:database-delete-element-word-query-through	This function deletes an element word query through for the specified database from the configuration.
admin:database-delete-field	This function deletes the field specification in the specified database from the configuration.
admin:database-delete-field-excluded-element	This function deletes the field excluded element specification in the specified database from the configuration.
admin:database-delete-field-included-element	This function deletes the field included element specification in the specified database from the configuration.
admin:database-delete-field-word-lexicon	This function deletes a word lexicon for the specified database from the configuration.
admin:database-delete-fragment-parent	This function deletes the specified fragment parent in the specified database from the configuration.
admin:database-delete-fragment-root	This function deletes the specified fragment root in the specified database from the configuration.
admin:database-delete-geospatial-element-attribute-pair-index	This function deletes a geospatial element attribute pair index in the specified database from the configuration.
admin:database-delete-geospatial-element-child-index	This function deletes a geospatial element child index for the specified database in the configuration.
admin:database-delete-geospatial-element-index	This function deletes a geospatial element index for the specified database in the configuration.
admin:database-delete-geospatial-element-pair-index	This function deletes a geospatial element pair index for the specified database from the configuration.
admin:database-delete-merge-blackout	This function deletes a merge blackout specification for a database from a configuration.

admin:database-delete-phrase-around	This function deletes a phrase around for the specified database from the configuration.
admin:database-delete-phrase-through	This function deletes a phrase through for the specified database from the configuration.
admin:database-delete-range-element-attribute-index	This function deletes a range element attribute index for the specified database in the configuration.
admin:database-delete-range-element-index	This function deletes a range element index for the specified database in the configuration.
admin:database-delete-word-lexicon	This function deletes a word lexicon for the specified database from the configuration.
admin:database-delete-word-query-excluded-element	This function deletes the word query excluded element specification in the specified database from the configuration.
admin:database-delete-word-query-included-element	This function deletes the word query included element specification in the specified database from the configuration.
admin:database-detach-forest	This function detaches the specified forest from the specified database.
admin:database-element-attribute-word-lexicon	This function constructs an element attribute word lexicon specification.
admin:database-element-word-lexicon	This function constructs an element word lexicon specification.
admin:database-element-word-query-through	This function constructs an element word query through specification.
admin:database-excluded-element	This function constructs an excluded element specification.
admin:database-field	This function constructs a field specification.
admin:database-fragment-parent	This function constructs a fragment parent specification.
admin:database-fragment-root	This function constructs a fragment root specification.
admin:database-geospatial-element-attribute-pair-index	This function constructs a geospatial element attribute pair index specification.
admin:database-geospatial-element-child-index	This function constructs a geospatial element child index specification.

admin:database-geospatial-element-index	This function constructs a geospatial element index specification.
admin:database-geospatial-element-pair-index	This function constructs a geospatial element pair index specification.
admin:database-get-attached-forests	This function returns the attached forest IDs for the specified database from the configuration.
admin:database-get-attribute-value-positions	This function returns the attribute value positions setting for the specified database from the configuration.
admin:database-get-backups	This function returns the scheduled backups for the specified database from the configuration.
admin:database-get-collection-lexicon	This function returns the collection lexicon setting for the specified database from the configuration.
admin:database-get-directory-creation	This function returns the directory creation setting for the specified database from the configuration.
admin:database-get-element-attribute-word-lexicons	This function returns the element attribute word lexicons specification(s) for the specified database from the configuration.
admin:database-get-element-value-positions	This function returns the element value positions setting for the specified database from the configuration.
admin:database-get-element-word-lexicons	This function returns the element word lexicons specification(s) for the specified database from the configuration.
admin:database-get-element-word-positions	This function returns the element word positions setting for the specified database from the configuration.
admin:database-get-element-word-query-throughs	This function returns the element word query throughs specification(s) for the specified database from the configuration.
admin:database-get-enabled	This function returns the enabled value for the specified database from the configuration.
admin:database-get-expunge-locks	This function returns the expunge locks setting for the specified database from the configuration.

admin:database-get-fast-case-sensitive-searches	This function returns the fast case sensitive searches setting for the specified database from the configuration.
admin:database-get-fast-diacritic-sensitive-searches	This function returns the fast diacritic sensitive searches setting for the specified database from the configuration.
admin:database-get-fast-element-character-searches	This function returns the fast element character searches setting for the specified database from the configuration.
admin:database-get-fast-element-phrase-searches	This function returns the fast element phrase searches setting for the specified database from the configuration.
admin:database-get-fast-element-trailing-wildcard-searches	This function returns the trailing wildcard searches setting for the specified database from the configuration.
admin:database-get-fast-element-word-searches	This function returns the fast element word searches setting for the specified database from the configuration.
admin:database-get-fast-phrase-searches	This function returns the fast phrase searches setting for the specified database from the configuration.
admin:database-get-fast-reverse-searches	This function returns the fast reverse searches setting for the specified database from the configuration.
admin:database-get-field	This function returns the field specification for the specified database from the configuration.
admin:database-get-field-excluded-elements	This function returns the field excluded elements specification for the specified database from the configuration.
admin:database-get-field-fast-case-sensitive-searches	This function returns true if the fast case sensitive searches setting for the specified field is enabled.
admin:database-get-field-fast-diacritic-sensitive-searches	This function returns true if the fast diacritic sensitive searches setting for the specified field is enabled.
admin:database-get-field-fast-phrase-searches	This function returns true if the fast phrase searches setting for the specified field is enabled.

admin:database-get-field-include-document-root	This function returns the field include document root setting for the specified field from the configuration.
admin:database-get-field-included-elements	This function returns the fields included elements specification for the specified database from the configuration.
admin:database-get-field-one-character-searches	This function returns true if the one character searches setting for the specified field is enabled.
admin:database-get-field-stemmed-searches	This function returns stemmed searches setting for the specified field if configured.
admin:database-get-field-three-character-searches	This function returns true if the three character searches setting for the specified field is enabled.
admin:database-get-field-three-character-word-positions	This function returns true if the three character word positions setting for the specified field is enabled.
admin:database-get-field-trailing-wildcard-searches	This function returns true if the trailing wildcard searches setting for the specified field is enabled.
admin:database-get-field-trailing-wildcard-word-positions	This function returns true if the trailing wildcard word positions setting for the specified field is enabled.
admin:database-get-field-two-character-searches	This function returns true if the two character searches setting for the specified field is enabled.
admin:database-get-field-word-lexicons	This function returns the word lexicons specification(s) for the specified database from the configuration.
admin:database-get-field-word-searches	This function returns true if the word searches setting for the specified field is enabled.
admin:database-get-fields	This function returns the fields specification(s) for the specified database from the configuration.
admin:database-get-format-compatibility	This function returns the format compatibility setting for the specified database from the configuration.
admin:database-get-fragment-parents	This function returns the fragment parents specification for the specified database from the configuration.
admin:database-get-fragment-roots	This function returns the fragment roots specification for the specified database from the configuration.

admin:database-get-geospatial-element-attribute-pair-indexes	This function returns the geospatial element attribute pair indexes specification(s) for the specified database from the configuration.
admin:database-get-geospatial-element-child-indexes	This function returns the geospatial element child indexes specification(s) for the specified database from the configuration.
admin:database-get-geospatial-element-indexes	This function returns the geospatial element indexes specification(s) for the specified database from the configuration.
admin:database-get-geospatial-element-pair-indexes	This function returns the geospatial element pair indexes specification(s) for the specified database from the configuration.
admin:database-get-id	This function returns the ID for the specified database from the configuration.
admin:database-get-in-memory-limit	This function returns the in memory limit setting for the specified database from the configuration.
admin:database-get-in-memory-list-size	This function returns the im memory list size setting for the specified database from the configuration.
admin:database-get-in-memory-range-index-size	This function returns the in memory range index size setting for the specified database from the configuration.
admin:database-get-in-memory-reverse-index-size	This function returns the in memory reverse index size setting for the specified database from the configuration.
admin:database-get-in-memory-tree-size	This function returns the in memory tree size setting for the specified database from the configuration.
admin:database-get-index-detection	This function returns the index detection setting for the specified database from the configuration.
admin:database-get-inherit-collections	This function returns the inherit collections setting for the specified database from the configuration.
admin:database-get-inherit-permissions	This function returns the inherit positions setting for the specified database from the configuration.
admin:database-get-inherit-quality	This function returns the inherit quality setting for the specified database from the configuration.

admin:database-get-journal-size	This function returns the journal size setting for the specified database from the configuration.
admin:database-get-language	This function returns the language for the specified database from the configuration.
admin:database-get-maintain-directory-last-modified	This function returns the maintain directory last modified setting for the specified database from the configuration.
admin:database-get-maintain-last-modified	This function returns the maintain last modified setting for the specified database from the configuration.
admin:database-get-merge-blackouts	This function returns the merge blackouts specification for the specified database from the configuration.
admin:database-get-merge-enable	This function returns the merge enable setting for the specified database from the configuration.
admin:database-get-merge-max-size	This function returns the merge max size setting for the specified database from the configuration.
admin:database-get-merge-min-ratio	This function returns the merge min ratio setting for the specified database from the configuration.
admin:database-get-merge-min-size	This function returns the merge min size setting for the specified database from the configuration.
admin:database-get-merge-timestamp	This function returns the merge timestamp setting for the specified database from the configuration.
admin:database-get-name	This function returns the name for the specified database from the configuration.
admin:database-get-one-character-searches	This function returns the one character searches setting for the specified database from the configuration.
admin:database-get-phrase-arounds	This function returns the phrase arounds specification(s) for the specified database from the configuration.
admin:database-get-phrase-throughs	This function returns the phrase throughs specification(s) for the specified database from the configuration.
admin:database-get-positions-list-max-size	This function returns the positions list max size setting for the specified database from the configuration.
admin:database-get-preallocate-journals	This function returns the preallocate journals setting for the specified database from the configuration.

admin:database-get-preload-mapped-data	This function returns the preload mapped data setting for the specified database from the configuration.
admin:database-get-range-element-attribute-indexes	This function returns the range element attribute indexes specification(s) for the specified database from the configuration.
admin:database-get-range-element-indexes	This function returns the range element indexes specification(s) for the specified database from the configuration.
admin:database-get-reindexer-enable	This function returns the reindexer enable setting for the specified database from the configuration.
admin:database-get-reindexer-throttle	This function returns the reindexer throttle setting for the specified database from the configuration.
admin:database-get-reindexer-timestamp	This function returns the reindexer timestamp setting for the specified database from the configuration.
admin:database-get-schema-database	This function returns the ID of the schema database for the specified database from the configuration.
admin:database-get-security-database	This function returns the ID of the security database for the specified database from the configuration.
admin:database-get-stemmed-searches	This function returns the stemmed searches setting for the specified database from the configuration.
admin:database-get-three-character-searches	This function returns the three character searches setting for the specified database from the configuration.
admin:database-get-three-character-word-positions	This function returns the three character word positions setting for the specified database from the configuration.
admin:database-get-trailing-wildcard-searches	This function returns the trailing wildcard searches setting for the specified database from the configuration.
admin:database-get-trailing-wildcard-word-positions	This function returns the trailing wildcard word positions setting for the specified database from the configuration.
admin:database-get-triggers-database	This function returns the ID of the triggers database for the specified database from the configuration.

admin:database-get-two-character-searches	This function returns the two character searches setting for the specified database from the configuration.
admin:database-get-uri-lexicon	This function returns the URI lexicon setting for the specified database from the configuration.
admin:database-get-word-lexicons	This function returns the word lexicons specification(s) for the specified database from the configuration.
admin:database-get-word-positions	This function returns the word positions setting for the specified database from the configuration.
admin:database-get-word-query-excluded-elements	This function returns the word query excluded elements setting for the specified database from the configuration.
admin:database-get-word-query-fast-case-sensitive-searches	This function returns the word query fast case sensitive searches setting for the specified database from the configuration.
admin:database-get-word-query-fast-diacritic-sensitive-searches	This function returns the word query fast diacritic sensitive searches setting for the specified database from the configuration.
admin:database-get-word-query-fast-phrase-searches	This function returns the word query fast phrase searches setting for the specified database from the configuration.
admin:database-get-word-query-include-document-root	This function returns the word query include document root setting for the specified database from the configuration.
admin:database-get-word-query-included-elements	This function returns the word query included elements setting for the specified database from the configuration.
admin:database-get-word-query-one-character-searches	This function returns the word query one character searches setting for the specified database from the configuration.
admin:database-get-word-query-stemmed-searches	This function returns the reindexer word query stemmed searches setting for the specified database from the configuration.

admin:database-get-word-query-three-character-searches	This function returns the word query three character searches setting for the specified database from the configuration.
admin:database-get-word-query-three-character-word-positions	This function returns the word query three character word positions setting for the specified database from the configuration.
admin:database-get-word-query-trailing-wildcard-searches	This function returns the word query trailing wildcard searches setting for the specified database from the configuration.
admin:database-get-word-query-trailing-wildcard-word-positions	This function returns the word query trailing wildcard word positions setting for the specified database from the configuration.
admin:database-get-word-query-two-character-searches	This function returns the word query two character searches setting for the specified database from the configuration.
admin:database-get-word-query-word-searches	This function returns the word query searches setting for the specified database from the configuration.
admin:database-get-word-searches	This function returns the word searches setting for the specified database from the configuration.
admin:database-included-element	This function constructs an included element specification.
admin:database-monthly-backup	This function constructs a monthly scheduled backup.
admin:database-one-time-backup	This function constructs a one-time backup.
admin:database-one-time-merge-blackout	This function constructs a one-time merge-blackout specification.
admin:database-phrase-around	This function constructs a phrase through specification.
admin:database-phrase-through	This function constructs a phrase through specification.
admin:database-range-element-attribute-index	This function constructs a range element attribute index specification.
admin:database-range-element-index	This function constructs a range element index specification.

admin:database-recurring-merge-blackout	This function constructs a merge-blackout specification.
admin:database-set-attribute-value-positions	This function sets the attribute value positions setting for the specified database in the configuration.
admin:database-set-collection-lexicon	This function sets the collection lexicon setting for the specified database in the configuration.
admin:database-set-directory-creation	This function sets the directory creation setting for the specified database in the configuration.
admin:database-set-element-value-positions	This function sets the element value positions setting for the specified database in the configuration.
admin:database-set-element-word-positions	This function sets the element word positions setting for the specified database in the configuration.
admin:database-set-enabled	This function sets the enabled value for the specified database in the configuration.
admin:database-set-expunge-locks	This function sets the expunge locks setting for the specified database in the configuration.
admin:database-set-fast-case-sensitive-searches	This function sets the fast case sensitive searches setting for the specified database in the configuration.
admin:database-set-fast-diacritic-sensitive-searches	This function sets the fast diacritic-sensitive searches setting for the specified database in the configuration.
admin:database-set-fast-element-character-searches	This function sets the fast element character searches setting for the specified database in the configuration.
admin:database-set-fast-element-phrase-searches	This function sets the fast element phrase searches setting for the specified database in the configuration.
admin:database-set-fast-element-trailing-wildcard-searches	This function sets the fast element trailing wildcard searches setting for the specified database in the configuration.
admin:database-set-fast-element-word-searches	This function sets the element word searches setting for the specified database in the configuration.
admin:database-set-fast-phrase-searches	This function sets the fast phrase searches setting for the specified database in the configuration.
admin:database-set-fast-reverse-searches	This function sets the fast reverse searches setting for the specified database in the configuration.

admin:database-set-field-fast-case-sensitive-searches	This function sets the field fast case sensitive searches setting for the specified field in the configuration.
admin:database-set-field-fast-diacritic-sensitive-searches	This function sets the field fast diacritic sensitive searches setting for the specified field in the configuration.
admin:database-set-field-fast-phrase-searches	This function sets the field fast phrase searches setting for the specified field in the configuration.
admin:database-set-field-include-document-root	This function sets the field include document root setting for the specified field in the configuration.
admin:database-set-field-name	This function sets the field name setting for the specified field in the configuration.
admin:database-set-field-one-character-searches	This function sets the field one character searches setting for the specified field in the configuration.
admin:database-set-field-stemmed-searches	This function sets the field stemmed searches setting for the specified field in the configuration.
admin:database-set-field-three-character-searches	This function sets the field three character searches setting for the specified field in the configuration.
admin:database-set-field-three-character-word-positions	This function sets the field three character word positions setting for the specified field in the configuration.
admin:database-set-field-trailing-wildcard-searches	This function sets the field trailing wildcard searches setting for the specified database in the configuration.
admin:database-set-field-trailing-wildcard-word-positions	This function sets the field trailing wildcard word positions setting for the specified field in the configuration.
admin:database-set-field-two-character-searches	This function sets the field two character searches setting for the specified field in the configuration.
admin:database-set-field-word-searches	This function sets the field word searches setting for the specified field in the configuration.
admin:database-set-format-compatibility	This function sets the format cpmpatibility setting for the specified database in the configuration.
admin:database-set-in-memory-limit	This function sets the in-memory limit setting for the specified database in the configuration.

admin:database-set-in-memory-list-size	This function sets the in-memory list size setting for the specified database in the configuration.
admin:database-set-in-memory-range-index-size	This function sets the in-memory range index size setting for the specified database in the configuration.
admin:database-set-in-memory-reverse-index-size	This function sets the in-memory range reverse index size setting for the specified database in the configuration.
admin:database-set-in-memory-tree-size	This function sets the in-memory tree size setting for the specified database in the configuration.
admin:database-set-index-detection	This function sets the index detection setting for the specified database in the configuration.
admin:database-set-inherit-collections	This function sets the inherit collections setting for the specified database in the configuration.
admin:database-set-inherit-permissions	This function sets the inherit permissions setting for the specified database in the configuration.
admin:database-set-inherit-quality	This function sets the inherit quality setting for the specified database in the configuration.
admin:database-set-journal-size	This function sets the journal size setting for the specified database in the configuration.
admin:database-set-language	This function sets the language for the specified database in the configuration.
admin:database-set-maintain-directory-last-modified	This function sets the maintain directory last modified setting for the specified database in the configuration.
admin:database-set-maintain-last-modified	This function sets the maintain last modified setting for the specified database in the configuration.
admin:database-set-merge-enable	This function sets the merge enable setting for the specified database in the configuration.
admin:database-set-merge-max-size	This function sets the merge max size setting for the specified database in the configuration.
admin:database-set-merge-min-ratio	This function sets the merge min ratio setting for the specified database in the configuration.
admin:database-set-merge-min-size	This function sets the merge minimum size setting for the specified database in the configuration.

admin:database-set-merge-timestamp	This function sets the merge timestamp setting for the specified database in the configuration.
admin:database-set-name	This function changes the name of the database with the specified ID to the specified name.
admin:database-set-one-character-searches	This function sets the one character searches setting for the specified database in the configuration.
admin:database-set-positions-list-max-size	This function sets the positions list max size setting for the specified database in the configuration.
admin:database-set-preallocate-journals	This function sets the preallocate journals setting for the specified database in the configuration.
admin:database-set-preload-mapped-data	This function sets the preload mapped data setting for the specified database in the configuration.
admin:database-set-reindexer-enable	This function sets the reindexer enable setting for the specified database in the configuration.
admin:database-set-reindexer-throttle	This function sets the reindexer throttle setting for the specified database in the configuration.
admin:database-set-reindexer-timestamp	This function sets the reindexer timestamp setting for the specified database in the configuration.
admin:database-set-schema-database	This function sets the schema database for a database to the specified database in the configuration.
admin:database-set-security-database	This function sets the security database for a database to the specified database in the configuration.
admin:database-set-stemmed-searches	This function sets the stemmed searches setting for the specified database in the configuration.
admin:database-set-three-character-searches	This function sets the three character searches setting for the specified database in the configuration.
admin:database-set-three-character-word-positions	This function sets the three character word positions setting for the specified database in the configuration.
admin:database-set-trailing-wildcard-searches	This function sets the trailing wildcard searches setting for the specified database in the configuration.
admin:database-set-trailing-wildcard-word-positions	This function sets the trailing wildcard word positions setting for the specified database in the configuration.

admin:database-set-triggers-database	This function sets the triggers database to the specified database ID for the specified database in the configuration.
admin:database-set-two-character-searches	This function sets the two character searches setting for the specified database in the configuration.
admin:database-set-uri-lexicon	This function sets the URI lexicon setting for the specified database in the configuration.
admin:database-set-word-positions	This function sets the word positions setting for the specified database in the configuration.
admin:database-set-word-query-fast-case-sensitive-searches	This function returns the word query fast case sensitive searches setting for the specified database from the configuration.
admin:database-set-word-query-fast-diacritic-sensitive-searches	This function sets the word query fast diacritic sensitive searches setting for the specified database in the configuration.
admin:database-set-word-query-fast-phrase-searches	This function sets the word query fast phrase searches setting for the specified database in the configuration.
admin:database-set-word-query-include-document-root	This function sets the word query include document root setting for the specified field in the configuration.
admin:database-set-word-query-one-character-searches	This function sets the word query one character searches setting for the specified field in the configuration.
admin:database-set-word-query-stemmed-searches	This function sets the word query stemmed searches setting for the specified database in the configuration.
admin:database-set-word-query-three-character-searches	This function sets the word query three character searches setting for the specified database in the configuration.
admin:database-set-word-query-three-character-word-positions	This function sets the word query three character word positions setting for the specified database in the configuration.
admin:database-set-word-query-trailing-wildcard-searches	This function sets the word query trailing wildcard searches setting for the specified database in the configuration.

admin:database-set-word-query-trailing-wildcard-word-positions	This function sets the word query trailing wildcard word positions setting for the specified database in the configuration.
admin:database-set-word-query-two-character-searches	This function sets the word query two character searches setting for the specified database in the configuration.
admin:database-set-word-query-word-searches	This function sets the word query word searches setting for the specified database in the configuration.
admin:database-set-word-searches	This function sets the word searches setting for the specified database in the configuration.
admin:database-weekly-backup	This function constructs a weekly scheduled backup.
admin:database-word-lexicon	This function constructs a word lexicon specification.
admin:forest-add-backup	This function adds scheduled backup specifications for a forest to a configuration.
admin:forest-add-failover-host	This function adds a failover host to the list of failover hosts for the specified forest in the specified configuration.
admin:forest-copy	This function creates a new forest specification with the same settings as the forest with the specified ID.
admin:forest-create	This function creates a new forest configuration.
admin:forest-delete	This function deletes the configuration for the specified forest from the configuration.
admin:forest-delete-backup	This function deletes scheduled backup specifications for a forest from a configuration.
admin:forest-delete-failover-host	This function deletes the specified failover host(s) from the failover-host list in the specified configuration.
admin:forest-get-backups	This function returns the scheduled backups for the specified forest from the configuration.
admin:forest-get-data-directory	This function returns the name of the data directory of the specified forest.
admin:forest-get-enabled	This function returns the enabled state of the specified forest.

admin:forest-get-failover-enable	This function returns the state of whether failover is enabled for the specified forest.
admin:forest-get-failover-hosts	This function returns the forest IDs of the hosts defined as failover hosts for this forest.
admin:forest-get-host	This function returns the ID of the host in which the specicified forest resides.
admin:forest-get-id	This function returns the ID of the forest with the specified name, from the specified configuration.
admin:forest-get-name	This function returns the name(s) of the specified forest(s), given the forest ID(s).
admin:forest-get-updates-allowed	This function returns the state of whether updates are allowed for the specified forest.
admin:forest-monthly-backup	This function constructs a monthly scheduled backup.
admin:forest-one-time-backup	This function constructs a one-time backup.
admin:forest-set-enabled	This function sets the enabled state for a forest configuration.
admin:forest-set-failover-enable	This function sets the forest failover enabled state for a forest configuration.
admin:forest-set-host	This function sets a forest configuration to a new host.
admin:forest-set-updates-allowed	This function sets whether updates are allowed for a forest configuration.
admin:forest-weekly-backup	This function constructs a weekly scheduled backup.
admin:get-appserver-ids	This function returns all the appserver IDs from the configuration.
admin:get-configuration	Loads the admin configuration into memory for use by other functions in the Admin module.
admin:get-database-ids	This function returns all the database IDs from the configuration.
admin:get-forest-ids	This function returns all the forest IDs from the configuration.
admin:get-group-ids	This function returns all the group IDs from the configuration.
admin:get-host-ids	This function returns all the host IDs from the configuration.

admin:group-add-namespace	Add one or more namespaces to a Group configuration, which will predefine the namespace(s) for all requests evaluated against any App Server in the Group.
admin:group-add-schema	This function adds a schema binding definition to the existing schema binding definitions in the configuration for the specified Group.
admin:group-add-trace-event	This function adds trace events to the configuration.
admin:group-copy	This function creates a new group specification with the same settings as the group with the specified ID.
admin:group-create	This function creates a new group with the specified name in the configuration.
admin:group-delete	This function deletes a group in the configuration.
admin:group-delete-namespace	This function deletes the specified namespaces from the configuration for the specified group.
admin:group-delete-schema	This function deletes a schema binding definition to the existing schema binding definitions in the configuration for the specified Group.
admin:group-delete-trace-event	This function deletes the specified trace events from the configuration.
admin:group-disable-audit-event-type	This function changes the audit event type(s) enabled setting for the audit configuration.
admin:group-enable-audit-event-type	This function changes the audit event type(s) enabled setting for the audit configuration.
admin:group-get-appserver-ids	This function returns the IDs of all appservers belonging to the group.
admin:group-get-audit-enabled	This function returns the value for the audit enabled setting from the specified group.
admin:group-get-audit-event-type-enabled	This function returns the audit event type's enabled setting for the audit configuration.
admin:group-get-audit-excluded-roles	This function returns the roles excluded from auditing.
admin:group-get-audit-excluded-uris	This function returns the uris excluded from auditing.

admin:group-get-audit-excluded-users	This function returns the users excluded from auditing.
admin:group-get-audit-included-roles	This function returns the roles included from auditing.
admin:group-get-audit-included-uris	This function returns the uris included from auditing.
admin:group-get-audit-included-users	This function returns the users included from auditing.
admin:group-get-audit-outcome-restriction	This function returns whether auditing events are restricted by a success or failure outcome.
admin:group-get-compressed-tree-cache-partitions	This function returns the value for the compressed tree cache partitions setting from the specified group.
admin:group-get-compressed-tree-cache-size	This function returns the value for the compressed tree cache size setting from the specified group.
admin:group-get-expanded-tree-cache-partitions	This function returns the value for the expanded tree cache partitions setting from the specified group.
admin:group-get-expanded-tree-cache-size	This function returns the value for the expanded tree cache size setting from the specified group.
admin:group-get-failover-enable	This function returns the value for the failover enable setting from the specified group.
admin:group-get-file-log-level	This function returns the value for the file log level setting from the specified group.
admin:group-get-host-ids	This function returns the IDs of all hosts belonging to the group.
admin:group-get-host-initial-timeout	This function returns the value for the host initial timeout setting from the specified group.
admin:group-get-host-timeout	This function returns the value for the host timeout setting from the specified group.
admin:group-get-http-timeout	This function returns the value for the http timeout setting from the specified group.
admin:group-get-http-user-agent	This function returns the value for the http user agent setting from the specified group.
admin:group-get-httpserver-ids	This function returns the IDs of all httpservers belonging to the group.

admin:group-get-id	This function returns the ID of the group.
admin:group-get-keep-audit-files	This function returns the value for the keep audit files setting from the specified group.
admin:group-get-keep-log-files	This function returns the value for the keep log files setting from the specified group.
admin:group-get-list-cache-partitions	This function returns the value for the list cache partitions setting from the specified group.
admin:group-get-list-cache-size	This function returns the value for the list cache size setting from the specified group.
admin:group-get-name	This function returns the name of the specified group.
admin:group-get-namespaces	This function returns the value of any namespace definitions predefined for the specified group.
admin:group-get-retry-timeout	This function returns the value for the number of seconds a request will retry before timing out.
admin:group-get-rotate-audit-files	This function returns the value for the rotate audit files setting from the specified group.
admin:group-get-rotate-log-files	This function returns the value for the rotate log files setting from the specified group.
admin:group-get-schemas	This function returns the value of any schemas definitions predefined for the specified group.
admin:group-get-smtp-relay	This function returns the value for the smtp relay setting from the specified group.
admin:group-get-smtp-timeout	This function returns the value for the smtp timeout setting from the specified group.
admin:group-get-system-log-level	This function returns the value for the system log level setting from the specified group.
admin:group-get-taskserver-id	This function returns the ID of of the taskserver belonging to the group.
admin:group-get-trace-events	This function returns the value of any trace events activated for the specified group.
admin:group-get-trace-events-activated	This function returns the value for the trace events activated setting from the specified group.
admin:group-get-webdavserver-ids	This function returns the IDs of all webdavservers belonging to the group.

admin:group-get-xdbcserver-ids	This function returns the IDs of all xdbcservers belonging to the group.
admin:group-get-xdqp-timeout	This function returns the value for the xdqp timeout setting from the specified group.
admin:group-namespace	This function constructs a namespace element with the specified prefix and URI.
admin:group-schema	This function constructs a schema element with the specified prefix and URI.
admin:group-set-audit-enabled	This function changes the audit enabled setting for the group in the configuration.
admin:group-set-audit-outcome-restriction	This function restricts the audit configuration by auditing events only if they are "success" or "failure" events.
admin:group-set-audit-role-restriction	This function restricts the audit configuration by excluding or including by role.
admin:group-set-audit-uri-restriction	This function restricts the audit configuration by excluding or including by document uri(s).
admin:group-set-audit-user-restriction	This function restricts the audit configuration by excluding or including by user.
admin:group-set-compressed-tree-cache-partitions	This function changes the compressed tree cache partitions setting of the group with the specified ID to the specified value.
admin:group-set-compressed-tree-cache-size	This function changes the compressed tree cache size setting of the group with the specified ID to the specified value.
admin:group-set-expanded-tree-cache-partitions	This function changes the expanded tree cache partitions setting of the group with the specified ID to the specified value.
admin:group-set-expanded-tree-cache-size	This function changes the expanded tree cache size setting of the group with the specified ID to the specified value.
admin:group-set-failover-enable	This function changes the failover enable setting for the group in the configuration.

admin:group-set-file-log-level	This function changes the host file log level setting for the group in the configuration.
admin:group-set-host-initial-timeout	This function changes the host initial timeout setting (the time the cluster will wait for a host to come online during cluster startup) for the group in the configuration.
admin:group-set-host-timeout	This function changes the host timeout setting (the timeout for communication between hosts) for the group in the configuration.
admin:group-set-http-timeout	This function changes the HTTP timeout setting for the group in the configuration.
admin:group-set-http-user-agent	This function changes the HTTP User-Agent setting for the group in the configuration.
admin:group-set-keep-audit-files	This function changes the keep audit files setting for the group in the configuration.
admin:group-set-keep-log-files	This function changes the keep log files setting for the group in the configuration.
admin:group-set-list-cache-partitions	This function changes the list cache partitions setting of the group with the specified ID to the specified value.
admin:group-set-list-cache-size	This function changes the list cache size setting of the group with the specified ID to the specified value.
admin:group-set-name	This function changes the name of the group with the specified ID to the specified name.
admin:group-set-retry-timeout	This function changes the the number of seconds a request will retry before timing out.
admin:group-set-rotate-audit-files	This function changes the rotate audit files setting for the group in the configuration.
admin:group-set-rotate-log-files	This function changes the rotate log files setting for the group in the configuration.
admin:group-set-smtp-relay	This function changes the SMTP relay setting for the group in the configuration.
admin:group-set-smtp-timeout	This function changes the SMTP timeout setting for the group in the configuration.

admin:group-set-system-log-level	This function changes the host system log level setting for the group in the configuration.
admin:group-set-trace-events-activated	This function changes the value for trace events in the group configuration.
admin:group-set-xdqp-timeout	This function changes the XDQP timeout setting (the timeout for communication between data nodes and evaluator nodes) for the group in the configuration.
admin:group-trace-event	This function constructs an event element for the specified event name.
admin:host-get-group	This function returns the group ID for the host with the specified ID.
admin:host-get-id	This function return the ID for the specified host from the configuration.
admin:host-get-name	This function returns the name for the host with the specified ID.
admin:host-get-port	This function returns the bind port for the host with the specified ID.
admin:host-set-group	This function changes the group to which an existing host belongs to the newly specified value.
admin:host-set-name	This function changes the name of an existing host to the newly specified value.
admin:host-set-port	This function changes the bind port value for the host to the newly specified value.
admin:http-server-create	This function creates a new HTTP App Server with the specified name, root, and port in the configuration.
admin:mimetype	This function constructs a mimetype specification.
admin:mimetypes-add	This function adds mimetypes to the configuration.
admin:mimetypes-delete	This function deletes mimetypes from the configuration.
admin:mimetypes-get	This function returns all the mimetypes from the configuration.
admin:restart-hosts	This function restarts MarkLogic Server for the specified hosts.
admin:save-configuration	This function saves a configuration specification to the cluster configuration files.

admin:save-configuration-without-restart	This function saves a configuration specification to the cluster configuration files, without restarting MarkLogic Server.
admin:taskserver-get-debug-allow	This function returns the value for the debug-allow setting configured on the task server for the specified group.
admin:taskserver-get-debug-threads	This function returns the number of debug threads configured on the task server for the specified group.
admin:taskserver-get-default-time-limit	This function returns the default time limit configured on the task server for the specified group.
admin:taskserver-get-log-errors	This function returns the value for the log-errors setting configured on the task server for the specified group.
admin:taskserver-get-max-time-limit	This function returns the maximum time limit configured on the task server for the specified group.
admin:taskserver-get-name	This function returns the name of the task server for the specified group from the configuration.
admin:taskserver-get-post-commit-trigger-depth	This function returns the maximum post-commit trigger depth configured on the task server for the specified group.
admin:taskserver-get-pre-commit-trigger-depth	This function returns the maximum pre-commit trigger depth configured on the task server for the specified group.
admin:taskserver-get-pre-commit-trigger-limit	This function returns the pre-commit trigger limit configured on the task server for the specified group.
admin:taskserver-get-profile-allow	This function returns the value for the profile-allow setting configured on the task server for the specified group.
admin:taskserver-get-queue-size	This function returns the number queue size configured on the task server for the specified group.
admin:taskserver-get-threads	This function returns the number of threads configured on the task server for the specified group.
admin:taskserver-set-debug-allow	This function sets the value for the debug allow setting for the task server in the configuration.

admin:taskserver-set-debug-threads	This function sets the value in the configuration of the maximum number of debug threads for the specified task server.
admin:taskserver-set-default-time-limit	This function sets the task server default time limit in the configuration.
admin:taskserver-set-log-errors	This function sets the value for the log errors setting for the task server in the configuration.
admin:taskserver-set-max-time-limit	This function sets the task server max time limit in the configuration.
admin:taskserver-set-post-commit-trigger-depth	This function sets the value for the task server post-commit trigger depth in the configuration.
admin:taskserver-set-pre-commit-trigger-depth	This function sets the value for the task server pre-commit trigger depth in the configuration.
admin:taskserver-set-pre-commit-trigger-limit	This function sets the value for the task server pre-commit trigger depth in the configuration.
admin:taskserver-set-profile-allow	This function sets the value for the profile allow setting for the task server in the configuration.
admin:taskserver-set-queue-size	This function sets the value in the configuration of the maximum queue size for the specified task server.
admin:taskserver-set-threads	This function sets the value in the configuration of the maximum number of threads for the specified task server.
admin:webdav-server-create	This function creates a new WebDAV App Server with the specified name, library, and port in the configuration.
admin:xdbc-server-create	This function creates a new XDBC App Server with the specified name, root, and port in the configuration.
alert:action-get-description	This function returns the description of a given action.
alert:action-get-module	This function returns the module of a given action.
alert:action-get-module-db	This function returns the module database of a given action.
alert:action-get-module-root	This function returns the module root of a given action.
alert:action-get-name	This function returns the name of a given action.
alert:action-get-options	This function returns the options of a given action.

alert:action-insert	This function inserts the xml representing the action into the collection.
alert:action-remove	This function removes the named action from the database or throws an exception if the action does not exist.
alert:action-set-description	This function returns the action with the description of the action updated.
alert:action-set-module	This function returns the action with the module of the action updated.
alert:action-set-module-db	This function sets the module database of a given action.
alert:action-set-module-root	This function sets the module root of a given action.
alert:action-set-name	This function returns the action with the name of the action updated.
alert:action-set-options	This function returns the action with the options of the action updated.
alert:config-delete	Remove an alerting configuration identified by the specified URI.
alert:config-get	Gets the config associated with the specified URI.
alert:config-get-cpf-domain-ids	This function provides convenient access to the specified sub-element within an alerting config.
alert:config-get-cpf-domain-names	This function provides convenient access to the specified sub-element within an alerting config.
alert:config-get-description	This function provides convenient access to the specified sub-element within an alerting config.
alert:config-get-id	This function provides convenient access to the specified sub-element within an alerting config.
alert:config-get-name	This function provides convenient access to the specified sub-element within an alerting config.
alert:config-get-options	This function provides convenient access to the specified sub-element within an alerting config.
alert:config-get-trigger-ids	This function provides convenient access to the specified sub-element within an alerting config.

alert:config-get-uri	This function provides convenient access to the specified sub-element within an alerting config.
alert:config-insert	Inserts a config into the database.
alert:config-set-cpf-domain-ids	This function provides convenient access to the specified sub-element within an alerting config.
alert:config-set-cpf-domain-names	This function provides convenient access to the specified sub-element within an alerting config.
alert:config-set-description	This function provides convenient access to the specified sub-element within an alerting config.
alert:config-set-name	This function provides convenient access to the specified sub-element within an alerting config.
alert:config-set-options	This function provides convenient access to the specified sub-element within an alerting config.
alert:config-set-trigger-ids	This function provides convenient access to the specified sub-element within an alerting config.
alert:config-set-uri	This function provides convenient access to the specified sub-element within an alerting config.
alert:config-set-uri	This function provides convenient access to the specified sub-element within an alerting config.
alert:create-triggers	Create triggers that invoke the standard alerting trigger module.
alert:find-matching-rules	Returns a list of all rules associated with the specified config that match the specified document.
alert:get-actions	This function retrieves all the named actions in the specified config URI.
alert:get-all-rules	This function returns all rules visible to the current user.
alert:get-my-rules	This function returns all rules associated with the current user.
alert:invoke-matching-actions	Finds the rules that match the specified document and invokes their associated actions.
alert:make-action	This function creates the xml representing an action.
alert:make-config	Create an alerting configuration associated with a particular URI.
alert:make-log-action	Create a standard logging action named "log".

alert:make-rule	This function creates the XML representing a rule.
alert:remove-triggers	Remove triggers whose IDs are listed in the config.
alert:rule-action-query	This function creates a query to find rules with any of the specified actions.
alert:rule-get-action	This function returns the action of a given rule.
alert:rule-get-description	This function returns the description of a given rule.
alert:rule-get-id	This function returns the ID of a given rule.
alert:rule-get-name	This function returns the name of a given rule.
alert:rule-get-options	This function returns the options of a given rule.
alert:rule-get-query	Get the cts:query corresponding to the rule's query expression.
alert:rule-get-user-id	This function returns the user ID of a given rule.
alert:rule-id-query	This function creates a query to find rules with any of the specified IDs.
alert:rule-insert	This function inserts rule into the database associated with the specified alerting configuration.
alert:rule-name-query	This function creates a query to find rules with any of the specified names.
alert:rule-remove	This function removes the XML representing the rule from the collection.
alert:rule-set-action	This function returns the rule with the action updated.
alert:rule-set-description	This function returns the rule with the description of the rule updated.
alert:rule-set-name	This function returns the rule with the name of the rule updated.
alert:rule-set-options	This function returns the rule with the options of the rule updated.
alert:rule-set-query	Set the cts:query corresponding to the rule's query expression.
alert:rule-set-user-id	This function returns the rule with the user ID updated.
alert:rule-user-id-query	This function creates a query to find rules with any of the specified user IDs.

alert:spawn-matching-actions		Finds the rules that match the specified document and spawns their associated actions.
cpf:check-transition		Verify that the current transition is the correct one for the document.
cpf:document-get-error		Fetch a trace of the error that caused the document's processing to fail, if any.
cpf:document-get-last-updated		Determine the date and time of the last update to the document's content, if any.
cpf:document-get-processing-status		Determine the document's current processing status, if any.
cpf:document-get-state		Determine the document's current state, if any.
cpf:document-set-error		Set the document's error trace to the given value.
cpf:document-set-last-updated		Set the date and time of the document's last update.
cpf:document-set-processing-status		Set the document's processing status to the given value.
cpf:document-set-state		Set the document's state to the given state.
cpf:failure		Concludes the state action in failure, advancing the state as defined by the state transition.
cpf:success		Concludes the action successfully, advancing the state as defined by the transition.
css:convert		Convert CSS text to an equivalent XML representation that is more suitable for analysis.
css:get		Fetch the CSS for the given document, be it embedded or linked.
cts:and-not-query		Returns a query specifying the set difference of the matches specified by two sub-queries.
	cts:and-not-query-negative-query	Returns the negative (second parameter) query used to construct the specified query.
	cts:and-not-query-positive-query	Returns the positive (first parameter) query used to construct the specified query.
cts:and-query		Returns a query specifying the intersection of the matches specified by the sub-queries.

	cts:and-query-options	Returns the options for the specified query.
	cts:and-query-queries	Returns a sequence of the queries that were used to construct the specified query.
cts:box		Returns a geospatial box value.
cts:box-east		Returns a box's eastern boundary.
cts:box-north		Returns a box's northern boundary.
cts:box-south		Returns a box's southern boundary.
cts:box-west		Returns a box's western boundary.
cts:circle		Returns a geospatial circle value.
cts:circle-center		Returns a circle's center point.
cts:circle-radius		Returns a circle's radius.
cts:classify		Classifies a sequence of nodes based on training data.
cts:collection-match		Returns values from the collection lexicon that match the specified wildcard pattern.
cts:collection-query		Returns a query matching documents in the collections with the given URIs.
	cts:collection-query-uris	Returns the URIs used to construct the specified query.
cts:collections		Returns values from the collection lexicon.
cts:confidence		Returns the confidence of a node, or of the context node if no node is provided.
cts:contains		Returns true if any of a sequence of nodes matches a query.
cts:deregister		Deregister a registered query, explicitly releasing the associated resources.
cts:directory-query		Returns a query matching documents in the directories with the given URIs.
	cts:directory-query-depth	Returns the depth used to construct the specified query.
	cts:directory-query-uris	Returns the URIs used to construct the specified query.
cts:distance		Returns the distance (in miles) between two points.

cts:document-query		Returns a query matching documents with the given URIs.
	cts:document-query-uris	Returns the URIs used to construct the specified query.
cts:element-attribute-pair-geospatial-boxes		Returns boxes derived from the specified element point lexicon(s).
cts:element-attribute-pair-geospatial-query		Returns a cts:query matching elements by name which has specific attributes representing latitude and longitude values for a point contained within the given geographic box, circle, or polygon, or equal to the given point.
	cts:element-attribute-pair-geospatial-query-element-name	Returns the QNames used to construct the specified query.
	cts:element-attribute-pair-geospatial-query-latitude-name	Returns the QNames used to construct the specified query.
	cts:element-attribute-pair-geospatial-query-longitude-name	Returns the QNames used to construct the specified query.
	cts:element-attribute-pair-geospatial-query-options	Returns the options for the specified query.
	cts:element-attribute-pair-geospatial-query-region	Returns the geographical regions with which the specified query was constructed.

	cts:element-attribute-pair-geospatial-query-weight	Returns the weight with which the specified query was constructed.
cts:element-attribute-pair-geospatial-value-match		Returns values from the specified element attribute pair geospatial value lexicon(s) that match the specified wildcard pattern.
cts:element-attribute-pair-geospatial-values		Returns values from the specified element-attribute-pair geospatial value lexicon(s).
cts:element-attribute-range-query		Returns a cts:query matching elements by name with a range-index entry equal a given value.
	cts:element-attribute-range-query-attribute-name	Returns the QNames used to construct the specified query.
	cts:element-attribute-range-query-element-name	Returns the QNames used to construct the specified query.
	cts:element-attribute-range-query-operator	Returns the operator used to construct the specified query.
	cts:element-attribute-range-query-options	Returns the options for the specified query.
	cts:element-attribute-range-query-value	Returns the value used to construct the specified query.
	cts:element-attribute-range-query-weight	Returns the weight with which the specified query was constructed.
cts:element-attribute-value-co-occurrences		Returns value co-occurrences from the specified element or element-attribute value lexicon(s).

cts:element-attribute-value-geospatial-co-occurrences		Returns value co-occurrences from the specified element-attribute value lexicon with the specified geospatial lexicon.
cts:element-attribute-value-match		Returns values from the specified element-attribute value lexicon(s) that match the specified pattern.
cts:element-attribute-value-query		Returns a query matching elements by name with attributes by name with text content equal a given phrase.
	cts:element-attribute-value-query-attribute-name	Returns the attribute QNames used to construct the specified query.
	cts:element-attribute-value-query-element-name	Returns the element QNames used to construct the specified query.
	cts:element-attribute-value-query-options	Returns the options for the specified query.
	cts:element-attribute-value-query-text	Returns the text used to construct the specified query.
	cts:element-attribute-value-query-weight	Returns the weight with which the specified query was constructed.
cts:element-attribute-value-query-attribute-name		Returns the attribute QNames used to construct the specified query.
cts:element-attribute-value-query-element-name		Returns the element QNames used to construct the specified query.
cts:element-attribute-value-query-options		Returns the options for the specified query.
cts:element-attribute-value-query-text		Returns the text used to construct the specified query.

cts:element-attribute-value-query-weight		Returns the weight with which the specified query was constructed.
	cts:element-attribute-word-query-attribute-name	Returns the attribute QNames used to construct the specified query.
	cts:element-attribute-word-query-element-name	Returns the element QNames used to construct the specified query.
	cts:element-attribute-word-query-options	Returns the options for the specified query.
	cts:element-attribute-word-query-text	Returns the text used to construct the specified query.
	cts:element-attribute-word-query-weight	Returns the weight with which the specified query was constructed.
cts:element-attribute-words		Returns words from the specified element-attribute word lexicon(s).
cts:element-child-geospatial-boxes		Returns boxes derived from the specified element point lexicon(s).
cts:element-child-geospatial-query		Returns a cts:query matching elements by name which has specific element children representing latitude and longitude values for a point contained within the given geographic box, circle, or polygon, or equal to the given point.
	cts:element-child-geospatial-query-child-name	Returns the QNames used to construct the specified query.

	cts:element-child-geospatial-query-element-name	Returns the QNames used to construct the specified query.
	cts:element-child-geospatial-query-options	Returns the options for the specified query.
	cts:element-child-geospatial-query-region	Returns the geographical regions with which the specified query was constructed.
	cts:element-child-geospatial-query-weight	Returns the weight with which the specified query was constructed.
cts:element-geospatial-value-match		Returns values from the specified element geospatial value lexicon(s) that match the specified wildcard pattern.
cts:element-geospatial-values		Returns values from the specified element geospatial value lexicon(s).
cts:element-pair-geospatial-boxes		Returns boxes derived from the specified element point lexicon(s).
cts:element-pair-geospatial-query		Returns a cts:query matching elements by name which has specific element children representing latitude and longitude values for a point contained within the given geographic box, circle, or polygon, or equal to the given point.
	cts:element-pair-geospatial-query-element-name	Returns the QNames used to construct the specified query.
	cts:element-pair-geospatial-query-latitude-name	Returns the QNames used to construct the specified query.

	cts:element-pair-geospatial-query-longitude-name	Returns the QNames used to construct the specified query.
	cts:element-pair-geospatial-query-options	Returns the options for the specified query.
	cts:element-pair-geospatial-query-region	Returns the geographical regions with which the specified query was constructed.
	cts:element-pair-geospatial-query-weight	Returns the weight with which the specified query was constructed.
cts:element-pair-geospatial-value-match		Returns values from the specified element pair geospatial value lexicon(s) that match the specified wildcard pattern.
cts:element-pair-geospatial-values		Returns values from the specified element-pair geospatial value lexicon(s).
cts:element-query		Returns a cts:query matching elements by name with the content constrained by the given cts:query in the second parameter.
	cts:element-query-element-name	Returns the QNames used to construct the specified query.
	cts:element-query-query	Returns the query used to construct the element query.
cts:element-range-query		Returns a cts:query matching elements by name with a range-index entry equal a given value.
	cts:element-range-query-element-name	Returns the QNames used to construct the specified query.
	cts:element-range-query-operator	Returns the operator used to construct the specified query.

	cts:element-range-query-options	Returns the options for the specified query.
	cts:element-range-query-value	Returns the value used to construct the specified query.
	cts:element-range-query-weight	Returns the weight with which the specified query was constructed.
cts:element-value-co-occurrences		Returns value co-occurrences (that is, pairs of values, both of which appear in the same fragment) from the specified element value lexicon(s).
cts:element-value-geospatial-co-occurrences		Returns value co-occurrences from the specified element value lexicon with the specified geospatial lexicon.
cts:element-value-match		Returns values from the specified element value lexicon(s) that match the specified wildcard pattern.
cts:element-value-query		Returns a query matching elements by name with text content equal a given phrase.
	cts:element-value-query-element-name	Returns the QNames used to construct the specified query.
	cts:element-value-query-options	Returns the options for the specified query.
	cts:element-value-query-text	Returns the text used to construct the specified query.
	cts:element-value-query-weight	Returns the weight with which the specified query was constructed.
cts:element-value-ranges		Returns value ranges from the specified element value lexicon(s).
cts:element-values		Returns values from the specified element value lexicon(s).

cts:element-word-match		Returns words from the specified element word lexicon(s) that match a wildcard pattern.
cts:element-word-query		Returns a query matching elements by name with text content containing a given phrase.
	cts:element-word-query-element-name	Returns the QNames used to construct the specified query.
	cts:element-word-query-options	Returns the options for the specified query.
	cts:element-word-query-text	Returns the text used to construct the specified query.
	cts:element-word-query-weight	Returns the weight with which the specified query was constructed.
cts:element-words		Returns words from the specified element word lexicon.
cts:entity-highlight		Returns a copy of the node, replacing any entities found with the specified expression.
cts:field-word-match		Returns words from the specified field word lexicon(s) that match a wildcard pattern.
cts:field-word-query		Returns a query matching text content containing a given phrase in the specified field.
	cts:field-word-query-field-name	Returns the names used to construct the specified cts:field-word-query.
	cts:field-word-query-options	Returns the options for the specified cts:field-word-query.
	cts:field-word-query-text	Returns the text used to construct the specified cts:field-word-query.
	cts:field-word-query-weight	Returns the weight with which the specified query was constructed.
cts:field-words		Returns words from the specified field word lexicon.
cts:fitness		Returns the fitness of a node, or of the context node if no node is provided.

cts:frequency		Returns an integer representing the number of times in which a particular value occurs in a value lexicon lookup (for example, cts:element-values).
cts:geospatial-co-occurrences		Returns value co-occurrences from the geospatial lexicons.
cts:highlight		Returns a copy of the node, replacing any text matching the query with the specified expression.
cts:near-query		Returns a query matching all of the specified queries, where the matches occur within the specified distance from each other.
	cts:near-query-distance	Returns the distance used to construct the near query.
	cts:near-query-options	Returns the options for the specified query.
	cts:near-query-queries	Returns the query sequence used to construct the near query.
	cts:near-query-weight	Returns the weight with which the specified query was constructed.
cts:not-query		Returns a query specifying the matches not specified by its sub-query.
	cts:not-query-query	Returns the query used to construct the specified query.
	cts:not-query-weight	Returns the weight with which the specified query was constructed.
cts:or-query		Returns a query specifying the union of the matches specified by the sub-queries.
	cts:or-query-queries	Returns a sequence of the queries that were used to construct the specified query.
cts:point		Returns a point value.
cts:point-latitude		Returns a point's latitude value.
cts:point-longitude		Returns a point's longitude value.
cts:polygon		Returns a geospatial polygon value.
cts:polygon-vertices		Returns a polygon's vertices.

cts:quality		Returns the quality of a node, or of the context node if no node is provided.
cts:query		Creates a query.
cts:register		Register a query for later use.
cts:registered-query		Returns a query matching fragments specified by previously registered queries (see cts:register).
	cts:registered-query-ids	Returns the registered query identifiers used to construct the specified query.
	cts:registered-query-options	Returns the options for the specified query.
	cts:registered-query-weight	Returns the weight with which the specified query was constructed.
cts:remainder		Returns an estimated search result size for a node, or of the context node if no node is provided.
cts:reverse-query		Returns a query matching the model nodes.
	cts:reverse-query-nodes	Returns the nodes used to construct the specified query.
	cts:reverse-query-weight	Returns the weight with which the specified query was constructed.
cts:score		Returns the score of a node, or of the context node if no node is provided.
cts:search		Returns a relevance-ordered sequence of nodes specified by a given query.
cts:similar-query		Returns a query matching nodes similar to the model nodes.
	cts:similar-query-nodes	Returns the nodes used to construct the specified query.
	cts:similar-query-weight	Returns the weight with which the specified query was constructed.
cts:stem		Returns the stem(s) for a word.
cts:thresholds		Compute precision, recall, the F measure, and thresholds for the classes computed by the classifier, by comparing with the labels for the same set.
cts:tokenize		Tokenizes text into words, punctuation, and spaces.

cts:train		Produces a set of classifiers from a list of labeled training documents.
cts:uri-match		Returns values from the URI lexicon that match the specified wildcard pattern.
cts:uris		Returns values from the URI lexicon.
cts:word-match		Returns words from the word lexicon that match the wildcard pattern.
cts:word-query		Returns a query matching text content containing a given phrase.
	cts:word-query-options	Returns the options for the specified query.
	cts:word-query-text	Returns the text used to construct the specified query.
	cts:word-query-weight	Returns the weight with which the specified query was constructed.
cts:words		Returns words from the word lexicon.
cvt:basename		Return the filename part of the URI, cutting off any query strings or fragments.
cvt:basepath		Return the base path of the URI, cutting off the filename.
cvt:destination-uri		Construct the destination URI from the source URI using the following rules: The path prefix of the destination URI is the same as the source URI's.
cvt:part-uri		Construct the URI for the part using the following rules: The path prefix of the part URI is the same source URI's, followed by a subdirectory name.
cvt:save-converted-documents		Save a set of converted documents, with appropriate links.
dbg:attach		Attach to a request and stop it for debugging.
dbg:attached		Return the request ID's of attached requests in a given server.
dbg:break		Set a breakpoint at the given expression ID.
dbg:breakpoints		Returns a sequence of expression ID's representing existing breakpoints for the given request.

dbg:clear	Clear a breakpoint at the given expression ID.
dbg:connect	Connect to a Server (http, xdbc, or task) for debugging.
dbg:continue	Continue evaluation of the request.
dbg:detach	Detach from a stopped request.
dbg:disconnect	End the debugging of a server.
dbg:eval	Evaluate a string as an XQuery for debugging.
dbg:expr	Returns a description/representation of a given expression.
dbg:finish	Continue evaluation of the request until the end of the current function.
dbg:function	Returns the expression ID representing the function defined in a module with a given name.
dbg:invoke	Invoke a module for debugging.
dbg:line	Returns a sequence of expression ID's found on a given line of a stopped request.
dbg:next	Continue evaluation of the request until the beginning or end of an expression that is not a descendant of the current expression.
dbg:out	Continue evaluation of the request until the end of the current expression.
dbg:stack	Return the stack trace for a given request.
dbg:status	Return the debugging status of given requests.
dbg:step	Continue evaluation of the request until the beginning or end of an expression.
dbg:stop	Placing this call in XQuery will instruct the evaluator to stop a request for debugging.
dbg:stopped	Return the request ID's of stopped requests in a given server.
dbg:value	Evaluate an expression in the context of the identified stopped request.
dbg:wait	Wait until at least one of the given requests stops or all complete evaluating.

dbk:convert	Convert XHTML to DocBook lite vocabulary, if possible.
dom:add-permissions	Add permissions to the domain.
dom:add-pipeline	Add another pipeline to the set of pipelines bound to the domain.
dom:collection	Return the name of the collection in which domains are stored.
dom:configuration-create	Create a new CPF configuration.
dom:configuration-get	Returns the CPF configuration.
dom:configuration-set-default-domain	Set a new default domain for the CPF configuration.
dom:configuration-set-evaluation-context	Set a new context for the CPF configuration.
dom:configuration-set-permissions	Set new permissions for the CPF configuration.
dom:configuration-set-restart-user	Set a new restart user for the CPF configuration.
dom:create	Create a new content processing domain, along with the triggers that perform work in that domain.
dom:domain-scope	Create a domain scope element.
dom:domains	Return all the domains.
dom:evaluation-context	Create an evaluation context element.
dom:get	Find a particular domain.
dom:remove	Remove the domain and any associated triggers.
dom:remove-permissions	Remove permissions to the domain.
dom:remove-pipeline	Remove the association between a pipeline and the domain.
dom:set-description	Set the description of the domain.
dom:set-domain-scope	Set the scope of the domain.
dom:set-evaluation-context	Set the evaluation context of the domain.
dom:set-name	Set the name of the domain to something else.
dom:set-permissions	Set the permissions of the domain.
dom:set-pipelines	Bind a new set of pipelines to the domain.

entity:enrich	Returns the entity-enriched XML for the given XML node.
excel:clean	Clean up any conversion artifacts or other infelicities, putting each sheet into its own div element.
fn:abs	Returns the absolute value of $arg.
fn:adjust-date-to-timezone	Adjusts an xs:date value to a specific timezone, or to no timezone at all.
fn:adjust-dateTime-to-timezone	Adjusts an xs:dateTime value to a specific timezone, or to no timezone at all.
fn:adjust-time-to-timezone	Adjusts an xs:time value to a specific timezone, or to no timezone at all.
fn:avg	Returns the average of the values in the input sequence $arg, that is, the sum of the values divided by the number of values.
fn:base-uri	Returns the value of the base-uri property for the specified node.
fn:boolean	Computes the effective boolean value of the sequence $arg.
fn:ceiling	Returns the smallest (closest to negative infinity) number with no fractional part that is not less than the value of $arg.
fn:codepoint-equal	Returns true if the specified parameters are the same Unicode code point, otherwise returns false.
fn:codepoints-to-string	Creates an xs:string from a sequence of Unicode code points.
fn:collection	Returns all of the documents that belong to the specified collection(s).
fn:compare	Returns -1, 0, or 1, depending on whether the value of the $comparand1 is respectively less than, equal to, or greater than the value of $comparand2, according to the rules of the collation that is used.
fn:concat	Returns the xs:string that is the concatenation of the values of the specified parameters.

fn:contains	Returns true if the first parameter contains the string from the second parameter, otherwise returns false.
fn:count	Returns the number of items in the value of $arg.
fn:current-date	Returns xs:date(fn:current-dateTime()).
fn:current-dateTime	Returns the current dateTime value (with timezone) from the dynamic context.
fn:current-time	Returns xs:time(fn:current-dateTime()).
fn:data	Takes a sequence of items and returns a sequence of atomic values.
fn:day-from-date	Returns an xs:integer between 1 and 31, both inclusive, representing the day component in the localized value of $arg.
fn:day-from-dateTime	Returns an xs:integer between 1 and 31, both inclusive, representing the day component in the localized value of $arg.
fn:days-from-duration	Returns an xs:integer representing the days component in the canonical lexical representation of the value of $arg.
fn:deep-equal	This function assesses whether two sequences are deep-equal to each other.
fn:default-collation	Returns the value of the default collation property from the static context.
fn:distinct-nodes	[0.9-ml only] Returns the sequence resulting from removing from the input sequence all but one of a set of nodes that have the same identity as one another.
fn:distinct-values	Returns the sequence that results from removing from $arg all but one of a set of values that are eq to one other.
fn:doc	Returns the document(s) stored in the database at the specified URI(s).
fn:doc-available	If fn:doc($uri) returns a document node, this function returns true.
fn:document-uri	Returns the value of the document-uri property for the specified node.

fn:empty	If the value of $arg is the empty sequence, the function returns true; otherwise, the function returns false.
fn:encode-for-uri	Invertible function that escapes characters required to be escaped inside path segments of URIs.
fn:ends-with	Returns true if the first parameter ends with the string from the second parameter, otherwise returns false.
fn:error	[1.0 and 1.0-ml only, 0.9-ml has a different signature] Throw the given error.
fn:escape-html-uri	%-escapes everything except printable ASCII characters.
fn:escape-uri	This is a May 2003 function, and is only available in compatibility mode (XQuery 0.9-ML)--it has been replaced with fn:encode-for-uri, fn:iri-to-uri, and fn:escape-html-uri.
fn:exactly-one	Returns $arg if it contains exactly one item.
fn:exists	If the value of $arg is not the empty sequence, the function returns true; otherwise, the function returns false.
fn:expanded-QName	[0.9-ml only, use fn:QName instead] Returns an xs:QName with the namespace URI given in $paramURI and the local name in $paramLocal.
fn:false	Returns the xs:boolean value false.
fn:floor	Returns the largest (closest to positive infinity) number with no fractional part that is not greater than the value of $arg.
fn:hours-from-dateTime	Returns an xs:integer between 0 and 23, both inclusive, representing the hours component in the localized value of $arg.
fn:hours-from-duration	Returns an xs:integer representing the hours component in the canonical lexical representation of the value of $arg.
fn:hours-from-time	Returns an xs:integer between 0 and 23, both inclusive, representing the value of the hours component in the localized value of $arg.

fn:id	Returns the sequence of element nodes that have an ID value matching the value of one or more of the IDREF values supplied in $arg.
fn:idref	Returns the sequence of element or attribute nodes that have an IDREF value matching the value of one or more of the ID values supplied in $arg.
fn:implicit-timezone	Returns the value of the implicit timezone property from the dynamic context.
fn:in-scope-prefixes	Returns the prefixes of the in-scope namespaces for $element.
fn:index-of	Returns a sequence of positive integers giving the positions within the sequence $seqParam of items that are equal to $srchParam.
fn:insert-before	Returns a new sequence constructed from the value of $target with the value of $inserts inserted at the position specified by the value of $position.
fn:iri-to-uri	Idempotent function that escapes non-URI characters.
fn:lang	This function tests whether the language of $node, or the context node if the second argument is omitted, as specified by xml:lang attributes is the same as, or is a sublanguage of, the language specified by $testlang.
fn:last	Returns the context size from the dynamic context.
fn:local-name	Returns the local part of the name of $arg as an xs:string that will either be the zero-length string or will have the lexical form of an xs:NCName.
fn:local-name-from-QName	Returns an xs:NCName representing the local part of $arg.
fn:lower-case	Returns the specified string converting all of the characters to lower-case characters.
fn:matches	Returns true if the specified $input matches the specified $pattern, otherwise returns false.
fn:max	Selects an item from the input sequence $arg whose value is greater than or equal to the value of every other item in the input sequence.

fn:min	Selects an item from the input sequence $arg whose value is less than or equal to the value of every other item in the input sequence.
fn:minutes-from-dateTime	Returns an xs:integer value between 0 and 59, both inclusive, representing the minute component in the localized value of $arg.
fn:minutes-from-duration	Returns an xs:integer representing the minutes component in the canonical lexical representation of the value of $arg.
fn:minutes-from-time	Returns an xs:integer value between 0 to 59, both inclusive, representing the value of the minutes component in the localized value of $arg.
fn:month-from-date	Returns an xs:integer between 1 and 12, both inclusive, representing the month component in the localized value of $arg.
fn:month-from-dateTime	Returns an xs:integer between 1 and 12, both inclusive, representing the month component in the localized value of $arg.
fn:months-from-duration	Returns an xs:integer representing the months component in the canonical lexical representation of the value of $arg.
fn:name	Returns the name of a node, as an xs:string that is either the zero-length string, or has the lexical form of an xs:QName.
fn:namespace-uri	Returns the namespace URI of the xs:QName of $arg.
fn:namespace-uri-for-prefix	Returns the namespace URI of one of the in-scope namespaces for $element, identified by its namespace prefix.
fn:namespace-uri-from-QName	Returns the namespace URI for $arg as an xs:string.
fn:nilled	Summary: Returns an xs:boolean indicating whether the argument node is "nilled".

fn:node-kind	[0.9-ml only, use xdmp:node-kind in 1.0 and 1.0-ml] Returns an xs:string representing the node's kind: either "document", "element", "attribute", "text", "namespace", "processing-instruction", "binary", or "comment".
fn:node-name	Returns an expanded-QName for node kinds that can have names.
fn:normalize-space	Returns the specified string with normalized whitespace, which strips off any leading or trailing whitespace and replaces any other sequences of more than one whitespace characters with a single space character (#x20).
fn:normalize-unicode	Return the argument normalized according to the normalization criteria for a normalization form identified by the value of $normalizationForm.
fn:not	Returns true if the effective boolean value is false, and false if the effective boolean value is true.
fn:number	Returns the value indicated by $arg or, if $arg is not specified, the context item after atomization, converted to an xs:double.
fn:one-or-more	Returns $arg if it contains one or more items.
fn:position	Returns the context position from the dynamic context.
fn:prefix-from-QName	Returns an xs:NCName representing the prefix of $arg.
fn:QName	Returns an xs:QName with the namespace URI given in $paramURI.
fn:remove	Returns a new sequence constructed from the value of $target with the item at the position specified by the value of $position removed.
fn:replace	Returns a string constructed by replacing the specified $pattern on the $input string with the specified $replacement string.

fn:resolve-QName	Returns an xs:QName value (that is, an expanded QName) by taking an xs:string that has the lexical form of an xs:QName (a string in the form "prefix:local-name" or "local-name") and resolving it using the in-scope namespaces for a given element.
fn:resolve-uri	Resolves a relative URI against an absolute URI.
fn:reverse	Reverses the order of items in a sequence.
fn:root	Returns the root of the tree to which $arg belongs.
fn:round	Returns the number with no fractional part that is closest to the argument.
fn:round-half-to-even	The value returned is the nearest (that is, numerically closest) numeric to $arg that is a multiple of ten to the power of minus $precision.
fn:seconds-from-dateTime	Returns an xs:decimal value between 0 and 60.999..., both inclusive representing the seconds and fractional seconds in the localized value of $arg.
fn:seconds-from-duration	Returns an xs:decimal representing the seconds component in the canonical lexical representation of the value of $arg.
fn:seconds-from-time	Returns an xs:decimal value between 0 and 60.999..., both inclusive, representing the seconds and fractional seconds in the localized value of $arg.
fn:starts-with	Returns true if the first parameter starts with the string from the second parameter, otherwise returns false.
fn:static-base-uri	Returns the value of the base-uri property from the static context.
fn:string	Returns the value of $arg represented as an xs:string.
fn:string-join	Returns an xs:string created by concatenating the members of the $parameter1 sequence using $parameter2 as a separator.
fn:string-length	Returns an integer representing the length of the specified string.

fn:string-pad	[0.9-ml only] Returns a string representing the $padString concatenated with itself the number of times specifed in $padCount.
fn:string-to-codepoints	Returns the sequence of Unicode code points that constitute an xs:string.
fn:subsequence	Returns the contiguous sequence of items in the value of $sourceSeq beginning at the position indicated by the value of $startingLoc and continuing for the number of items indicated by the value of $length.
fn:substring	Returns a substring starting from the $startingLoc and continuing for $length characters.
fn:substring-after	Returns the substring created by taking all of the input characters that occur after the specified $after characters.
fn:substring-before	Returns the substring created by taking all of the input characters that occur before the specified $before characters.
fn:subtract-dateTimes-yielding-dayTimeDuration	[0.9-ml only, use the minus operator (-) instead] Returns the xdt:dayTimeDuration that corresponds to the difference between the normalized value of $srcval1 and the normalized value of $srcval2.
fn:subtract-dateTimes-yielding-yearMonthDuration	[0.9-ml only, use the minus operator (-) instead] Returns the xdt:yearMonthDuration hat corresponds to the difference between the normalized value of $srcval1 and the normalized value of $srcval2.
fn:sum	Returns a value obtained by adding together the values in $arg.
fn:timezone-from-date	Returns the timezone component of $arg if any.
fn:timezone-from-dateTime	Returns the timezone component of $arg if any.
fn:timezone-from-time	Returns the timezone component of $arg if any.
fn:tokenize	Returns a sequence of strings contructed by breaking the specified input into substrings separated by the specified $pattern.

fn:trace	Return the input $value unchanged and, if $label is the name of an enabled server event, emit that server event to the server log file (ErrorLog.txt) with $value as its data.
fn:translate	Returns a string where every character in $src that occurs in some position in the $mapString is translated into the $transString character in the corresponding location of the $mapString character.
fn:true	Returns the xs:boolean value true.
fn:unordered	Returns the items of $sourceSeq in an implementation dependent order.
fn:upper-case	Returns the specified string converting all of the characters to upper-case characters.
fn:year-from-date	Returns an xs:integer representing the year component in the localized value of $arg.
fn:year-from-dateTime	Returns an xs:integer representing the year component in the localized value of $arg.
fn:years-from-duration	Returns an xs:integer representing the years component in the canonical lexical representation of the value of $arg.
fn:zero-or-one	Returns $arg if it contains zero or one items.
geo:box	Create a cts:point value from an element representing a box in one of the supported markup vocabularies.
geo:circle	Create a cts:circle value from a radius and an element representing a point in one of the supported markup vocabularies.
geo:geospatial-query	Returns a cts:query matching points within given regions.
geo:geospatial-query-from-elements	Returns a cts:query matching points within given regions.
geo:interior-polygon	Create a sequence of cts:polygon values from a polygon element in one of the supported markup vocabularies.
geo:point	Create a cts:point value from an element representing a point in one of the supported markup vocabularies.

geo:polygon	Create a cts:polygon value from a sequence of point elements in one of the supported markup vocabularies.
geo:polygon	Create a cts:polygon value from a polygon element in one of the supported markup vocabularies.
georss:circle	Create a cts:circle value from a radius and GeoRSS point element.
georss:geospatial-query	Returns a cts:query matching points within given regions.
georss:point	Create a cts:point value from a GeoRSS point element.
gml:box	Create a cts:box value from a GML Envelope element.
gml:circle	Create a cts:circle value from a radius and GML Point element.
gml:geospatial-query	Returns a cts:query matching points within given regions.
gml:geospatial-query-from-elements	Returns a cts:query matching points within given regions.
gml:interior-polygon	Create a sequence of cts:polygon values from a GML Polygon element.
gml:point	Create a cts:point value from a GML Point element.
gml:polygon	Create a cts:polygon value from a sequence of GML Point elements.
gml:polygon	Create a cts:polygon value from a GML Polygon element.
kml:box	Create a cts:point value from a KML LatLongBox element.
kml:circle	Create a cts:circle value from a radius and KML Point or Location element.
kml:geospatial-query	Returns a cts:query matching points within given regions.
kml:geospatial-query-from-elements	Returns a cts:query matching points within given regions.
kml:interior-polygon	Create a sequence of cts:polygon values from a KML Polygon element.

kml:point	Create a cts:point value from a KML Point or Location element.
kml:polygon	Create a cts:polygon value from a sequence of KML Point or Location elements.
kml:polygon	Create a cts:polygon value from a KML Polygon element.
lnk:create	Create a link between the two given documents with the given role labels and strength.
lnk:from	Find and return all the links from the given document to some other.
lnk:get	Find and return the link between the two documents, if any.
lnk:insert	Insert the given link.
lnk:remove	Remove the link between the two given documents and return the removed link.
lnk:to	Find and return all the links to the given document from some other.
map:clear	Clear a map.
map:count	Returns the number of entries used in the map.
map:delete	Delete a value from a map.
map:get	Get a value from a map.
map:keys	Get the keys used in the map.
map:map	Creates a map.
map:put	Put a value into a map at the given key.
math:acos	Returns the arc cosine of x, in radians, in the range from 0 to pi (inclusive).
math:asin	Returns the arc sine of x, in radians, in the range from -pi/2 to +pi/2 (inclusive).
math:atan	Returns the arc tangent of x, in radians.
math:atan2	Returns the arc tangent of y/x, in radians, in the range from -pi/2 to +pi/2 (inclusive), using the signs of y and x to determine the apropriate quadrant.
math:ceil	Returns the smallest integer greater than or equal to x.

math:cos	Returns the cosine of x, in the range from -1 to +1 (inclusive).
math:cosh	Returns the hyperbolic cosine of x.
math:exp	Returns e to the xth power.
math:fabs	Returns the absolute value of x.
math:floor	Returns the largest integer less than or equal to x.
math:fmod	Returns the remainder of x/y.
math:frexp	Returns x broken up into mantissa and exponent, where $x = mantissa*2^{exponent}$.
math:ldexp	Returns $x*2^{i}$.
math:log	Returns the base-e logarithm of x.
math:log10	Returns the base-10 logarithm of x.
math:modf	Returns x broken up into fraction and integer.
math:pow	Returns x^{y}.
math:sin	Returns the sine of x, in the range from -1 to +1 (inclusive).
math:sinh	Returns the hyperbolic sine of x.
math:sqrt	Returns the square root of x.
math:tan	Returns the tangent of x.
math:tanh	Returns the hyperbolic tangent of x, in the range from -1 to +1 (inclusive).
mcgm:circle	Create a cts:circle value from a radius and MCGM Dot element.
mcgm:geospatial-query	Returns a cts:query matching points within given regions.
mcgm:geospatial-query-from-elements	Returns a cts:query matching points within given regions.
mcgm:point	Create a cts:point value from a MCGM Dot element.
mcgm:polygon	Create a cts:polygon value from a sequence of MCGM Dot elements.
msword:clean	Clean up any conversion artifacts or other infelicities.
ooxml:package-parts	This function returns the documents within the zip package.

ooxml:package-parts-insert	This function inserts one document in the database for each part at the specified URI.
ooxml:package-uris	This function returns the list of files in the zip package.
ooxml:runs-merge	This function updates document or paragraph node(s) (from a Word 2007 document) so that all similar runs are merged, retaining formatting, and removing text split across elements.
p:action	Construct an action element.
p:collection	Return the name of the collection in which pipelines are stored.
p:condition	Construct a condition element.
p:create	Create a new content processing pipeline.
p:execute	Construct a execute element.
p:get	Find a particular pipeline.
p:get-by-id	Find a particular pipeline.
p:insert	Insert a fully constructed content processing pipeline, returning its unique id.
p:pipelines	Return all the pipelines.
p:remove	Remove the named pipeline.
p:state-transition	Construct a new state transition element.
p:status-transition	Construct a new status transition element.
pdf:clean	Clean up any conversion artifacts or other infelicities.
pdf:get-toc	Fetch the linked TOC, if any.
pdf:insert-toc-headers	Locate TOC anchors and make them properly refer to headers at the appropriate level.
pdf:make-toc	Clean and normalize the TOC produced by raw conversion.
ppt:clean	Clean up any conversion artifacts or other infelicities, putting each slide into its own div element.
prof:allowed	Returns the value of the Profile Allow setting for the App Server or Task Server upon which the target request is running.
prof:disable	Disable profiling for this request.

prof:enable	Enable profiling for this request.
prof:eval	Evaluate a string as an XQuery for profiling.
prof:invoke	Profiles and returns the result of evaluating a module at the given path.
prof:report	Return a prof:report node containing the current state of profiling statistics for the given request.
prof:reset	Clear any accumulated profiling statistics for the requests.
prof:value	Evaluate an expression in the context of the current evaluating statement and return the profiling report for its evaluation.
sec:amp-add-roles	Adds the roles ($role-names) to the list of roles granted to the amp ($namespace, $local-name, $document-uri).
sec:amp-doc-collections	Returns a sequence of strings corresponding to the collection uri's that amps belong to.
sec:amp-doc-permissions	Returns a sequence of permission elements that all newly created amp documents receive.
sec:amp-get-roles	Returns a sequence of role names for the roles directly assigned to the amp ($namespace, $local-name, $document-uri).
sec:amp-remove-roles	Removes a role ($role-name) from the set of roles included by the amp ($namespace, $local-name, $document-uri).
sec:amp-set-roles	Assigns the amp identified by $namespace, $local-name and $document-uri to have the roles identified by $roles-names.
sec:amps-collection	Returns a string corresponding to the uri for the amps collection.
sec:check-admin	Throws an error if the current user does not have the admin role.
sec:collection-add-permissions	Add the permissions $permissions to the protected collection identified by $uri.

sec:collection-get-permissions	Returns a sequence of permission elements corresponding to the current permissions granted to the protected collection identified by $uri.
sec:collection-remove-permissions	Removes the permissions $permissions from the protected collection identified by $uri.
sec:collection-set-permissions	Sets the permissions of a protected collection identified by $uri to $permissions.
sec:collections-collection	Returns a string corresponding to the uri for the protected collections collection.
sec:create-amp	Creates a new amp in the system database for the context database.
sec:create-privilege	Creates a new privilege and returns the new privilege-id.
sec:create-role	Creates a new role in the system database for the context database.
sec:create-user	Creates a new user in the system database for the context database.
sec:create-user-with-role	Creates a new user in the system database for the context database.
sec:get-amp	Returns an sec:amp element corresponding to an amp identified by ($namespace, $local-name, $document-uri).
sec:get-collection	Gets the security document corresponding to a protected collection with uri equal to $uri.
sec:get-distinct-permissions	Returns a sequence of permission elements made up of a concatenation of $output-perms and the distinct permission elements of $input-perms.
sec:get-privilege	Returns a sec:privilege element corresponding to a privilege identified by ($action,$kind).
sec:get-role-ids	Returns sequence of unique sec:role-id's that corresponds to the sequence of role names $role-names.
sec:get-role-names	Returns sequence of unique sec:role-name's that corresponds to the sequence of role IDs $role-ids.
sec:get-unique-elem-id	Returns a unique id for a given security element, $elem.

sec:get-user-names	Returns sequence of unique sec:user-name's that corresponds to the sequence of user IDs $user-ids.
sec:priv-doc-collections	Returns a sequence of strings corresponding to the collection uri's that privileges belong to.
sec:priv-doc-permissions	Returns a sequence of permission elements that all newly created privilege documents receive.
sec:privilege-add-roles	Adds the roles ($role-names) to the list of roles assigned to the privilege ($action,$kind).
sec:privilege-get-roles	Returns a sequence of role names for the roles assigned to the privilege ($action,$kind).
sec:privilege-remove-roles	Removes roles ($role-names) from the roles assigned to the privilege ($action,$kind).
sec:privilege-set-name	Changes the sec:privilege-name of a sec:privilege to $new-privilege-name.
sec:privilege-set-roles	Assigns the privilege ($action,$kind) to have the roles identified by $role-names.
sec:privileges-collection	Returns a string corresponding to the uri for the privileges collection.
sec:protect-collection	Protects a collection $uri with the given permissions ($permissions).
sec:remove-amp	Removes the amp ($namespace, $local-name, $document-uri, $database) and returns true after completion.
sec:remove-privilege	Removes the privilege identified by ($action,$kind).
sec:remove-role	Removes the role ($role-name).
sec:remove-role-from-amps	Removes references to the role ($role-name) from all amps.
sec:remove-role-from-privileges	Removes references to the role ($role-name) from all privileges.
sec:remove-role-from-role	Removes references to the role ($role-name) from other roles.
sec:remove-role-from-users	Removes references to the role ($role-name) from all users.
sec:remove-user	Removes the user with name $user-name.

sec:role-add-roles	Adds the roles ($new-roles) to the set of roles included by the role ($role-name).
sec:role-doc-collections	Returns a sequence of strings corresponding to the collection uri's that roles belong to.
sec:role-doc-permissions	Returns a sequence of permission elements that all newly created role documents receive.
sec:role-get-default-collections	Returns a sequence of strings correspondinig to the uri's of the role's default collections.
sec:role-get-default-permissions	Returns a sequence of permission elements correspondinig to the role's default permissions.
sec:role-get-description	Returns the description for the specified role.
sec:role-get-roles	Returns a sequence of role names for the roles directly assigned to the given role ($role-name).
sec:role-privileges	Returns a set of privilege elements corresponding to all privileges that a role has.
sec:role-remove-roles	Removes the roles ($role-names) from the set of roles included by the role ($role-name).
sec:role-set-default-collections	Sets the default collections of a role with name $role-name to $collections.
sec:role-set-default-permissions	Sets the default permissions for a role with name $role-name.
sec:role-set-description	Changes the description of the role identified by $role-name to $description.
sec:role-set-name	Changes the sec:role-name of a role from $role-name to $new-role-name.
sec:role-set-roles	Assigns roles (named $role-names) to be the set of included roles for the role ($role-name).
sec:roles-collection	Returns a string corresponding to the uri for the roles collection.
sec:security-collection	Returns a string corresponding to the uri for the Security collection.
sec:security-installed	Returns fn:true() if security has been installed on the current database.

sec:security-namespace	Returns a string corresponding to the uri of the security namespace.
sec:security-version	Returns the current version of the security database.
sec:set-realm	Changes the realm of this security database to $realm.
sec:uid-for-name	Returns the uids for the named user or () if no such user exists.
sec:unprotect-collection	Removes the protection of a collection $uri.
sec:user-add-roles	Adds the roles ($role-names) to the list of roles granted to the user ($user-name).
sec:user-doc-collections	Returns a sequence of strings corresponding to the collection uri's that users belong to.
sec:user-doc-permissions	Returns a sequence of permission elements that all newly created user documents receive.
sec:user-get-default-collections	Returns a sequence of strings correspondinig to the uri's of the user's default collections.
sec:user-get-default-permissions	Returns a sequence of permission elements correspondinig to the user's default permissions.
sec:user-get-description	Returns the user's description.
sec:user-get-roles	Returns a sequence of role names for the roles directly assigned to the user ($user-name).
sec:user-privileges	Returns a set of privilege elements corresponding to all privileges that a user has.
sec:user-remove-roles	Removes the roles ($role-names) from the list of roles granted to the user ($user-name).
sec:user-set-default-collections	Sets the default collections of a user with name $user-name to $collections.
sec:user-set-default-permissions	Sets the default permissions for a user with name $user-name.
sec:user-set-description	Changes the description of the user identified by $user-name to $description.
sec:user-set-name	Changes the name of the user from $user-name to $new-user-name.
sec:user-set-password	Changes the password for the user identified by $user-name to $password.

sec:user-set-roles	Assigns the user with name $user-name to have the roles identified by $role-names.
sec:users-collection	Returns a string corresponding to the uri for the users collection.
spell:add-word	Add the word $word to the dictionary at $uri.
spell:insert	Load the words in $dict into the dictionary at $uri.
spell:is-correct	Returns true() if the specified word is spelled correctly, otherwise returns false().
spell:load	Add the words from the file specified in $path to the dictionary at $uri.
spell:remove-word	Remove the word $word from the dictionary at $uri.
spell:suggest	Suggests a list of spellings for a word.
thsr:add-synonym	Adds a synonym to the specified thesaurus entry.
thsr:expand	Returns a query that searches for all the query strings specified in $query and their synonyms as found in $entries.
thsr:insert	Load the entries in $thsr into the thesaurus at $uri.
thsr:load	Load the file specified in $path to the thesaurus at $uri.
thsr:lookup	Returns all entries for term $term in the thesaurus document(s) at $uri.
thsr:query-lookup	Returns a sequence of all entries that are found by looking up terms in the query and/or subqueries of $query in the thesaurus document(s) at $uri.
thsr:remove-entry	Removes all entries that exactly match $entry from the thesaurus documents(s) at $uri.
thsr:remove-synonym	Removes synonym $synonym from thesaurus entry $entry.
thsr:remove-term	Removes all entries with term $term from the thesaurus document(s) at $uri.
thsr:set-entry	Adds the entry $entry to the thesaurus at $uri.
trgr:any-property-content	Returns the representation of an all-properties part to a triggering event.
trgr:collection-scope	Returns the representation of a collection scope.

trgr:create-trigger	Creates a new trigger in the context database.
trgr:directory-scope	Returns the representation of a directory scope.
trgr:document-content	Returns the representation of a document part to a triggering event.
trgr:document-scope	Returns the representation of a document scope.
trgr:get-trigger	Returns the xml representation of the trigger named $trigger-name.
trgr:get-trigger-by-id	Returns the xml representation of the trigger that has a trigger-id of $trigger-id.
trgr:post-commit	Returns the representation of a post-commit trigger timing.
trgr:pre-commit	Returns the representation of a pre-commit trigger timing.
trgr:property-content	Returns the representation of a property part to a triggering event.
trgr:remove-trigger	Remove the trigger named $trigger-name.
trgr:trigger-add-permissions	Add $permissions to the set of permissions on the trigger named $trigger.
trgr:trigger-data-event	Returns the representation of a triggering event.
trgr:trigger-database-online-event	Returns the representation of a database coming online event.
trgr:trigger-disable	Disable the trigger named $trigger-name.
trgr:trigger-enable	Enable the trigger named $trigger-name.
trgr:trigger-get-permissions	Get the set of permissions of the trigger named $trigger-name.
trgr:trigger-module	Returns the representation of a trigger module invocation.
trgr:trigger-remove-permissions	Remove $permissions from the set of permissions on the trigger named $trigger-name.
trgr:trigger-set-description	Sets the description of the trigger nameds $trigger-name to $description.
trgr:trigger-set-event	Assigned the trigger named $trigger-name the new triggering event defined in $event.

trgr:trigger-set-module	Assigned the trigger named $trigger-name the new execution module defined in $module.
trgr:trigger-set-name	Changes the name of the trigger from $user-name to $new-user-name.
trgr:trigger-set-permissions	Set the permissions on the trigger to the new set of permissions in $permissions.
trgr:trigger-set-recursive	Sets the recursive setting of the identified trigger.
xdmp:access	Returns whether a given action on the specified document URI would succeed.
xdmp:add-response-header	Adds an HTTP response header field.
xdmp:amp	Returns the amp ID for the specified amp.
xdmp:amp-roles	Returns the set of all roles assigned to an amp, including roles directly assigned to the amp and roles inherited by other roles.
xdmp:architecture	Returns the hardware architecture upon which MarkLogic Server is running.
xdmp:base64-decode	Converts base64-encoded string to plaintext.
xdmp:base64-encode	Converts plaintext into base64-encoded string.
xdmp:can-grant-roles	Tests whether a user can grant or revoke a set of roles.
xdmp:castable-as	Returns true if a value is castable.
xdmp:collation-canonical-uri	Returns the canonical URI for the given URI, if it represents a valid collation.
xdmp:collection-delete	Deletes from the database every document in a collection.
xdmp:collection-locks	Returns locks of documents in a collection.
xdmp:collection-properties	Returns a sequence of properties documents, one for each document in the specified collection(s) that has a corresponding properties document.
xdmp:database	Returns the the ID of the database named in the the parameter.
xdmp:database-backup	Starts an asynchronous backup of the specified list of forests to the backup data directory.

xdmp:database-backup-cancel	Cancels an outstanding backup job with the specified job ID, returning true if the cancel operation is successful, false if the cancel operation is not successful.
xdmp:database-backup-purge	Purge old backups from a directory.
xdmp:database-backup-status	Checks the status of the outstanding backup job with the specified job ID.
xdmp:database-backup-validate	Validates that the specified list of forests can be backed up to the backup data directory.
xdmp:database-forests	Returns a sequence of forest IDs in the specified database.
xdmp:database-name	Return the name of the database with the given ID.
xdmp:database-restore	Starts an asynchronous restore of the specified list of forests from the backup data directory.
xdmp:database-restore-cancel	Cancels an outstanding restore job with the specified job ID, returning true if the cancel operation is successful, false if the cancel operation is not successful.
xdmp:database-restore-status	Checks the status of the outstanding restore job with the specified job ID.
xdmp:database-restore-validate	Validates that the specified list of forests can be restored from the backup data directory.
xdmp:databases	Returns a sequence of the IDs of all the databases in the system.
xdmp:default-collections	Returns the collections any new document would get if the current user were to insert a document without specifying the collections.
xdmp:default-permissions	Returns the permissions any new document would get if the current user were to insert a document without specifying the default permissions.
xdmp:describe	Returns a string representing the description of a given item sequence.

xdmp:diacritic-less	Returns the specified string, converting all of the characters with diacritics to characters without diacritics.
xdmp:directory	Returns the documents in a directory.
xdmp:directory-create	Creates a directory.
xdmp:directory-delete	Deletes a directory and its children from the database.
xdmp:directory-locks	Returns locks of documents in a directory.
xdmp:directory-properties	Returns a sequence of properties documents, one for each document in the specified directory that has a corresponding properties document.
xdmp:document-add-collections	Adds the named document to the given collections.
xdmp:document-add-permissions	Adds the given permissions to the given document or directory.
xdmp:document-add-properties	Adds a sequence of properties to the properties of a document.
xdmp:document-delete	Deletes a document from the database.
xdmp:document-forest	Returns the forest ID of the forest in which a document (or a lock or a property) with the specified URI is stored.
xdmp:document-get	Returns the document in the file specified by $location.
xdmp:document-get-collections	Returns the collections to which a given document belongs.
xdmp:document-get-permissions	Returns the permissions to a given document.
xdmp:document-get-properties	Returns the property values for a document's property.
xdmp:document-get-quality	Returns the quality of the specified document if the document exists.
xdmp:document-insert	Inserts a new document into the database if a document with the specified URI does not already exist.
xdmp:document-load	Inserts a new document with the specified URI.
xdmp:document-locks	Returns the locks for one or more documents or directories.

xdmp:document-properties	Returns a sequence of properties documents, one for each of the specified documents that has a corresponding properties document.
xdmp:document-remove-collections	Removes the named document from the given collections.
xdmp:document-remove-permissions	Removes the given permissions from the named document or directory.
xdmp:document-remove-properties	Removes a sequence of properties from the properties of a document.
xdmp:document-set-collections	Sets the named document to belong to the given collections, replacing any previously set collections on the named document.
xdmp:document-set-permissions	Sets the permissions on the named document (or directory) to the given permissions, replacing any permissions previously set on the document (or directory).
xdmp:document-set-properties	Sets the properties of a document to the given sequence of elements, replacing any properties that already exist on the document.
xdmp:document-set-property	Sets a property on a document.
xdmp:document-set-quality	Sets the quality of the document with the given URI.
xdmp:email	Send an email in an XQuery program.
xdmp:estimate	Returns the number of fragments selected by an expression.
xdmp:eval	Returns the result of evaluating a string as an XQuery module.
xdmp:eval-in	[DEPRECATED: use xdmp:eval with the database option instead] Returns the result of evaluating a string as an XQuery module in a given database.
xdmp:excel-convert	Converts a Microsoft Excel document to XHTML.
xdmp:exists	Returns true if any fragment is selected by an expression, false if no fragments are selected.
xdmp:filesystem-directory	Performs a directory listing of the given file pathname.
xdmp:filesystem-file	Reads a file from the filesystem.

xdmp:forest	Returns the the ID of the forest specified as the parameter.
xdmp:forest-backup	Backs up forest data files.
xdmp:forest-clear	Clears forest data files.
xdmp:forest-counts	Returns detailed forest statistics for a given forest.
xdmp:forest-databases	Returns the database ID corresponding to the database to which the specified forest belongs.
xdmp:forest-name	Return the name of the forest with the given id.
xdmp:forest-restart	Restarts a forest.
xdmp:forest-restore	Restores forest data files.
xdmp:forest-status	Returns the status of a forest.
xdmp:forests	Returns a sequence of the IDs of all the forests in the system.
xdmp:get	[DEPRECATED: use xdmp:document-get instead] Returns the document in the XML file specified by $path.
xdmp:get-current-roles	Returns all the current roles, both assigned and inherited by the current user and any received from amps.
xdmp:get-current-user	Returns the name of the current user.
xdmp:get-request-body	Returns the POST or PUT body of this request, if it is not application/x-www-form-urlencoded.
xdmp:get-request-client-address	Returns as a string the internet address of the client from which the HTTP server request is issued.
xdmp:get-request-field	Returns the value of a named request field.
xdmp:get-request-field-content-type	This function is used to extract the content type from the request field.
xdmp:get-request-field-filename	Returns a list of filenames from a multipart request for the field name specified.
xdmp:get-request-field-names	Returns a sequence of the request field names.
xdmp:get-request-header	Returns the value of a named request header.
xdmp:get-request-header-names	Returns a sequence of request header names.

xdmp:get-request-method	Returns the HTTP request method.
xdmp:get-request-path	Returns the HTTP request path.
xdmp:get-request-user	Returns the id of the current user.
xdmp:get-request-username	Returns the username from the Authorization header of this App Server request.
xdmp:get-response-code	Returns two nodes, the first containing the HTTP response code and the second containing the HTTP response message.
xdmp:get-response-encoding	Returns the encoding that the response from this server is in.
xdmp:get-session-field	Returns the value of a named HTTP session field.
xdmp:get-session-field-names	Returns a sequence of the HTTP session field names.
xdmp:group	Returns the the ID of the group specified in the parameter.
xdmp:group-hosts	Returns the the IDs of all hosts beloning to the group with the given ID.
xdmp:group-name	Returns the the name of the group with the given ID.
xdmp:group-servers	Returns the the IDs of all App Servers belonging to the group with the given ID.
xdmp:groups	Returns a sequence of the IDs of all the groups in the system.
xdmp:has-privilege	Tests whether the current user has at least one of a given set of privileges.
xdmp:hash32	Returns the 32-bit hash of a string.
xdmp:hash64	Returns the 64-bit hash of a string.
xdmp:hex-to-integer	Parses a hexadecimal string, returning an integer.
xdmp:host	Returns the the ID of the host named in the parameter.
xdmp:host-name	Returns the the name of the host ID specified as the parameter.
xdmp:host-status	Returns the status of a host.
xdmp:hosts	Returns a sequence of the IDs of all the hosts in the system.

xdmp:http-delete	Sends an http DELETE request to the http server specified in the URI to delete the specified resource.
xdmp:http-get	Sends the http GET method to the specified URI.
xdmp:http-head	Sends the http HEAD method to the specified URI.
xdmp:http-options	Sends the http OPTIONS method to the specified URI.
xdmp:http-post	Sends the http POST request to the server.
xdmp:http-put	Sends an HTTP PUT request to an HTTP server.
xdmp:integer-to-hex	Returns a hexadecimal representation of an integer.
xdmp:integer-to-octal	Returns an octal representation of an integer.
xdmp:invoke	Returns the result of evaluating a module at the given path.
xdmp:invoke-in	[DEPRECATED: use xdmp:invoke with the database option instead] Returns the result of evaluating a module at the given path.
xdmp:load	[DEPRECATED: use xdmp:document-load instead] Inserts a new document from the XML file at $path if a document with the specified URI does not already exist.
xdmp:lock-acquire	Acquire a lock on a document or directory for an extended amount of time.
xdmp:lock-release	Unlock a document or directory.
xdmp:log	Logs a debug message to the log file <install_dir>/Logs/ErrorLog.txt.
xdmp:log-level	Retrieves the current server log level.
xdmp:login	Logs in a user on an application server that is using application-level authentication and deposits a session cookie.
xdmp:logout	Sets the current user to the default user defined in application-level authentication.
xdmp:md5	Calculates the md5 hash of the given argument.
xdmp:merge	Starts merging the forests of the database, subject to specified options.
xdmp:merge-cancel	Cancel the merge with the specified merge ID on a forest with the specified forest ID.

xdmp:merging	Returns the forest IDs of any currently merging database forests.
xdmp:modules-database	Returns the database ID of the modules database.
xdmp:modules-root	Returns the current root path for modules.
xdmp:node-database	Returns the database id where the parameter is stored.
xdmp:node-delete	Deletes a node from the database.
xdmp:node-insert-after	Adds an immediately following sibling to a node.
xdmp:node-insert-before	Adds an immediately preceding sibling to a node.
xdmp:node-insert-child	Adds a new last child to a node.
xdmp:node-kind	Returns an xs:string representing the node's kind: either "document", "element", "attribute", "text", "namespace", "processing-instruction", "binary", or "comment".
xdmp:node-replace	Replaces a node.
xdmp:node-uri	Returns the document-uri property of the parameter or its ancestor.
xdmp:octal-to-integer	Parses an octal string, returning an integer.
xdmp:path	Returns a string whose value corresponds to the path of the node.
xdmp:pdf-convert	Converts a PDF file to XHTML.
xdmp:permission	Returns a permission element in the security namespace corresponding to the named role and capability given.
xdmp:platform	Returns the operating-system platform upon which MarkLogic Server is running ("solaris", "winnt", or "linux").
xdmp:powerpoint-convert	Converts a Microsoft Powerpoint document to XHTML.
xdmp:privilege	Returns the privilege ID for the specified privilege name.
xdmp:privilege-roles	Returns the set of all roles that have a given privilege.
xdmp:product-edition	Returns the current Mark Logic product edition.
xdmp:query-meters	Returns the current value of the resource meters for this query sequence.

xdmp:query-trace	Enables or disables tracing of this query.
xdmp:quote	Returns the unevaluated serialized representation of the input parameter as a string.
xdmp:random	Returns a random unsigned integer between 0 and a number up to 64 bits long.
xdmp:redirect-response	Redirects the App Server response to a given location.
xdmp:request	Returns the unique key of the current request.
xdmp:request-cancel	Cancel the request with the given host, server, and request IDs.
xdmp:request-status	Returns the status of a running request.
xdmp:request-timestamp	Returns the system timestamp for this request if the request is a query statement.
xdmp:restart	Restart servers on hosts.
xdmp:rethrow	Rethrow the currently caught error.
xdmp:role	Returns the role ID for the specified role name.
xdmp:role-roles	Returns the set of all roles inherited by a given role, including roles directly assigned to the role and roles inherited from other roles.
xdmp:save	Serializes a node as text and saves it to a file.
xdmp:schema-database	Returns the database ID of the schema database associated with the current database.
xdmp:security-assert	Tests whether the current user has at least one of a given set of privileges.
xdmp:security-database	Returns the database ID of the security database associated with the current database.
xdmp:server	Returns the the ID(s) of the App Server specified in the parameter.
xdmp:server-name	Return the name of the App Server with the given ID.
xdmp:server-status	Returns the status of an app-server on a host.
xdmp:servers	Returns a sequence of the IDs of all the App Servers in the system.
xdmp:set	Set the value of a variable to the specified expression.

xdmp:set-request-time-limit	Changes the time limit for an actively running request to the specified value.
xdmp:set-response-code	Sets the response code and message.
xdmp:set-response-content-type	Sets the response content-type.
xdmp:set-response-encoding	Sets the response encoding.
xdmp:set-session-field	Sets the value of a named HTTP session field.
xdmp:shutdown	Shutdown servers on hosts.
xdmp:sleep	Delays for a specific amount of time.
xdmp:spawn	Place the specified module on the task queue for evaluation.
xdmp:spawn-in	[DEPRECATED: use xdmp:spawn with the database option instead] Place the specified module on the task queue for evaluation.
xdmp:strftime	Formats a dateTime value using POSIX strftime.
xdmp:subbinary	Returns a binary node made up of a subset of the given binary node.
xdmp:tidy	Run tidy on the specified html document to convert the document to well-formed and clean XHTML.
xdmp:trace	Signal a trace event.
xdmp:triggers-database	Returns the database ID of the triggers database associated with the current database.
xdmp:unpath	Evaluate a string as an XPath and return the corresponding node(s).
xdmp:unquote	Parses a string as XML, returning one or more document nodes.
xdmp:uri-content-type	Returns the content type of the given URI as matched in the mimetypes configuration.
xdmp:uri-format	Returns the format of the given URI as matched in the mimetypes configuration.
xdmp:uri-is-file	Returns true if a given URI refers to a file which exists on the current application server.
xdmp:url-decode	Converts URL-encoded string to plaintext.

xdmp:url-encode	Converts plaintext into URL-encoded string.
xdmp:user	Returns the user ID for the specified user name.
xdmp:user-last-login	Returns the last-login node for the specified user ID.
xdmp:user-roles	Returns all roles assigned to a user, including roles directly assigned to the user and roles inherited by other roles.
xdmp:value	Evaluate an expression in the context of the current evaluating statement.
xdmp:version	Returns the current MarkLogic Server version.
xdmp:with-namespaces	Evaluates the expression in the context of a specific set of namespace bindings.
xdmp:word-convert	Converts a Microsoft Word document to XHTML.
xdmp:xquery-version	Returns the XQuery language version of the calling module.
xdmp:zip-create	Create a zip file from a list of nodes.
xdmp:zip-get	Get a named file from a zip document.
xdmp:zip-manifest	Return a manifest for this zip file.
xhtml:add-lists	Infer numbered or bulleted lists and insert appropriate markup.
xhtml:clean	Clean up the XHTML: pruning empty spans, consolidating adjacent spans, etc.
xhtml:restructure	Turn an XHTML with flat structure into one with div structure based on the header elements.
xinc:link-expand	This function performs a single level expansion of a single XInclude reference.
xinc:link-references	This function returns a list of all the distinct URIs of documents referenced (either directly or indirectly) in the expansion of the node.
xinc:node-expand	This function recursively examines the node for XInclude references and expands them, following the rules of the XInclude specification.
xp:dereference	This function resolves an XPointer in the context of a particular node.

Appendix II

XQuery Glossary (Non-Normative)

atomic value

An atomic value is a value in the value space of an atomic type, as defined in XML Schema:
http://www.w3.org/TR/xquery/#XMLSchema

atomization

Atomization of a sequence is defined as the result of invoking the `fn:data` function on the sequence, as defined in XQuery 1.0 and XPath 2.0 Functions and Operators.
http://www.w3.org/TR/xquery/#FunctionsAndOperators

available collections

Available collections. This is a mapping of strings onto sequences of nodes. The string represents the absolute URI of a resource. The sequence of nodes represents the result of the `fn:collection` function when that URI is supplied as the argument.

available documents

Available documents. This is a mapping of strings onto document nodes.

The string represents the absolute URI of a resource. The document node is the root of a tree that represents that resource using the data model.
http://www.w3.org/TR/xquery/#dt-datamodel
The document node is returned by the fn:doc function when applied to that URI.

axis step

An axis step returns a sequence of nodes that are reachable from the context node via a specified axis. Such a step has two parts: an axis, which defines the "direction of movement" for the step, and a node test, which selects nodes based on their kind, name, and/or type annotation.
Node Test:
http://www.w3.org/TR/xquery/#dt-node-test
Type Annotation:
http://www.w3.org/TR/xquery/#dt-type-annotation

base URI

Base URI. This is an absolute URI, used when necessary in the resolution of relative URIs (for example, by the fn:resolve-uri function.)

base URI declaration

A base URI declaration specifies the base URI property of the static context. The base URI property is used when resolving relative URIs within a module.
BaseURI:
http://www.w3.org/TR/xquery/#dt-base-uri
Static Context:
http://www.w3.org/TR/xquery/#dt-static-context

Module:
http://www.w3.org/TR/xquery/#dt-module

binding sequence

The value of the expression associated with a variable in a for clause is called the binding sequence for that variable.

boundary-space declaration

A boundary-space declaration sets the boundary-space policy in the static context, overriding any implementation-defined default. Boundary-space policy controls whether boundary whitespace is preserved by element constructors during processing of the query.
Boundary space policy:
http://www.w3.org/TR/xquery/#dt-boundary-space-policy
Static Context:
http://www.w3.org/TR/xquery/#dt-static-context
boundary whitespace:
http://www.w3.org/TR/xquery/#dt-boundary-whitespace

boundary-space policy

Boundary-space policy. This component controls the processing of boundary whitespace by direct element constructors.
boundary whitespace:
http://www.w3.org/TR/xquery/#dt-boundary-whitespace
direct element constructors:
http://www.w3.org/TR/xquery/#dt-direct-elem-const

boundary whitespace

Boundary whitespace is a sequence of consecutive whitespace characters within the content of a direct element constructor, that is delimited at each end either by the start or end of the content, or by a DirectConstructor, or by an EnclosedExpr. For this purpose, characters generated by character references such as   or by CdataSections are not considered to be whitespace characters.

direct element constructors:
http://www.w3.org/TR/xquery/#dt-direct-elem-const
DirectConstructor:
http://www.w3.org/TR/xquery/#doc-xquery-DirectConstructor
EnclosedExpr:
http://www.w3.org/TR/xquery/#doc-xquery-EnclosedExpr
character reference:
http://www.w3.org/TR/xquery/#dt-character-reference
CdataSection:
http://www.w3.org/TR/xquery/#doc-xquery-CdataSection

built-in function

The built-in functions supported by XQuery are defined in XQuery 1.0 and
XPath 2.0 Functions and Operators.
XQuery 1.0 and XPath 2.0 Functions and Operators:
http://www.w3.org/TR/xquery/#FunctionsAndOperators

character reference

A character reference is an XML-style reference to a Unicode character,
identified by its decimal or hexadecimal code point.
Unicode:
http://www.w3.org/TR/xquery/#Unicode

collation

A collation is a specification of the manner in which strings and URIs are
compared and, by extension, ordered. For a more complete definition of
collation, see XQuery 1.0 and XPath 2.0 Functions and Operators.
XQuery 1.0 and XPath 2.0 Functions and Operators:
http://www.w3.org/TR/xquery/#FunctionsAndOperators

comma operator

One way to construct a sequence is by using the comma operator, which evaluates each of its operands and concatenates the resulting sequences, in order, into a single result sequence.

computed element constructor

A computed element constructor creates an element node, allowing both the name and the content of the node to be computed.

construction declaration

A construction declaration sets the construction mode in the static context, overriding any implementation-defined default.
construction mode:
http://www.w3.org/TR/xquery/#dt-construction-mode
static context:
http://www.w3.org/TR/xquery/#dt-static-context

construction mode

Construction mode. The construction mode governs the behavior of element and document node constructors. If construction mode is `preserve`, the type of a constructed element node is `xs:anyType`, and all attribute and element nodes copied during node construction retain their original types. If construction mode is strip, the type of a constructed element node is `xs:untyped`; all element nodes copied during node construction receive the type `xs:untyped`, and all attribute nodes copied during node construction receive the type `xs:untypedAtomic`.

constructor function

The constructor function for a given type is used to convert instances of other atomic types into the given type. The semantics of the constructor function call T($arg) are defined to be equivalent to the expression `(($arg) cast as T?)`.

content expression

The final part of a computed constructor is an expression enclosed in braces, called the content expression of the constructor, that generates the content of the node.

context item

The context item is the item currently being processed. An item is either an atomic value or a node.

context item static type

Context item static type. This component defines the static type of the context item within the scope of a given expression.
static type:
http://www.w3.org/TR/xquery/#dt-static-type

context node

When the context item is a node, it can also be referred to as the context node.

context position

The context position is the position of the context item within the sequence of items currently being processed.

context size

The context size is the number of items in the sequence of items currently being processed.

copy-namespaces declaration

A copy-namespaces declaration sets the value of copy-namespaces mode in the static context, overriding any implementation-defined default. Copy-namespaces mode controls the namespace bindings that are assigned when an existing element node is copied by an element constructor or document constructor.
copy-namespaces mode:
http://www.w3.org/TR/xquery/#dt-copy-namespaces-mode
static context:
http://www.w3.org/TR/xquery/#dt-static-context

copy-namespaces mode

Copy-namespaces mode. This component controls the namespace bindings that are assigned when an existing element node is copied by an element constructor, as described in Direct Element Constructors. Its value consists of two parts: preserve or no-preserve, and inherit or no-inherit.
Direct Element Constructors:
http://www.w3.org/TR/xquery/#id-element-constructor

current dateTime

Current dateTime. This information represents an implementation-dependent point in time during the processing of a query, and includes an explicit timezone. It can be retrieved by the fn:current-dateTime function. If invoked multiple times during the execution of a query, this function always returns the same result.
implementation-dependent:

http://www.w3.org/TR/xquery/#dt-implementation-dependent

data model

XQuery operates on the abstract, logical structure of an XML document, rather than its surface syntax. This logical structure, known as the data model, is defined in XQuery/XPath Data Model (XDM).
XQuery/XPath Data Model (XDM):
http://www.w3.org/TR/xquery/#datamodel

data model schema

For a given node in an XDM instance, the data model schema is defined as the schema from which the type annotation of that node was derived.
XDM instance:
http://www.w3.org/TR/xquery/#dt-data-model-instance
Type annotation:
http://www.w3.org/TR/xquery/#dt-type-annotation

default collation

Default collation. This identifies one of the collations in statically known collations as the collation to be used by functions and operators for comparing and ordering values of type xs:string and xs:anyURI (and types derived from them) when no explicit collation is specified.
statically known collations:
http://www.w3.org/TR/xquery/#dt-static-collations

default collation declaration

A default collation declaration sets the value of the default collation in the static context, overriding any implementation-defined default.
default collation:
http://www.w3.org/TR/xquery/#dt-def-collation

static context:
http://www.w3.org/TR/xquery/#dt-static-context

default collection

Default collection. This is the sequence of nodes that would result from calling the fn:collection function with no arguments.

default element/type namespace

Default element/type namespace. This is a namespace URI or "none". The namespace URI, if present, is used for any unprefixed QName appearing in a position where an element or type name is expected.

default function namespace

Default function namespace. This is a namespace URI or "none". The namespace URI, if present, is used for any unprefixed QName appearing in a position where a function name is expected.

default order for empty sequences

Default order for empty sequences. This component controls the processing of empty sequences and NaN values as ordering keys in an order by clause in a FLWOR expression.

delimiting terminal symbol

The delimiting terminal symbols are: S, "-", (comma), (semi-colon), (colon), "::", ":=", "!=", "?", "?>", "/", "//", "/>", (dot), "..", StringLiteral, "(", "(#", ")", "[", "]", "]]>", "{", "}", "@", "$", "*", "#)", "+", "<", "<!--", "<![CDATA[", "<?", "</", "<<", "<=", "=", ">", "-->", ">=", ">>", "|"
S:

http://www.w3.org/TR/xquery/#prod-xquery-S
StringLiteral:
http://www.w3.org/TR/xquery/#prod-xquery-StringLiteral

direct element constructor

A direct element constructor is a form of element constructor in which the name of the constructed element is a constant.

document order

Informally, document order is the order in which nodes appear in the XML serialization of a document.

dynamic context

The dynamic context of an expression is defined as information that is available at the time the expression is evaluated.

dynamic error

A dynamic error is an error that must be detected during the dynamic evaluation phase and may be detected during the static analysis phase. Numeric overflow is an example of a dynamic error.

dynamic evaluation phase

The dynamic evaluation phase is the phase during which the value of an expression is computed.

dynamic type

A dynamic type is associated with each value as it is computed. The

dynamic type of a value may be more specific than the static type of the expression that computed it (for example, the static type of an expression might be xs:integer*, denoting a sequence of zero or more integers, but at evaluation time its value may have the dynamic type xs:integer, denoting exactly one integer.)
Static type:
http://www.w3.org/TR/xquery/#dt-static-type

effective boolean value

The effective boolean value of a value is defined as the result of applying the fn:boolean function to the value, as defined in [XQuery 1.0 and XPath 2.0 Functions and Operators].
XQuery 1.0 and XPath 2.0 Functions and Operators:
http://www.w3.org/TR/xquery/#FunctionsAndOperators

effective case

The effective case in a typeswitch expression is the first case clause such that the value of the operand expression matches the SequenceType in the case clause, using the rules of SequenceType matching.
SequenceType:
http://www.w3.org/TR/xquery/#prod-xquery-SequenceType

empty order declaration

An empty order declaration sets the default order for empty sequences in the static context, overriding any implementation-defined default. This declaration controls the processing of empty sequences and NaN values as ordering keys in an order by clause in a FLWOR expression.
default order for empty sequences:
http://www.w3.org/TR/xquery/#dt-default-empty-order
static context:
http://www.w3.org/TR/xquery/#dt-static-context

empty sequence

A sequence containing zero items is called an empty sequence.

encoding declaration

If present, a version declaration may optionally include an encoding declaration. The value of the string literal following the keyword encoding is an encoding name, and must conform to the definition of EncName specified in [XML 1.0][err:XQST0087]. The purpose of an encoding declaration is to allow the writer of a query to provide a string that indicates how the query is encoded, such as "UTF-8", "UTF-16", or "US-ASCII".

error value

In addition to its identifying QName, a dynamic error may also carry a descriptive string and one or more additional values called error values.

expanded QName

An expanded QName consists of an optional namespace URI and a local name. An expanded QName also retains its original namespace prefix (if any), to facilitate casting the expanded QName into a string.

expression context

The expression context for a given expression consists of all the information that can affect the result of the expression.

extension expression

An extension expression is an expression whose semantics are

implementation-defined.
implementation-defined:
http://www.w3.org/TR/xquery/#dt-implementation-defined

external function

External functions are functions that are implemented outside the query environment.

filter expression

A filter expression consists simply of a primary expression followed by zero or more predicates. The result of the filter expression consists of the items returned by the primary expression, filtered by applying each predicate in turn, working from left to right.
Predicates:
http://www.w3.org/TR/xquery/#dt-predicate

focus

The first three components of the dynamic context (context item, context position, and context size) are called the focus of the expression.
Dynamic context:
http://www.w3.org/TR/xquery/#dt-dynamic-context

Full Axis Feature

A conforming XQuery implementation that supports the Full Axis Feature MUST support all the optional axes.
Optional axes:
http://www.w3.org/TR/xquery/#dt-optional-axis

function depends

A function f1 depends on a variable $y or a function f2 if a reference to $y or f2 appears in the body of f1, or if there exists a variable $z or a function f3 such that f1 depends on $z or f3 and $z or f3 depends on $y or f2.
Depends:
http://www.w3.org/TR/xquery/#dt-variable-depends

function implementation

Function implementations. Each function in function signatures has a function implementation that enables the function to map instances of its parameter types into an instance of its result type. For a user-defined function, the function implementation is an XQuery expression. For a built-in function or external function, the function implementation is implementation-dependent.
Function signatures:
http://www.w3.org/TR/xquery/#dt-function-signature
user-defined function:
http://www.w3.org/TR/xquery/#dt-udf
built-in function:
http://www.w3.org/TR/xquery/#dt-built-in-function
external function:
http://www.w3.org/TR/xquery/#dt-external-function
implementation-dependent:
http://www.w3.org/TR/xquery/#dt-implementation-dependent

function signature

Function signatures. This component defines the set of functions that are available to be called from within an expression. Each function is uniquely identified by its expanded QName and its arity (number of parameters).
Expanded QName:
http://www.w3.org/TR/xquery/#dt-expanded-qname

Gregorian

In the operator mapping tables, the term Gregorian refers to the types xs:gYearMonth, xs:gYear, xs:gMonthDay, xs:gDay, and xs:gMonth.

ignorable whitespace

Ignorable whitespace consists of any whitespace characters that may occur between terminals, unless these characters occur in the context of a production marked with a ws:explicit annotation, in which case they can occur only where explicitly specified.

implementation defined

Implementation-defined indicates an aspect that may differ between implementations, but must be specified by the implementor for each particular implementation.

implementation dependent

Implementation-dependent indicates an aspect that may differ between implementations, is not specified by this or any W3C specification, and is not required to be specified by the implementor for any particular implementation.

implicit timezone

Implicit timezone. This is the timezone to be used when a date, time, or dateTime value that does not have a timezone is used in a comparison or arithmetic operation. The implicit timezone is an implementation-defined value of type xs:dayTimeDuration.

initializing expression

If a variable declaration includes an expression, the expression is called an initializing expression.

in-scope attribute declarations

In-scope attribute declarations. Each attribute declaration is identified either by an expanded QName (for a top-level attribute declaration) or by an implementation-dependent attribute identifier (for a local attribute declaration). If the Schema Import Feature is supported, in-scope attribute declarations include all attribute declarations found in imported schemas.

in-scope element declarations

In-scope element declarations. Each element declaration is identified either by an expanded QName (for a top-level element declaration) or by an implementation-dependent element identifier (for a local element declaration). If the Schema Import Feature is supported, in-scope element declarations include all element declarations found in imported schemas.

in-scope namespaces

The in-scope namespaces property of an element node is a set of namespace bindings, each of which associates a namespace prefix with a URI, thus defining the set of namespace prefixes that are available for interpreting QNames within the scope of the element. For a given element, one namespace binding may have an empty prefix; the URI of this namespace binding is the default namespace within the scope of the element.

in-scope schema definitions

In-scope schema definitions. This is a generic term for all the element declarations, attribute declarations, and schema type definitions that are in scope during processing of an expression.

in-scope schema type

In-scope schema types. Each schema type definition is identified either by an expanded QName (for a named type) or by an implementation-dependent type identifier (for an anonymous type). If the Schema Import Feature is supported, in-scope schema types also include all type definitions found in imported schemas.

in-scope variables

In-scope variables. This is a set of (expanded QName, type) pairs. It defines the set of variables that are available for reference within an expression. The expanded QName is the name of the variable, and the type is the static type of the variable.

item

An item is either an atomic value or a node.

kind test

An alternative form of a node test called a kind test can select nodes based on their kind, name, and type annotation.

library module

A module that does not contain a Query Body is called a library module. A library module consists of a module declaration followed by a Prolog.

literal

A literal is a direct syntactic representation of an atomic value.

main module

A main module consists of a Prolog followed by a Query Body.

may

MAY means that an item is truly optional.

module

A module is a fragment of XQuery code that conforms to the Module grammar and can independently undergo the static analysis phase. Each module is either a main module or a library module.

module declaration

A module declaration serves to identify a module as a library module. A module declaration begins with the keyword module and contains a namespace prefix and a URILiteral.

module directly depends

A module M1 directly depends on another module M2 (different from M1) if a variable or function declared in M1 depends on a variable or function declared in M2.

module feature

A conforming XQuery implementation that supports the Module Feature allows a query Prolog to contain a Module Import and allows library modules to be created.

module import

A module import imports the function declarations and variable declarations from one or more library modules into the function signatures and in-scope variables of the importing module.

must

MUST means that the item is an absolute requirement of the specification.

name expression

When an expression is used to specify the name of a constructed node, that expression is called the name expression of the constructor.

namespace declaration

A namespace declaration declares a namespace prefix and associates it with a namespace URI, adding the (prefix, URI) pair to the set of statically known namespaces.

namespace declaration attribute

A namespace declaration attribute is used inside a direct element constructor. Its purpose is to bind a namespace prefix or to set the default element/type namespace for the constructed element node, including its attributes.

namespace-sensitive

A value is namespace-sensitive if it includes an item whose dynamic type is xs:QName or xs:NOTATION or is derived by restriction from xs:QName or xs:NOTATION.

name test

A node test that consists only of a QName or a Wildcard is called a name test.

node

A node is an instance of one of the node kinds defined in XQuery/XPath Data Model (XDM).

node test

A node test is a condition that must be true for each node selected by a step.

non-delimiting terminal symbol

The non-delimiting terminal symbols are: IntegerLiteral, NCName, QName, DecimalLiteral, DoubleLiteral, "ancestor", "ancestor-or-self", "and", "as", "ascending", "at", "attribute", "base-uri", "boundary-space", "by", "case", "cast", "castable", "child", "collation", "comment", "construction", "copy-namespaces", "declare", "default", "descendant", "descendant-or-self", "descending", "div", "document", "document-node", "element", "else", "empty", "empty-sequence", "encoding", "eq", "every", "except", "external", "following", "following-sibling", "for", "function", "ge", "greatest", "gt", "idiv", "if", "import", "in", "inherit", "instance", "intersect", "is", "item", "lax", "le", "least", "let", "lt", "mod", "module", "namespace", "ne",

"node", "no-inherit", "no-preserve", "of", "option", "or", "order",
"ordered", "ordering", "parent", "preceding", "preceding-sibling",
"preserve", "processing-instruction", "return", "satisfies", "schema",
"schema-attribute", "schema-element", "self", "some", "stable",
"strict", "strip", "text", "then", "to", "treat", "typeswitch", "union",
"unordered", "validate", "variable", "version", "where", "xquery"

numeric

When referring to a type, the term numeric denotes the types
`xs:integer`, `xs:decimal`, `xs:float`, and `xs:double`.

numeric predicate

A predicate whose predicate expression returns a numeric type is called a
numeric predicate.

operator function

For each operator and valid combination of operand types, the operator
mapping tables specify a result type and an operator function that
implements the semantics of the operator for the given types.

optional axis

The following axes are designated as optional axes: `ancestor`,
`ancestor-or-self`, `following`, `following-sibling`,
`preceding`, and `preceding-sibling`.

option declaration

An option declaration declares an option that affects the behavior of a
particular implementation. Each option consists of an identifying QName
and a StringLiteral.

ordering mode

Ordering mode. Ordering mode, which has the value ordered or unordered, affects the ordering of the result sequence returned by certain path expressions, union, intersect, and except expressions, and FLWOR expressions that have no order by clause.

ordering mode declaration

An ordering mode declaration sets the ordering mode in the static context, overriding any implementation-defined default.

path expression

A path expression can be used to locate nodes within trees. A path expression consists of a series of one or more steps, separated by "/" or "//", and optionally beginning with "/" or "//".

pragma

A pragma is denoted by the delimiters (# and #), and consists of an identifying QName followed by implementation-defined content.

predefined entity reference

A predefined entity reference is a short sequence of characters, beginning with an ampersand, that represents a single character that might otherwise have syntactic significance.

predicate

A predicate consists of an expression, called a predicate expression, enclosed in square brackets. A predicate serves to filter a sequence, retaining some items and discarding others.

primary expression

Primary expressions are the basic primitives of the language. They include literals, variable references, context item expressions, constructors, and function calls. A primary expression may also be created by enclosing any expression in parentheses, which is sometimes helpful in controlling the precedence of operators.

principal node kind

Every axis has a principal node kind. If an axis can contain elements, then the principal node kind is element; otherwise, it is the kind of nodes that the axis can contain.

Prolog

A Prolog is a series of declarations and imports that define the processing environment for the module that contains the Prolog.

QName

Lexically, a QName consists of an optional namespace prefix and a local name. If the namespace prefix is present, it is separated from the local name by a colon.

query

A query consists of one or more modules.

query body

The Query Body, if present, consists of an expression that defines the result of the query.

reverse document order

The node ordering that is the reverse of document order is called reverse document order.

schema import

A schema import imports the element declarations, attribute declarations, and type definitions from a schema into the in-scope schema definitions.

schema import feature

The Schema Import Feature permits the query Prolog to contain a schema import.

schema type

A schema type is a type that is (or could be) defined using the facilities of XML Schema.

schema validation feature

The Schema Validation Feature permits a query to contain a validate expression.

sequence

A sequence is an ordered collection of zero or more items.

sequence type

A sequence type is a type that can be expressed using the SequenceType syntax. Sequence types are used whenever it is necessary to refer to a type in an XQuery expression. The term sequence type suggests that this syntax is used to describe the type of an XQuery value, which is always a sequence.

SequenceType matching

During evaluation of an expression, it is sometimes necessary to determine whether a value with a known dynamic type "matches" an expected sequence type. This process is known as SequenceType matching.

serialization

Serialization is the process of converting an XDM instance into a sequence of octets.

serialization feature

A conforming XQuery implementation that supports the Serialization Feature MUST provide means for serializing the result of a query.

setter

Setters are declarations that set the value of some property that affects query processing, such as construction mode, ordering mode, or default collation.

should

SHOULD means that there may exist valid reasons in particular circumstances to ignore a particular item, but the full implications must be understood and carefully weighed before choosing a different course.

singleton

A sequence containing exactly one item is called a singleton.

stable

Document order is stable, which means that the relative order of two nodes will not change during the processing of a given query, even if this order is implementation-dependent.

statically known collations

Statically known collations. This is an implementation-defined set of (URI, collation) pairs. It defines the names of the collations that are available for use in processing queries and expressions.

statically known collections

Statically known collections. This is a mapping from strings onto types. The string represents the absolute URI of a resource that is potentially available using the fn:collection function. The type is the type of the sequence of nodes that would result from calling the fn:collection function with this URI as its argument.

statically known default collection type

Statically known default collection type. This is the type of the sequence of nodes that would result from calling the fn:collection function with no arguments.

statically known documents

Statically known documents. This is a mapping from strings onto types. The string represents the absolute URI of a resource that is potentially available using the fn:doc function. The type is the static type of a call to fn:doc with the given URI as its literal argument.

statically known namespaces

Statically known namespaces. This is a set of (prefix, URI) pairs that define all the namespaces that are known during static processing of a given expression.

static analysis phase

The static analysis phase depends on the expression itself and on the static context. The static analysis phase does not depend on input data (other than schemas).

static context

The static context of an expression is the information that is available during static analysis of the expression, prior to its evaluation.

static error

A static error is an error that must be detected during the static analysis phase. A syntax error is an example of a static error.

static type

The static type of an expression is a type such that, when the expression is evaluated, the resulting value will always conform to the static type.

static typing extension

A static typing extension is an implementation-defined type inference rule that infers a more precise static type than that inferred by the type inference rules in

static typing feature

The Static Typing Feature provides support for the static semantics defined in XQuery 1.0 and XPath 2.0 Formal Semantics, and requires implementations to detect and report type errors during the static analysis phase.
XQuery 1.0 and XPath 2.0 Formal Semantics:
http://www.w3.org/TR/xquery/#XQueryFormalSemantics

step

A step is a part of a path expression that generates a sequence of items and then filters the sequence by zero or more predicates. The value of the step consists of those items that satisfy the predicates, working from left to right. A step may be either an axis step or a filter expression.

string value

The string value of a node is a string and can be extracted by applying the fn:string function to the node.

substitution group

Substitution group headed by a given element (called the head element) consists of the set of elements that can be substituted for the head element without affecting the outcome of schema validation.

subtype substitution

The use of a value whose dynamic type is derived from an expected type is known as subtype substitution.

symbol

Each rule in the grammar defines one symbol, using the following format:
```
symbol ::= expression
```

symbol separators

Whitespace and Comments function as symbol separators. For the most part, they are not mentioned in the grammar, and may occur between any two terminal symbols mentioned in the grammar, except where that is forbidden by the /* ws: explicit */ annotation in the EBNF, or by the /* xgs: xml-version */ annotation.

target namespace

Each imported schema or module is identified by its target namespace, which is the namespace of the objects (such as elements or functions) that are defined by the schema or module.

terminal

A terminal is a symbol or string or pattern that can appear in the right-hand side of a rule, but never appears on the left hand side in the main grammar, although it may appear on the left-hand side of a rule in the grammar for terminals.

type annotation

Each element node and attribute node in an XDM instance has a type annotation (referred to in [XQuery/XPath Data Model (XDM)] as its type-name property.) The type annotation of a node is a schema type that describes the relationship between the string value of the node and its typed value.

typed value

The typed value of a node is a sequence of atomic values and can be extracted by applying the fn:data function to the node.

type error

A type error may be raised during the static analysis phase or the dynamic evaluation phase. During the static analysis phase, a type error occurs when the static type of an expression does not match the expected type of the context in which the expression occurs. During the dynamic evaluation phase, a type error occurs when the dynamic type of a value does not match the expected type of the context in which the value occurs.

type promotion

Under certain circumstances, an atomic value can be promoted from one type to another. Type promotion is used in evaluating function calls, order by clauses, and operators that accept numeric or string operands.

URI

Within this specification, the term URI refers to a Universal Resource Identifier as defined in RFC3986 and extended in RFC3987 with the new name IRI.
RFC3986 & RFC3987:

http://www.w3.org/TR/xquery/#RFC3986
http://www.w3.org/TR/xquery/#RFC3987

user-defined function

For a user-defined function, the function declaration includes an expression called the function body that defines how the result of the function is computed from its parameters.

value

In the data model, a value is always a sequence.

variable depends

A variable $x depends on a variable $y or a function f2 if a reference to $y or f2 appears in the initializing expression of $x, or if there exists a variable $z or a function f3 such that $x depends on $z or f3 and $z or f3 depends on $y or f2.

variable reference

A variable reference is a QName preceded by a $-sign.

variable values

Variable values. This is a set of (expanded QName, value) pairs. It contains the same expanded QNames as the in-scope variables in the static context for the expression. The expanded QName is the name of the variable and the value is the dynamic value of the variable, which includes its dynamic type.

version declaration

Any module may contain a version declaration. If present, the version declaration occurs at the beginning of the module and identifies the applicable XQuery syntax and semantics for the module.

warning

In addition to static errors, dynamic errors, and type errors, an XQuery implementation may raise warnings, either during the static analysis phase or the dynamic evaluation phase. The circumstances in which warnings are raised, and the ways in which warnings are handled, are implementation-defined.

whitespace

A whitespace character is any of the characters defined by http://www.w3.org/TR/REC-xml#NT-S

XDM instance

The term XDM instance is used, synonymously with the term value, to denote an unconstrained sequence of nodes and/or atomic values in the data model.

XPath 1.0 compatibility mode

XPath 1.0 compatibility mode. This component must be set by all host languages that include XPath 2.0 as a subset, indicating whether rules for compatibility with XPath 1.0 are in effect. XQuery sets the value of this component to false.

xs:anyAtomicType

xs:anyAtomicType is an atomic type that includes all atomic values (and no values that are not atomic). Its base type is xs:anySimpleType from which all simple types, including atomic, list, and union types, are derived. All primitive atomic types, such as xs:integer, xs:string, and xs:untypedAtomic, have xs:anyAtomicType as their base type.

xs:dayTimeDuration

xs:dayTimeDuration is derived by restriction from xs:duration. The lexical representation of xs:dayTimeDuration is restricted to contain only day, hour, minute, and second components.

xs:untyped

xs:untyped is used as the type annotation of an element node that has not been validated, or has been validated in skip mode.

xs:untypedAtomic

xs:untypedAtomic is an atomic type that is used to denote untyped atomic data, such as text that has not been assigned a more specific type.

xs:yearMonthDuration

xs:yearMonthDuration is derived by restriction from xs:duration. The lexical representation of xs:yearMonthDuration is restricted to contain only year and month components.

Appendix III

Reserved Function Names

The following names are not allowed as function names in an unprefixed form because expression syntax takes precedence.

- attribute
- comment
- document-node
- element
- empty-sequence
- if
- item
- node
- processing-instruction
- schema-attribute
- schema-element
- text
- typeswitch

Appendix IV
Precedence Order

This appendix defines built-in precedence among the operators of XQuery. These operators are summarized here to make clear the order of their precedence from lowest to highest. Operators that have a lower precedence number cannot be contained by operators with a higher precedence number. The associativity column indicates the order in which operators of equal precedence in an expression are applied.

#	Operator	Associativity
1	, (comma)	left-to-right
2	:= (assignment)	right-to-left
3	for, some, every, typeswitch, if	left-to-right
4	or	left-to-right
5	and	left-to-right
6	eq, ne, lt, le, gt, ge, =, !=, <, <=, >, >=, is, <<, >>	left-to-right
7	to	left-to-right
8	+, -	left-to-right
9	*, div, idiv, mod	left-to-right
10	union, |	left-to-right
11	intersect, except	left-to-right
12	instance of	left-to-right

13	treat	left-to-right
14	castable	left-to-right
15	cast	left-to-right
16	-(unary), +(unary)	right-to-left
17	?, *(OccurrenceIndicator), +(OccurrenceIndicator)	left-to-right
18	/, //	left-to-right
19	[ ], (), {}	left-to-right

Appendix V

Error Conditions

err:XPST0001

> It is a static error if analysis of an expression relies on some component of the static context that has not been assigned a value.

err:XPDY0002

> It is a dynamic error if evaluation of an expression relies on some part of the dynamic context that has not been assigned a value.

err:XPST0003

> It is a static error if an expression is not a valid instance of the grammar.

err:XPTY0004

> It is a type error if, during the static analysis phase, an expression is found to have a static type that is not appropriate for the context in which the expression occurs, or during the dynamic evaluation phase, the dynamic type of a value does not match a required type as specified by the matching rules.

err:XPST0005

> During the analysis phase, it is a static error if the static type assigned to an expression other than the expression () or data(()) is empty-sequence().

err:XPTY0006

> (Not currently used.)

err:XPTY0007

> (Not currently used.)

err:XPST0008

> It is a static error if an expression refers to an element name, attribute

name, schema type name, namespace prefix, or variable name that is not defined in the static context, except for an ElementName in an ElementTest or an AttributeName in an AttributeTest.

err:XQST0009
An implementation that does not support the Schema Import Feature must raise a static error if a Prolog contains a schema import.

err:XPST0010
An implementation must raise a static error if it encounters a reference to an axis that it does not support.

err:XQST0012
It is a static error if the set of definitions contained in all schemas imported by a Prolog do not satisfy the conditions for schema validity. For example, each definition must be valid, complete, and unique.

err:XQST0013
It is a static error if an implementation recognizes a pragma but determines that its content is invalid.

err:XQST0014
(Not currently used.)

err:XQST0015
(Not currently used.)

err:XQST0016
An implementation that does not support the Module Feature raises a static error if it encounters a module declaration or a module import.

err:XPST0017
It is a static error if the expanded QName and number of arguments in a function call do not match the name and arity of a function signature in the static context.

err:XPTY0018
It is a type error if the result of the last step in a path expression contains both nodes and atomic values.

err:XPTY0019
It is a type error if the result of a step (other than the last step) in a path expression contains an atomic value.

err:XPTY0020
It is a type error if, in an axis step, the context item is not a node.

err:XPDY0021

(Not currently used.)

err:XQST0022

It is a static error if the value of a namespace declaration attribute is not a URILiteral.

err:XQTY0023

(Not currently used.)

err:XQTY0024

It is a type error if the content sequence in an element constructor contains an attribute node following a node that is not an attribute node.

err:XQDY0025

It is a dynamic error if any attribute of a constructed element does not have a name that is distinct from the names of all other attributes of the constructed element.

err:XQDY0026

It is a dynamic error if the result of the content expression of a computed processing instruction constructor contains the string "?>".

err:XQDY0027

In a validate expression, it is a dynamic error if the root element information item in the PSVI resulting from validation does not have the expected validity property: valid if validation mode is strict, or either valid or notKnown if validation mode is lax.

err:XQTY0028

(Not currently used.)

err:XQDY0029

(Not currently used.)

err:XQTY0030

It is a type error if the argument of a validate expression does not evaluate to exactly one document or element node.

err:XQST0031

It is a static error if the version number specified in a version declaration is not supported by the implementation.

err:XQST0032

A static error is raised if a Prolog contains more than one base URI declaration.

err:XQST0033

It is a static error if a module contains multiple bindings for the same namespace prefix.

err:XQST0034

It is a static error if multiple functions declared or imported by a module have the number of arguments and their expanded QNames are equal (as defined by the eq operator).

err:XQST0035

It is a static error to import two schema components that both define the same name in the same symbol space and in the same scope.

err:XQST0036

It is a static error to import a module if the importing module's in-scope schema types do not include definitions for the schema type names that appear in the declarations of variables and functions (whether in an argument type or return type) that are present in the imported module and are referenced in the importing module.

err:XQST0037

(Not currently used.)

err:XQST0038

It is a static error if a Prolog contains more than one default collation declaration, or the value specified by a default collation declaration is not present in statically known collations.

err:XQST0039

It is a static error for a function declaration to have more than one parameter with the same name.

err:XQST0040

It is a static error if the attributes specified by a direct element constructor do not have distinct expanded QNames.

err:XQDY0041

It is a dynamic error if the value of the name expression in a computed processing instruction constructor cannot be cast to the type xs:NCName.

err:XQST0042

(Not currently used.)

err:XQST0043

(Not currently used.)

err:XQDY0044

It is a dynamic error if the node-name property of the node constructed by a computed attribute constructor is in the namespace http://www. w3.org/2000/xmlns/ (corresponding to namespace prefix xmlns), or is in no namespace and has local name xmlns.

err:XQST0045

It is a static error if the function name in a function declaration is in one of the following namespaces: http://www.w3.org/XML/1998/namespace, http://www.w3.org/2001/XMLSchema, http://www.w3.org/2001/ XMLSchema-instance, http://www.w3.org/2005/xpath-functions.

err:XQST0046

An implementation MAY raise a static error if the value of a URILiteral is of nonzero length and is not in the lexical space of xs:anyURI.

err:XQST0047

It is a static error if multiple module imports in the same Prolog specify the same target namespace.

err:XQST0048

It is a static error if a function or variable declared in a library module is not in the target namespace of the library module.

err:XQST0049

It is a static error if two or more variables declared or imported by a module have equal expanded QNames (as defined by the eq operator.)

err:XPDY0050

It is a dynamic error if the dynamic type of the operand of a treat expression does not match the sequence type specified by the treat expression. This error might also be raised by a path expression beginning with "/" or "//" if the context node is not in a tree that is rooted at a document node. This is because a leading "/" or "//" in a path expression is an abbreviation for an initial step that includes the clause treat as document-node().

err:XPST0051

It is a static error if a QName that is used as an AtomicType in a SequenceType is not defined in the in-scope schema types as an atomic type.

err:XQDY0052

(Not currently used.)

err:XQST0053

(Not currently used.)

err:XQST0054

It is a static error if a variable depends on itself.

err:XQST0055

It is a static error if a Prolog contains more than one copy-namespaces declaration.

err:XQST0056

(Not currently used.)

err:XQST0057

It is a static error if a schema import binds a namespace prefix but does not specify a target namespace other than a zero-length string.

err:XQST0058

It is a static error if multiple schema imports specify the same target namespace.

err:XQST0059

It is a static error if an implementation is unable to process a schema or module import by finding a schema or module with the specified target namespace.

err:XQST0060

It is a static error if the name of a function in a function declaration is not in a namespace (expanded QName has a null namespace URI).

err:XQDY0061

It is a dynamic error if the operand of a validate expression is a document node whose children do not consist of exactly one element node and zero or more comment and processing instruction nodes, in any order.

err:XQDY0062

(Not currently used.)

err:XQST0063

(Not currently used.)

err:XQDY0064

It is a dynamic error if the value of the name expression in a computed processing instruction constructor is equal to "XML" (in any combination of upper and lower case).

err:XQST0065

A static error is raised if a Prolog contains more than one ordering mode declaration.

err:XQST0066

A static error is raised if a Prolog contains more than one default element/type namespace declaration, or more than one default function namespace declaration.

err:XQST0067

A static error is raised if a Prolog contains more than one construction declaration.

err:XQST0068

A static error is raised if a Prolog contains more than one boundary-space declaration.

err:XQST0069

A static error is raised if a Prolog contains more than one empty order declaration.

err:XQST0070

A static error is raised if a namespace URI is bound to the predefined prefix xmlns, or if a namespace URI other than http://www.w3.org/XML/1998/namespace is bound to the prefix xml, or if the prefix xml is bound to a namespace URI other than http://www.w3.org/XML/1998/namespace.

err:XQST0071

A static error is raised if the namespace declaration attributes of a direct element constructor do not have distinct names.

err:XQDY0072

It is a dynamic error if the result of the content expression of a computed comment constructor contains two adjacent hyphens or ends with a hyphen.

err:XQST0073

It is a static error if the graph of module imports contains a cycle (that is, if there exists a sequence of modules M1 ... Mn such that each Mi imports Mi+1 and Mn imports M1), unless all the modules in the cycle share a common namespace.

err:XQDY0074

It is a dynamic error if the value of the name expression in a computed element or attribute constructor cannot be converted to an expanded QName (for example, because it contains a namespace prefix not found in statically known namespaces.)

err:XQST0075

An implementation that does not support the Validation Feature must raise a static error if it encounters a validate expression.

err:XQST0076

It is a static error if a collation subclause in an order by clause of a FLWOR expression does not identify a collation that is present in statically known collations.

err:XQST0077

(Not currently used.)

err:XQST0078

(Not currently used.)

err:XQST0079

It is a static error if an extension expression contains neither a pragma that is recognized by the implementation nor an expression enclosed in curly braces.

err:XPST0080

It is a static error if the target type of a cast or castable expression is xs:NOTATION or xs:anyAtomicType.

err:XPST0081

It is a static error if a QName used in a query contains a namespace prefix that cannot be expanded into a namespace URI by using the statically known namespaces.

err:XQST0082

(Not currently used.)

err:XPST0083

(Not currently used.)

err:XQDY0084

It is a dynamic error if the element validated by a validate statement does not have a top-level element declaration in the in-scope element declarations, if validation mode is strict.

err:XQST0085

It is a static error if the namespace URI in a namespace declaration attribute is a zero-length string, and the implementation does not support XML Names 1.1: http://www.w3.org/TR/xquery/#XMLNAMES11.

err:XQTY0086

It is a type error if the typed value of a copied element or attribute node is namespace-sensitive when construction mode is preserve and copy-namespaces mode is no-preserve.

err:XQST0087

It is a static error if the encoding specified in a Version Declaration does not conform to the definition of EncName specified in XML 1.0: http://www.w3.org/TR/xquery/#XML

err:XQST0088

It is a static error if the literal that specifies the target namespace in a module import or a module declaration is of zero length.

err:XQST0089

It is a static error if a variable bound in a for clause of a FLWOR expression, and its associated positional variable, do not have distinct names (expanded QNames).

err:XQST0090

It is a static error if a character reference does not identify a valid character in the version of XML that is in use.

err:XQDY0091

An implementation MAY raise a dynamic error if an xml:id error, as defined in http://www.w3.org/TR/xquery/#XMLID, is encountered during construction of an attribute named xml:id.

err:XQDY0092

An implementation MAY raise a dynamic error if a constructed attribute named xml:space has a value other than preserve or default.

err:XQST0093

It is a static error to import a module M1 if there exists a sequence of modules M1 ... Mi ... M1 such that each module directly depends on the next module in the sequence (informally, if M1 depends on itself through some chain of module dependencies.)

Appendix VI

Type Promotion and Operator Mapping
Type Promotion

Under certain circumstances, an atomic value can be promoted from one type to another. Type promotion is used in evaluating function calls, order by clauses, and operators that accept numeric or string operands. The following type promotions are permitted:

1. Numeric type promotion:
   a. A value of type xs:float (or any type derived by restriction from xs:float) can be promoted to the type xs:double. The result is the xs:double value that is the same as the original value.
   b. A value of type xs:decimal (or any type derived by restriction from xs:decimal) can be promoted to either of the types xs:float or xs:double. The result of this promotion is created by casting the original value to the required type. This kind of promotion may cause loss of precision.
2. URI type promotion: A value of type xs:anyURI (or any type derived by restriction from xs:anyURI) can be promoted to the type xs:string. The result of this promotion is created by casting the original value to the type xs:string.

   Note:

Since xs:anyURI values can be promoted to xs:string, functions and operators that compare strings using the default collation also compare xs:anyURI values using the default collation. This ensures that orderings that include strings, xs:anyURI values, or any combination of the two types are consistent and well-defined.

Note that type promotion is different from subtype substitution. For example:

- A function that expects a parameter $p of type xs:float can be invoked with a value of type xs:decimal. This is an example of type promotion. The value is actually converted to the expected type. Within the body of the function, $p instance of xs:decimal returns false.
- A function that expects a parameter $p of type xs:decimal can be invoked with a value of type xs:integer. This is an example of subtype substitution. The value retains its original type. Within the body of the function, $p instance of xs:integer returns true.

Operator Mapping

The operator mapping tables in this section list the combinations of types for which the various operators of XQuery are defined. [Definition: For each operator and valid combination of operand types, the operator mapping tables specify a result type and an operator function that implements the semantics of the operator for the given types.] The definitions of the operator functions are given in XQuery 1.0 and XPath 2.0 Functions and Operators: http://www.w3.org/TR/xquery/#FunctionsAndOperators. The result of an operator may be the raising of an error by its operator function, as defined in XQuery 1.0 and XPath 2.0 Functions and Operators: http://www.w3.org/TR/xquery/#FunctionsAndOperators. In some cases, the operator function does not implement the full semantics of a given operator. For the definition of each operator (including its behavior for empty sequences or sequences of length greater than one), see the descriptive material in the main part of this document. The and and or operators are defined directly in the main body of this document, and do not occur in the operator mapping tables.

If an operator in the operator mapping tables expects an operand of type ET, that operator can be applied to an operand of type AT if type AT can be converted to type ET by a combination of type promotion and subtype substitution. For example, a table entry indicates that the gt operator may be applied to two xs:date operands, returning xs:boolean. Therefore, the gt operator may also be applied to two (possibly different) subtypes of xs:date, also returning xs:boolean.

[Definition: When referring to a type, the term numeric denotes the types xs:integer, xs:decimal, xs:float, and xs:double.] An operator whose operands and result are designated as numeric might be thought of as representing four operators, one for each of the numeric types. For example, the numeric + operator might be thought of as representing the following four operators:

Operator	First operand type	Second operand type	Result type
+	xs:integer	xs:integer	xs:integer
+	xs:decimal	xs:decimal	xs:decimal
+	xs:float	xs:float	xs:float
+	xs:double	xs:double	xs:double

A numeric operator may be validly applied to an operand of type AT if type AT can be converted to any of the four numeric types by a combination of type promotion and subtype substitution. If the result type of an operator is listed as numeric, it means "the first type in the ordered list (xs:integer, xs:decimal, xs:float, xs:double) into which all operands can be converted by subtype substitution and type promotion." As an example, suppose that the type hatsize is derived from xs:integer and the type shoesize is derived from xs:float. Then if the + operator is invoked with operands of type hatsize and shoesize, it returns a result of type xs:float. Similarly, if + is invoked with two operands of type hatsize it returns a result of type xs:integer.

[Definition: In the operator mapping tables, the term Gregorian refers to the types xs:gYearMonth, xs:gYear, xs:gMonthDay, xs:gDay, and xs:gMonth.] For binary operators that accept two Gregorian-type operands, both operands must have the same type (for example, if one operand is of type xs:gDay, the other operand must be of type xs:gDay.)

Binary Operators

Operator	Type(A)	Type(B)	Function	Result type
A + B	numeric	numeric	op:numeric-add(A, B)	numeric

A + B	xs:date	xs:yearMonth Duration	op:add-yearMonth Duration-to-date (A, B)	xs:date
A + B	xs:yearMonth Duration	xs:date	op:add-yearMonth Duration-to-date (B, A)	xs:date
A + B	xs:date	xs:dayTime Duration	op:add-dayTime Duration-to-date (A, B)	xs:date
A + B	xs:dayTime Duration	xs:date	op:add-dayTime Duration-to-date (B, A)	xs:date
A + B	xs:time	xs:dayTime Duration	op:add-dayTime Duration-to-time (A, B)	xs:time
A + B	xs:dayTime Duration	xs:time	op:add-dayTime Duration-to-time (B, A)	xs:time
A + B	xs:dateTime	xs:yearMonth Duration	op:add-yearMonth Duration-to-dateTime(A, B)	xs:date Time
A + B	xs:yearMonth Duration	xs:dateTime	op:add-yearMonth Duration-to-dateTime(B, A)	xs:date Time
A + B	xs:dateTime	xs:dayTime Duration	op:add-dayTime Duration-to-dateTime(A, B)	xs:date Time
A + B	xs:dayTime Duration	xs:dateTime	op:add-dayTime Duration-to-dateTime(B, A)	xs:date Time
A + B	xs:yearMonth Duration	xs:yearMonth Duration	op:add-year MonthDurations (A, B)	xs:year Month Duration

378

A + B	xs:dayTime Duration	xs:dayTime Duration	op:add-dayTime Durations(A, B)	xs:day Time Duration
A - B	numeric	numeric	op:numeric-subtract(A, B)	numeric
A - B	xs:date	xs:date	op:subtract-dates(A, B)	xs:day Time Duration
A - B	xs:date	xs:yearMonth Duration	op:subtract-yearMonth Duration-from-date(A, B)	xs:date
A - B	xs:date	xs:dayTime Duration	op:subtract-dayTime Duration-from-date(A, B)	xs:date
A - B	xs:time	xs:time	op:subtract-times(A, B)	xs:day Time Duration
A - B	xs:time	xs:dayTime Duration	op:subtract-dayTime Duration-from-time(A, B)	xs:time
A - B	xs:dateTime	xs:dateTime	op:subtract-dateTimes(A, B)	xs:day Time Duration
A - B	xs:dateTime	xs:yearMonth Duration	op:subtract-yearMonth Duration-from-dateTime(A, B)	xs:date Time
A - B	xs:dateTime	xs:dayTime Duration	op:subtract-dayTime Duration-from-dateTime(A, B)	xs:date Time

A - B	xs:yearMonth Duration	xs:yearMonth Duration	op:subtract-yearMonth Durations(A, B)	xs:yearMonth Duration
A - B	xs:dayTime Duration	xs:dayTime Duration	op:subtract-dayTime Durations(A, B)	xs:dayTime Duration
A * B	numeric	numeric	op:numeric-multiply(A, B)	numeric
A * B	xs:yearMonth Duration	numeric	op:multiply-yearMonth Duration(A, B)	xs:yearMonth Duration
A * B	numeric	xs:yearMonth Duration	op:multiply-yearMonth Duration(B, A)	xs:yearMonth Duration
A * B	xs:dayTime Duration	numeric	op:multiply-dayTime Duration(A, B)	xs:dayTime Duration
A * B	numeric	xs:dayTime Duration	op:multiply-dayTime Duration(B, A)	xs:dayTime Duration
A idiv B	numeric	numeric	op:numeric-integer-divide (A, B)	xs:integer
A div B	numeric	numeric	op:numeric-divide(A, B)	numeric; but xs:decimal if both operands are xs:integer
A div B	xs:yearMonth Duration	numeric	op:divide-yearMonth Duration(A, B)	xs:yearMonth Duration
A div B	xs:dayTime Duration	numeric	op:divide-dayTime Duration(A, B)	xs:dayTime Duration

A div B	xs:yearMonth Duration	xs:yearMonth Duration	op:divide-yearMonth Duration-by-yearMonth Duration (A, B)	xs:decimal
A div B	xs:dayTime Duration	xs:dayTime Duration	op:divide-dayTime Duration-by-dayTime Duration (A, B)	xs:decimal
A mod B	numeric	numeric	op:numeric-mod(A, B)	numeric
A eq B	numeric	numeric	op:numeric-equal(A, B)	xs:boolean
A eq B	xs:boolean	xs:boolean	op:boolean-equal(A, B)	xs:boolean
A eq B	xs:string	xs:string	op:numeric-equal(fn:compare (A, B), 0)	xs:boolean
A eq B	xs:date	xs:date	op:date-equal(A, B)	xs:boolean
A eq B	xs:time	xs:time	op:time-equal(A, B)	xs:boolean
A eq B	xs:dateTime	xs:dateTime	op:dateTime-equal(A, B)	xs:boolean
A eq B	xs:duration	xs:duration	op:duration-equal(A, B)	xs:boolean
A eq B	Gregorian	Gregorian	op:gYear-equal(A, B) etc.	xs:boolean
A eq B	xs:hexBinary	xs:hexBinary	op:hex-binary-equal(A, B)	xs:boolean
A eq B	xs:base64 Binary	xs:base64 Binary	op:base64-binary-equal(A, B)	xs:boolean

A eq B	xs:anyURI	xs:anyURI	op:numeric-equal(fn:compare (A, B), 0)	xs:boolean
A eq B	xs:QName	xs:QName	op:QName-equal(A, B)	xs:boolean
A eq B	xs:NOTATION	xs:NOTATION	op:NOTATION-equal(A, B)	xs:boolean
A ne B	numeric	numeric	fn:not(op:numeric-equal(A, B))	xs:boolean
A ne B	xs:boolean	xs:boolean	fn:not(op:boolean-equal(A, B))	xs:boolean
A ne B	xs:string	xs:string	fn:not(op:numeric-equal(fn:compare (A, B), 0))	xs:boolean
A ne B	xs:date	xs:date	fn:not(op:date-equal(A, B))	xs:boolean
A ne B	xs:time	xs:time	fn:not(op:time-equal(A, B))	xs:boolean
A ne B	xs:dateTime	xs:dateTime	fn:not(op:date Time-equal (A, B))	xs:boolean
A ne B	xs:duration	xs:duration	fn:not(op: duration-equal (A, B))	xs:boolean
A ne B	Gregorian	Gregorian	fn:not(op:gYear-equal(A, B)) etc.	xs:boolean
A ne B	xs:hexBinary	xs:hexBinary	fn:not(op:hex-binary-equal (A, B))	xs:boolean
A ne B	xs:base64 Binary	xs:base64 Binary	fn:not(op:base64-binary-equal (A, B))	xs:boolean

A ne B	xs:anyURI	xs:anyURI	fn:not(op: numericequal (fn:compare (A, B), 0))	xs:boolean
A ne B	xs:QName	xs:QName	fn:not(op:QName-equal(A, B))	xs:boolean
A ne B	xs:NOTATION	xs:NOTATION	fn:not(op: NOTATION-equal(A, B))	xs:boolean
A gt B	numeric	numeric	op:numeric-greater-than(A, B)	xs:boolean
A gt B	xs:boolean	xs:boolean	op:boolean-greater-than(A, B)	xs:boolean
A gt B	xs:string	xs:string	op:numeric-greater-than (fn:compare (A, B), 0)	xs:boolean
A gt B	xs:date	xs:date	op:date-greater-than(A, B)	xs:boolean
A gt B	xs:time	xs:time	op:time-greater-than(A, B)	xs:boolean
A gt B	xs:dateTime	xs:dateTime	op:dateTime-greater-than(A, B)	xs:boolean
A gt B	xs:yearMonth Duration	xs:yearMonth Duration	op:yearMonth Duration-greater-than(A, B)	xs:boolean
A gt B	xs:dayTime Duration	xs:dayTime Duration	op:dayTime Duration-greater-than(A, B)	xs:boolean
A gt B	xs:anyURI	xs:anyURI	op:numeric-greater-than (fn:compare (A, B), 0)	xs:boolean

A lt B	numeric	numeric	op:numeric-less-than(A, B)	xs:boolean
A lt B	xs:boolean	xs:boolean	op:boolean-less-than(A, B)	xs:boolean
A lt B	xs:string	xs:string	op:numeric-less-than(fn:compare (A, B), 0)	xs:boolean
A lt B	xs:date	xs:date	op:date-less-than(A, B)	xs:boolean
A lt B	xs:time	xs:time	op:time-less-than(A, B)	xs:boolean
A lt B	xs:dateTime	xs:dateTime	op:dateTime-less-than(A, B)	xs:boolean
A lt B	xs:yearMonth Duration	xs:yearMonth Duration	op:yearMonth Duration-less-than(A, B)	xs:boolean
A lt B	xs:dayTime Duration	xs:dayTime Duration	op:dayTime Duration-less-than(A, B)	xs:boolean
A lt B	xs:anyURI	xs:anyURI	op:numeric-less-than(fn:compare (A, B), 0)	xs:boolean
A ge B	numeric	numeric	op:numeric-greater-than (A, B) or op: numeric-equal (A, B)	xs:boolean
A ge B	xs:boolean	xs:boolean	fn:not(op:boolean-less-than(A, B))	xs:boolean
A ge B	xs:string	xs:string	op:numeric-greaterthan (fn:compare (A, B), -1)	xs:boolean

A ge B	xs:date	xs:date	fn:not(op:date-less-than(A, B))	xs:boolean
A ge B	xs:time	xs:time	fn:not(op:time-less-than(A, B))	xs:boolean
A ge B	xs:dateTime	xs:dateTime	fn:not(op:dateTime-less-than (A, B))	xs:boolean
A ge B	xs:yearMonth Duration	xs:yearMonth Duration	fn:not(op:year MonthDuration-less-than(A, B))	xs:boolean
A ge B	xs:dayTime Duration	xs:dayTime Duration	fn:not(op:dayTime Duration-less-than (A, B))	xs:boolean
A ge B	xs:anyURI	xs:anyURI	op:numeric-greater-than(fn:compare (A, B), -1)	xs:boolean
A le B	numeric	numeric	op:numeric-less-than(A, B) or op:numeric-equal (A, B)	xs:boolean
A le B	xs:boolean	xs:boolean	fn:not(op:boolean-greater-than (A, B))	xs:boolean
A le B	xs:string	xs:string	op:numeric-less-than(fn:compare (A, B), 1)	xs:boolean
A le B	xs:date	xs:date	fn:not(op:date-greater-than (A, B))	xs:boolean
A le B	xs:time	xs:time	fn:not(op:time-greater-than (A, B))	xs:boolean

A le B	xs:dateTime	xs:dateTime	fn:not(op:date Time-greater-than (A, B))	xs:boolean
A le B	xs:yearMonth Duration	xs:yearMonth Duration	fn:not(op:year MonthDuration-greater-than (A, B))	xs:boolean
A le B	xs:dayTime Duration	xs:dayTime Duration	fn:not(op:dayTime Duration-greater-than(A, B))	xs:boolean
A le B	xs:anyURI	xs:anyURI	op:numeric-less-than(fn:compare (A, B), 1)	xs:boolean
A is B	node()	node()	op:is-same-node (A, B)	xs:boolean
A << B	node()	node()	op:node-before (A, B)	xs:boolean
A >> B	node()	node()	op:node-after (A, B)	xs:boolean
A union B	node()*	node()*	op:union(A, B)	node()*
A | B	node()*	node()*	op:union(A, B)	node()*
A intersect B	node()*	node()*	op:intersect (A, B)	node()*
A except B	node()*	node()*	op:except(A, B)	node()*
A to B	xs:integer	xs:integer	op:to(A, B)	xs:integer*
A , B	item()*	item()*	op:concatenate (A, B)	item()*

Unary Operators

Operator	Operand type	Function	Result type
+ A	numeric	op:numeric-unary-plus(A)	numeric
- A	numeric	op:numeric-unary-minus(A)	numeric

Appendix VII

References
Normative References

RFC 2119

S. Bradner. *Key Words for use in RFCs to Indicate Requirement Levels.* IETF RFC 2119. See http://www.ietf.org/rfc/rfc2119.txt.

RFC2396

T. Berners-Lee, R. Fielding, and L. Masinter. Uniform Resource Identifiers (URI): Generic Syntax. IETF RFC 2396. See http://www.ietf.org/rfc/rfc2396.txt.

RFC3986

T. Berners-Lee, R. Fielding, and L. Masinter. Uniform Resource Identifiers (URI): Generic Syntax. IETF RFC 3986. See http://www.ietf.org/rfc/rfc3986.txt.

RFC3987

M. Duerst and M. Suignard. Internationalized Resource Identifiers (IRIs). IETF RFC 3987. See http://www.ietf.org/rfc/rfc3987.txt.

ISO/IEC 10646

ISO (International Organization for Standardization). ISO/IEC 10646:2003. Information technology — Universal Multiple-Octet Coded Character Set (UCS), as, from time to time, amended, replaced by a new edition, or expanded by the addition of new parts. [Geneva]: International Organization for Standardization. (See http://www.iso.org for the latest version.)

Unicode

The Unicode Consortium. The Unicode Standard Reading, Mass.: Addison-Wesley, 2003, as updated from time to time by the publication of new versions. See http://www.unicode.org/unicode/standard/ versions for the latest version and additional information on versions of the standard and of the Unicode Character Database. The version of Unicode to be used is implementation-defined, but implementations are recommended to use the latest Unicode version.

XML 1.0

World Wide Web Consortium. Extensible Markup Language (XML) 1.0. (Third Edition) W3C Recommendation. See http://www.w3.org/TR/REC-xml

XML 1.1

World Wide Web Consortium. Extensible Markup Language (XML) 1.1. W3C Recommendation. See http://www.w3.org/TR/xml11/

XML Base

World Wide Web Consortium. XML Base. W3C Recommendation. See http://www.w3.org/TR/xmlbase/

XML Names

World Wide Web Consortium. Namespaces in XML. W3C Recommendation. See http://www.w3.org/TR/REC-xml-names/

XML Names 1.1

World Wide Web Consortium. Namespaces in XML 1.1. W3C Recommendation. See http://www.w3.org/TR/xml-names11/

XML ID

World Wide Web Consortium. xml:id Version 1.0. W3C Recommendation. See http://www.w3.org/TR/xml-id/

XML Schema

World Wide Web Consortium. XML Schema, Parts 0, 1, and 2 (Second Edition). W3C Recommendation, 28 October 2004. See http://www.w3.org/TR/xmlschema-0/, http://www.w3.org/TR/xmlschema-1/, and http://www.w3.org/TR/xmlschema-2/.

XQuery/XPath Data Model (XDM)

World Wide Web Consortium. XQuery 1.0 and XPath 2.0 Data Model (XDM). W3C Recommendation, 23 Jan. 2007. See http://www.w3.org/

TR/xpath-datamodel/.

XQuery 1.0 and XPath 2.0 Formal Semantics

World Wide Web Consortium. XQuery 1.0 and XPath 2.0 Formal Semantics. W3C Recommendation, 23 Jan. 2007. See http://www.w3.org/TR/xquery-semantics/.

XQuery 1.0 and XPath 2.0 Functions and Operators

World Wide Web Consortium. XQuery 1.0 and XPath 2.0 Functions and Operators W3C Recommendation, 23 Jan. 2007. See http://www.w3.org/TR/xpath-functions/.

XSLT 2.0 and XQuery 1.0 Serialization

World Wide Web Consortium. XSLT 2.0 and XQuery 1.0 Serialization. W3C Recommendation, 23 Jan. 2007. See http://www.w3.org/TR/xslt-xquery-serialization/.

Non-normative References

XML Query 1.0 Requirements

World Wide Web Consortium. XML Query 1.0 Requirements. W3C Working Draft, 14 Nov 2003. See http://www.w3.org/TR/xquery-requirements/.

XPath 2.0

World Wide Web Consortium. XML Path Language (XPath) Version 2.0. W3C Recommendation, 23 Jan. 2007. See http://www.w3.org/TR/xpath20/.

XQueryX 1.0

World Wide Web Consortium. XQueryX, Version 1.0. W3C Recommendation, 23 Jan. 2007. See http://www.w3.org/TR/xqueryx/.

XSLT 2.0

World Wide Web Consortium. XSL Transformations (XSLT) 2.0. W3C Recommendation, 23 Jan. 2007. See http://www.w3.org/TR/xslt20/

Document Object Model

World Wide Web Consortium. Document Object Model (DOM) Level 3 Core Specification. W3C Recommendation, April 7, 2004. See http://www.w3.org/TR/DOM-Level-3-Core/.

XML Infoset

World Wide Web Consortium. XML Information Set. W3C Recommendation 24 October 2001. See http://www.w3.org/TR/xml-infoset/

XPath 1.0

World Wide Web Consortium. XML Path Language (XPath) Version 1.0. W3C Recommendation, Nov. 16, 1999. See http://www.w3.org/TR/xpath.html

XPointer

World Wide Web Consortium. XML Pointer Language (XPointer). W3C Last Call Working Draft 8 January 2001. See http://www.w3.org/TR/WD-xptr

XML Query Use Cases

World Wide Web Consortium. XML Query Use Cases. W3C Working Draft, 8 June 2006. See http://www.w3.org/TR/xquery-use-cases/.

XML 1.1 and Schema 1.0

World Wide Web Consortium. Processing XML 1.0 Documents with XML Schema 1.0 Processors. W3C Working Group Note, 11 May 2005. See http://www.w3.org/TR/xml11schema10/.

Uniform Resource Locators (URL)

Internet Engineering Task Force (IETF). Uniform Resource Locators (URL). Request For Comment No. 1738, Dec. 1994. See http://www.ietf.org/rfc/rfc1738.txt.

ODMG

Rick Cattell et al. The Object Database Standard: ODMG-93, Release 1.2. Morgan Kaufmann Publishers, San Francisco, 1996.

Quilt

Don Chamberlin, Jonathan Robie, and Daniela Florescu. Quilt: an XML Query Language for Heterogeneous Data Sources. In Lecture Notes in Computer Science, Springer-Verlag, Dec. 2000. Also available at http://www.almaden.ibm.com/cs/people/chamberlin/quilt_lncs.pdf. See also http://www.almaden.ibm.com/cs/people/chamberlin/quilt.html.

XML-QL

Alin Deutsch, Mary Fernandez, Daniela Florescu, Alon Levy, and Dan Suciu. A Query Language for XML.

SQL

International Organization for Standardization (ISO). Information Technology-Database Language SQL. Standard No. ISO/IEC 9075:2003. (Available from American National Standards Institute, New York, NY 10036, (212) 642-4900.)

XQL

J. Robie, J. Lapp, D. Schach. XML Query Language (XQL). See http://www.w3.org/TandS/QL/QL98/pp/xql.html.

Background Material

Character Model

World Wide Web Consortium. Character Model for the World Wide Web. W3C Working Draft. See http://www.w3.org/TR/charmod/.

XSLT 1.0

World Wide Web Consortium. XSL Transformations (XSLT) 1.0. W3C Recommendation. See http://www.w3.org/TR/xslt

Index

A

B

backup, 33, 34, 35, 39, 41, 42, 221, 222, 225, 232, 238, 239, 286, 287
binary, 21, 140, 207, 212, 271, 293, 295
box, 23, 28, 252, 253, 256, 257, 274, 275
browse, 51, 144
built-in types, 135, 153

C

calculation, 101, 106, 108, 162
category, 95, 99
character, 103, 115, 116, 121, 145, 175-177, 217, 220, 226, 229, 230, 231, 232, 233,
        234, 236-238, 268, 269, 271, 273, 274, 288
child, 65, 70, 130, 138, 194, 211, 222-224, 228, 256, 257, 293
children, 127, 128, 256, 257, 288
circle, 252, 253, 256, 257, 274, 275, 277
collection, 27, 31, 174, 189, 190, 191, 193, 196, 201, 203, 208-212, 225, 228, 233, 235,
        248, 250, 252, 265, 266, 278-284, 286-289
combine, 23, 24, 25, 69, 70, 86, 165
comment(), 140
compare, 48, 82, 108, 115, 175, 266
comparison, 84, 104, 106, 111, 113-115, 121
concat, 118, 266
concatenating, 118, 121, 272
conditionals, 59, 60
configuration, 36, 37, 38, 215, 216, 218-240, 243, 244, 246-250, 265, 295
construction, 111
contains, 115, 139, 149, 153, 154, 162, 173, 179, 252
content enrichment, 19, 22, 23, 28
convert, 91, 112, 121, 149, 182, 218, 277, 291, 312, 315, 319, 321, 322, 329
count, 26, 173, 174
counting, 96, 97, 101, 173, 177, 178, 179
create, 21, 24, 27, 33, -35, 37, 38, 39, 42, 47, 48, 57, 63, 76-78, 83, 86, 89, 98, 102, 144,
        149, 156, 167, 177, 181, 182, 186, 189, 190, 199, 200, 203, 209, 210,
        217-220, 224-226, 229-233, 241, 248, 264, 266, 271, 273, 275, 276, 288, 291,

duration, 153, 160, 162, 293, 294, 296, 298, 299, 300, 339, 357, 37-386

E

element, 37, 64-70, 74, 95, 123, 125, 126, 127, 128, 131, 133, 138-140, 143-146, 174,
        189-195, 247-254, 257, 258, 259, 269, 271, 274, 275, 279-286, 291, 292, 295-309,
        315, 319, 329, 331, 333, 334, 340, 343, 344, 345, 347, 348, 352-354, 357, 359,
        365-368, 370-373
element(), 140
empty , 85, 294, 322, 333, 336, 340, 344, 359, 365, 371, 376
enable, 37, 166, 175, 190, 191, 196, 242, 245, 251-253, 255, 256, 261, 262, 265, 266,
        267, 269, 305, 311, 386, 305, 311, 320, 338
ends-with, 115, 294
enrichment, 19, 21, 22, 23, 24, 25, 28
entity, 24, 25, 193, 246, 286, 292, 346
error, 133, 136, 137, 147, 148, 167, 168, 219, 235, 236, 237, 242, 243, 245, 272, 273,
        277, 294, 300, 305, 320, 351, 352, 354, 356, 365, 366-368, 370-373, 376
estimate, 173, 177, 178, 179, 315
expression, 50-52, 55, 57-60, 63, 65-68, 70, 73-78, 81, 83-85, 89, -93, 95-99, 105, 106,
        107, 112, 113, 115, -120, 125, 126, 127, 130, 131, 136, 137, 138, 140, 146, 148,
        149, 156-158, 160, 162, 165, 166, 167, 174, 178, 192, 193, 200, 203, 208, 210,
        212, 216, 217, 218, 220, 224, 226, 230, 231, 232, 235, 236, 276, 286, 287, 289,
        290, 305, 315, 320, 322, 327, 330, 333-338, 340, 341, 345-355, 359, 361, 365-373

F

facet, 21
failover, 21, 264, 265
file, 21, 34, 36, 47, 50, 51, 55-58, 60, 63, 66, 73, 75, 78, 81, 83, 84, 85, 101, 105, 136,
        138, 154, 156, 166, 182, 183, 185, 199-202, 204, 207, 208, 209, 225, 244, 267,
        268, 270, 271, 272, 300, 304, 310, 314, 315, 316, 318, 319, 320-322
filter, 21, 40, 63, 70, 74, 75, 78, 337, 346, 352
FLWOR, 73-78, 81, 89, 96, 99, 333, 335, 346, 372, 373
fn, 147, 148, 149, 177, 236, 238, 292, 293, 294-300, 308, 325, 326, 331, 333, 335, 350,
        351, 352, 354, 381, 382, 383, 384, 385, 386
folder, 50, 51, 58

M

Mac OS, 181, 184

managing, 19, 27, 34, 73

manipulation, 111

MarkLogic, 19, 20, 21, 23, 25, 26, 27, 28, 31-42, 140, 144, 147, 148, 149, 173, 174, 175, 177, 178, 181-186, 189-193, 195, 196, 199-208, 212, 215, 219, 224, 225, 226, 232, 235, 237, 238, 241, 271, 272, 312, 319, 322

markup   19, 20, 300-322, 390

matches, 84, 114, 115, 117, 140, 178, 181, 191, 277, 223, 224, 278, 287, 295, 335, 349

maximum, 133, 134, 136, 137, 139, 244-247, 272, 273

modules, 36, 147, 149, 150, 182, 199, 243, 246, 319, 343, 347, 371, 373

movie, 50, 51, 56-60, 101-103, 105-107, 154, 155-161, 165-168, 174, 178, 208, 209, 210-212

multiple, 19, 20, 23, 28, 69, 70, 75, 78, 92, 93, 175, 182, 184, 185, 298, 331, 368, 369, 370, 389

N

namespaces, 34, 143, 144, 145, 146, 147, 148, 150, 241, 243, 266, 295, 296, 298, 322, 331, 340, 343, 344, 351, 369, 370, 372, 373, 390

navigating, 123, 131

nested loop, 77, 78

node, 50, 57, 64, 65, 70, 74, 128, 130, 131, 138, 139, 140, 207, 209, 211, 212, 271, 278, 286, 287, 288, 292, 293, 295, 296, 297, 304, 305, 317, 319, 320, 321, 322, 325, 326, 328-334, 340, 341, 343-348, 350, 352, 354, 356, 357, 359, 366, 367, 369, 370, 373, 386

node(), 140, 211, 237, 369, 386

notification, 19, 26, 27, 28, 232

number, 26, 76, 81, 82, 83, 84, 85, 92, 93, 96, 97, 98, 99, 101, 103, 105, 104, 108, 123, 124, 126, 127, 129, 130, 133, 136, 144, 145, 162, 173, 177, 178, 210, 215, 218, 244, 245, 246, 247, 268, 270, 272, 273, 287, 292, 293, 294, 297, 298, 299, 302, 315, 322, 331, 338, 361, 366-368 numeric, 26, 67, 101, 103, 104, 105, 106, 108, 133, 298, 334, 345, 354, 375, 376, 377, 379, 380, 381, 382, 383, 384, 385, 386, 387

O

operating systems, 31, 32, 181, 183, 184
operation, 73, 185, 201, 211, 212, 313, 339
operator, 104, 105, 106, 133, 280, 284, 299, 325, 328, 329, 332, 335, 339, 345, 347, 354, 361, 368, 369, 375, 376, 377, 387, 391
order by, 73, 74, 75, 76, 90, 91, 93, 97, 98, 105, 106, 107, 112, 333, 335, 346, 354, 372, 375
outer joins, 84, 86
outermost, 125, 145
Oxygen XML Editor, 49

P

parent::, 128
parentheses, 68, 347
path, 25, 48, 50, 51, 57, 58, 63, 70, 123, 125, 126, 131, 143, 147, 149, 174, 182, 199, 201, 242, 245, 289, 294, 305, 310, 316, 317, 318, 319, 321, 325, 328, 332, 335, 344, 346, 352, 354, 356, 366, 369, 376, 390, 391, 392
pattern, 25, 55, 120, 191, 192, 193, 194, 195, 196, 278, 280, 281, 283, 284, 285, 286, 289, 295, 297, 299, 353
PDF, 20, 34, 149, 207, 304, 319, 392
percent, 106
performance, 20, 25, 31, 32, 34, 37, 177, 178
plain text, 20, 207
point, 23, 41, 101, 103, 162, 194, 215-220, 278, 279, 282, 283, 287, 292, 299-303, 328, 331
polygon, 23, 215, 216, 219, 220, 279, 282, 283, 287, 300-303
population, 81-83
position, 19, 37, 67, 68, 70, 116, 211, 251, 253-260, 262-295, 297, 299, 300, 330, 333, 337
positional, 67, 70, 373

PowerPoint, 149, 207, 319
preceding::, 128
preceding-sibling::, 128
predicate, 63, 64, 66, 67, 69, 70, 73, 337, 345, 346, 352
prefix, 113, 144, 145, 147, 148, 149, 150, 174, 182, 269, 289, 295, 296, 297, 298, 336, 340, 342, 343, 347, 351, 366, 368, 369, 370, 371, 372
privileges, 185, 201, 225, 307, 308, 309, 317, 320
programming, 20, 21, 28, 31, 36, 48, 50, 57, 58, 111, 116, 133, 141, 143, 149, 165, 167, 168, 173, 207

Q

QName, 149, 189, 193, 279-286, 294-298, 333, 336, 338, 340, 341, 344-347, 355, 366, 368, 369, 370, 372, 373, 382, 383

R

range, 23, 64, 76, 78, 189, 190, 191, 193, 195, 196, 218, 248, 250, 254, 256, 258, 261, 280, 284, 285, 302, 303
rearranging, 73
redundancy, 98, 149
references, 183, 184, 185, 200, 201, 307, 322, 327, 347, 389, 391
reindexer, 37, 262, 356
relevance, 25, 173, 178, 288
remainder, 173, 177, 178, 179, 288, 303
replace, 120, 121, 162, 182, 211, 294, 297, 319, 389
reporting, 20
restore, 33, 34, 41, 42, 313, 316
return, 58, 60, 64-69, 73-77, 83, 84, 85, 90, 91, 93, 97, 98, 105, 106, 107, 112-121, 126, 127, 129, 130, 136, 137, 138, 140, 146, 148, 149, 156-158, 160, 165-168, 174, 177, 178, 181, 182, 191-196, 203, 210
reverse, 76, 77, 78, 128, 252, 254, 259, 261, 288, 298, 223, 224, 233, 348
reverse query, 223, 224, 233
role, 19, 28, 56, 102, 225, 266, 267, 269, 302, 305-310, 312, 316, 319, 320, 322
RSS feeds, 20

S

synchronization, 21, 41
syntax 48, 50, 57, 68, 78, 123, 149, 167, 174, 184, 226, 332, 349, 351, 356, 359, 389
system memory, 37

T

text(), 140, 167
thesaurus, 25, 181-186, 201, 310
three-way joins, 83, 86
time, 20, 24-28, 38, 48, 50, 59, 60, 75, 133, 134, 136, 137, 139, 144, 153-160, 162, 165,
        166, 168, 173, 174, 177, 178, 179, 185, 242, 243, 244, 245, 246, 258, 270, 272,
        273, 277, 292, 293, 294, 296, 298, 299, 318, 321, 236, 331, 334, 335, 339, 378,
        379, 380, 391, 389, 390
title, 56, 57, 58, 59, 60, 96, 97, 98, 99, 101, 102, 105, 106, 107, 123, 124, 126, 127, 130,
146, 154-161, 166-168, 174, 178, 211
tokenization, 25
tokenize, 119, 288, 299
ToolKit, 20
trace, 236, 238, 266, 268, 271, 277, 290, 300, 320, 321
track, 73, 166
transaction, 21, 37, 41
transform, 20
transforming, 20, 73
two-way join, 83
type, 20, 23, 26, 36, 40, 42, 89, 90, 91, 92, 93, 101, 103, 104, 106, 108, 111-113, 121,
        128, 133, 135, 136, 138, 139, 140, 141, 153, 156, 158, 160, 162, 167, 168, 173,
        177, 179, 189-193, 195, 196, 207, 212, 215, 217, 218, 236, 244, 266, 271, 316,
        321, 325, 326, 329, 330, 332-335, 338, 339, 341, 343, 344, 345, 348-357, 365-
        369, 371, 372, 373, 375, 376, 377, 387

U

unit, 82-85, 101
UNIX, 32, 181, 183
upper case, 121, 182

Printed in the United Kingdom by
Lightning Source UK Ltd., Milton Keynes
141322UK00001B/60/P